T0113407

ALSO BY JAMES W. FINEGAN

Emerald Fairways and Foam-Flecked Seas:
*A Golfer's Pilgrimage to
the Courses of Ireland*

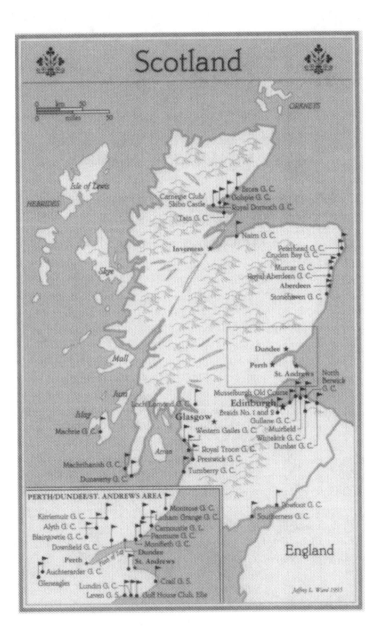

Scotland

Isle of Lewis

HEBRIDES

ORKNEYS

Carnegie Club/
Skibo Castle

Brora G. C.
Golspie G. C.
Royal Dornoch G. C.

Tain G. C.

Nairn G. C.

Inverness

Peterhead G. C.
Cruden Bay G. C.
Murcar G. C.
Royal Aberdeen G. C.
Aberdeen
Stonehaven G. C.

Skye

Mull

Jura

Islay

Dundee
Perth
St. Andrews
North
Berwick
G. C.

Loch Lomond G. C.

Musselburgh Old Course
Edinburgh
Braids No. 1 and 2
Gullane G. C.
Muirfield
Whitekirk G. C.
Dunbar G. C.

Glasgow

Western Gailes G. C.

Machrie G. C.

Arran

Royal Troon G. C.
Prestwick G. C.
Turnberry G. C.

Machrihanish G. C.

Dunaverty G. C.

Dowfoot G. C.
Southerness G. C.

England

Jeffrey L. Ward 1995

PERTH/DUNDEE/ST. ANDREWS AREA

Kirriemuir G. C.
Alyth G. C.
Blairgowrie G. C.
Downfield G. C.

Perth
Auchterarder G. C.
Gleneagles

Lundin G. C.
Leven G. S.

Montrose G. C.
Letham Grange G. C.
Carnoustie G. L.
Panmure G. C.
Monifieth G. C.
Dundee
St. Andrews

Firth of Tay

Crail G. S.
Golf House Club, Elie

Blasted Heaths
and
Blessed Greens

*A Golfer's Pilgrimage to
the Courses of Scotland*

JAMES W. FINEGAN

SIMON & SCHUSTER
NEW YORK   LONDON   TORONTO
SYDNEY   TOKYO   SINGAPORE

SIMON & SCHUSTER
Rockefeller Center
1230 Avenue of the Americas
New York, NY 10020

Designed by Brian Mulligan
Map design by Jeffrey L. Ward
Manufactured in the United States of America

10 9 8 7 6 5 4 3 2 1

Library of Congress Cataloging-In-Publication Data

Finegan, James W.
        Blasted heaths and blessed greens : a golfer's pilgramage to the
courses of Scotland / James W. Finegan.
            p.   cm.
        1. Golf courses—Scotland—Guidebooks. 2. Scotland—Guidebooks.
    I. Title.
    GV975.F556   1996
    196.352'06'8411—dc20   95-47187
                                                            CIP

ISBN 978-0-743-26484-6

For information regarding the special discounts for bulk purchases, please contact Simon &
Schuster Special Sales at 1-800-456-6798 or business@simonandschuster.com

For Harriet, my dear wife,
who has never struck a golf ball,
yet cherishes Scotland as deeply as do I

Contents

Introduction

Scotland is a tiny land—smaller, in fact, than the state of Maine—but it boasts more than 460 golf courses (120 of them with only nine holes). This book provides a look at some 60 of these 460. It also comments on 35 places to stay, 7 or 8 restaurants (a very thin list, because my wife and I generally find ourselves eating dinner at our hotel), and a number of nongolfing attractions in what is an enormously rich and varied, beautiful and hospitable country. Technically—only technically—Scotland is not a country, but you won't want to remind the Scots of that.

I have visited Scotland 21 times over the years, only once for a purpose other than golf. That was in 1952, when the ship on which I was serving, the aircraft carrier *Wasp*, lay anchored in the Firth of Clyde. This happy circumstance enabled a shipmate and me to work our way, lightweight golf bags over our shoulders, by train to St. Andrews.

Resplendent in our youthful ignorance, we told the porter at the Royal and Ancient Golf Club that we had come to play the Old Course and would like to change our clothes. He was polite but firm: Unless we were guests of a member, it would not be possible to admit us. He suggested we try the St. Andrews Golf Club, right over there—he pointed—just beyond the 18th green.

The St. Andrews club secretary directed us to a plain room at the top of the house. It contained no lockers. We hung our uniforms on pegs, speedily donned golf clothes, clattered down the three flights of stairs in our spikes, crossed The Links road and the 18th fairway, and paid our green fee. I believe it was 25 pence. There was no need for a starting time—in fact, there were no other players about on this mid-September afternoon, not on the first hole, nor the last.

Right from the outset I loved this ancient links, where some form of the game, however rudimentary, has been played for about 500 years, but I was utterly baffled by it: the vast double greens; the corresponding "double fairways"; the ferocious sandpits rearing their revetted faces in the most unexpected spots (such as the middle of the fairway); the heather and the gorse; and above all, the rippling, heaving, hummocky terrain.

I vowed to return one day, but that day did not come for almost 20 years—the twin priorities of earning a living and raising a family taking precedence. I finally got back to St. Andrews in late summer of 1971, this time with a wife and three children. Over the next 25 years, I returned to Scotland 19 more times, venturing farther and farther from the golfing shrines to play at places such as Golspie in the north and Powfoot in the south, at Dunbar in the east and Dunaverty in the west—indeed, just about everywhere I could find that there was good golf in a grand setting. My wife, who has never struck a ball, always accompanied me. She long ago discovered that golf courses, especially those near the sea, can be among the most beautiful places in the world.

This book is intended to be useful in three ways. First, the armchair traveler will experience vicariously the special and often simple pleasures of golf in Scotland. If that's your aim, I hope you'll let the book inspire you to make your own pilgrimage to these wonderful sites. Second, and rather more important, the book will help in planning such a trip, however long you have to tour or wherever your other purposes might take you in the land. I'm certain that after reading what's here, you will be able to choose courses to play and places to stay with confidence that both will prove rewarding and enjoyable. And lastly, it can function as a traveling companion, portable enough to pop into a suitcase and have at hand for ready reference throughout your trip.

Some Practical Advice

An appendix contains the addresses and phone numbers of the clubs, courses, and hotels described in the text. This information will be useful for those who intend to make their own reservations for starting times and accommodations.

It has become an axiom of golf holidays in Scotland that in season—May through October—tee times can be more difficult to pin down than hotel rooms. This is particularly true in the case of the fabled courses: the Old Course, Muirfield, Prestwick, Royal Troon, Turnberry, Gleneagles, Royal Dornoch. Prior to the worldwide golf boom, a letter was generally the accepted way to make arrangements. You wrote saying when you would like to play, and the club secretary wrote back confirming your request or, if this was not possible, suggesting another time. But with so many courses now offering starting times seven days a week, a phone call lets you learn straight off whether the date and time you have in mind are available, or if you should change your plans accordingly. You also have the opportunity in this conversation to find out the green fee, the deposit that may be required, the availability of caddies or pull-carts (golf carts as we know them are still extremely uncommon in Scotland), and any restrictions on women's play or on the admission of women to the dining room that may be in force. Once you have this information and have arranged a starting time, you may well want to write a confirming note to the secretary. This is the kind of courtesy that is often appreciated, for despite their "open-door" policy, most of the clubs at which you wish to play are private. In a manner of speaking.

The accessibility of Scottish golf courses comes as a surprise to many Americans. It is simply not that way in this country. You don't just drop in at Merion or at Oakland Hills or at Augusta National because you've a mind to. Without a member at your side, you cannot play at these private clubs. Not so in Scotland; clubs there welcome the visiting stranger. The green fees paid by outsiders are a major source of club revenue, sometimes *the* major source, and it is these tariffs, now steadily climbing, that make the members' dues so modest—on average a mere 10%–15% of what Americans pay annually to belong to a first-rate golf or country club. There is, of course, a *quid pro quo*: The Scottish courses are frequently crowded with non-members.

It is at the older and more prestigious clubs that one encounters substantial restrictions on visitors. Muirfield, for example, accepts visitors who are unaccompanied by a member on Tuesday and Thursday only. Women may play only with men and may not use the clubhouse facilities, which eliminates for them the chance to enjoy the famous five- or six-course lunch. At Prestwick, women are not permitted in the dining room, but are welcome in the visitors' bar, where a simple soup-and-sandwich lunch is served. Royal Troon is strictly for men—here women are not permitted to play the golf course. This, to my knowledge, is the only club in Scotland with such a totally exclusionary policy, though a number of clubs do have some restrictions on the times when women may play. These points are easily clarified with a phone call.

All that having been said, I nevertheless suspect that, on the whole, the attitude toward women on the golf course at the Scottish clubs will strike most Americans as considerably more enlightened than it is at home.

As for the green fees in Scotland, they used to be a negligible factor in a vacation budget. If you had decided to play, for instance, ten rounds of golf in 1971, the most it would have cost, *in total*, was £15. A round of golf on the Old Course was 75 pence then; in 1995 it was £55. At Muirfield in 1971, a round cost £1.50; in 1995, £55. At Turnberry it was £1.80; in 1995, £85. At Royal Dornoch it was 75 pence; in 1995, £35. Today the green fee in Scotland is scarcely a dismissable item.

If you plan to play ten rounds on courses that are of the highest rank, be prepared to set aside about £500, which, at the time this book went to press, translated to $800. In the unlikely event that you confined yourself to little-known courses, you would probably still spend something like $300. The law of supply and demand seems to be working in Scotland.

To give you some idea of the cost of accommodations, let me say that a room for two in season and generally with full Scottish breakfast, service, and taxes included, can range anywhere in 1996 from about £50 per night (say, Oatfield House, near Machrihanish) to £280 per night at Gleneagles. Between these two extremes are hotels such as Dornoch Castle, £86; Rufflets (St. Andrews), £130; and Cameron House (Loch Lomond), £180.

One final note: at some Scottish courses (the Old Course at St. Andrews is a prime example), there is a policy requiring visitors to present a current handicap card or a letter of introduction with handicap confirmation from their club professional. Only rarely is a golfer actually asked to produce either document, but it is prudent to carry them with you.

The Lure of Seaside Golf

There are two principal reasons for the powerful appeal of golf in Scotland: it is the birthplace of the game and thus full of history and lore; and it is the site of so many marvelous links courses. For all the undeniable charms—and merits—of Gleneagles and Loch Lomond, of the Duke's Course at St. Andrews and the Rosemount Course at Blairgowrie, they are unlikely, on their own, to compel us to cross an ocean. But to play around Gullane's noble hill or through the minefields of the Old Course's terrifying pot bunkers, along the dune-framed corridors of Royal Aberdeen or over the tumbling fairways of Royal Dornoch or off the pinnacle tees of Turnberry's Ailsa—ah, for those rare pleasures we would not simply span an ocean, we would circumnavigate the globe!

You will find the emphasis in this book on seaside golf, the earliest and the most natural form of the game. Of the 60 courses that are examined rather comprehensively here, 42 are links, laid out on the sand-based soil that serves as the buffer between the sea and the fertile stretches at a remove from the salt water.

Over tens of thousands of years this linksland evolved as the sea gradually receded, leaving behind sandy wastes which the winds fashioned into dunes, knolls, hollows, and gullies. Gradually, fertilized by the droppings of the gulls, grass began to grow in the hollows. It was a thick, close-growing mixture with stiff, erect blades—the key features of true links turf.

In time other vegetation—gorse, heather, broom—took root, now resulting in terrain that would sustain life. First the rabbits appeared, then the foxes. Then man came along with his sheep, and the animal tracks were widened into paths. These paths began to serve as a rude kind of fairway along which the shepherd might at first have propelled a stone with his crook. The closely grazed ground acted as a putting surface on which the stone, or a ball, could be rolled into a hole. And those places where the sheep huddled during nasty weather created what became the first bunkers. The noted course designer Sir Guy

Campbell summarized the development of the earliest golf
links in memorable language: "Nature was their architect, and
beast and man her contractors."

As it happened, nature did not endow the links with trees.
Oh, now and again a solitary, wind-warped excuse for a tree will
surface, even occasionally a spinney (there's a small grove of
pines near the 5th hole on the championship course at
Carnoustie), but generally the great links are treeless, present-
ing a severe, desolate kind of beauty. Encroaching limbs and
claustrophobic foliage have no place on a pure links. There is an
enticing spaciousness, an exhilarating sense of openness and
freedom about the great majority of seaside courses that is
rarely found in inland golf. To be abroad on a links in Scotland
is to return to the beginnings of the game.

Mindful of the fact that the British Open is contested only at
the sea, we will examine the Old Course, Muirfield, Carnoustie,
the Ailsa, Prestwick, and Royal Troon. It is on these links that
virtually all of the game's most storied figures—Old and Young
Tom Morris, Harry Vardon, James Braid, J. H. Taylor, Bobby
Jones, Walter Hagen, Gene Sarazen, Henry Cotton, Sam Snead,
Ben Hogan, Arnold Palmer, Gary Player, Jack Nicklaus, Tom
Watson, Seve Ballesteros—have scored some of their most notable triumphs. So we will look closely at these famous links.

But I suspect that this volume may be of more value—perhaps even of more interest—when we examine courses you may
have heard about but have only a hazy notion of (Cruden Bay
and Elie, for instance, or North Berwick, Nairn, and Machrihanish). And then there are the truly unheralded gems, some of
them just around the corner (Braids No. 1 is in the very heart
of Edinburgh), some of them in the shadow of renowned

courses (Panmure is not five minutes from Carnoustie), still others far off the beaten track (you have to take a nearly two-hour ferry ride to reach the isle of Islay, home of the remarkable Machrie links; and Brora is even farther north than Dornoch). But whether celebrated or unsung, they all (well, *almost* all—there are four or five courses that I am not an admirer of but that I think you would want to be acquainted with) promise a round of golf that could turn out, for you, to be at least thoroughly enjoyable and quite possibly the golfing experience of a lifetime.

In Praise of the White Markers

For very like 40 years I was what is generally considered a good club player. My handicap moved between 1 and 4, and I won a handful of club championships and a couple of senior club championships. I was always a short hitter, and today I'm an unreliable 8 who thinks that a 210-yard drive—on the flat and in the calm—is scarcely to be disdained.

I mention these things so you will have some idea whose hands you're in as you roam through Scotland. With me, you play from the white tees. Too often, it seems, descriptions of golf holes find the author back on the blues, tackling a course that measures 7,000 yards (or more), a layout with seven or eight two-shotters over 425 yards and a couple of par fives in the 580 neighborhood. I'm inclined to think that many readers of this book will be more comfortable swinging from the regular markers—overall course length averaging maybe 6,250 yards—with a fellow whose solid 3-wood travels 195 yards and whose 5-iron can be counted on for 150 yards. Besides, it's virtually impossible for a visitor to get permission to use the back tees (often called the medal tees) in Scotland; those are reserved for members in competitions.

The Simple Scheme of It

I've organized the book as though you and I had the luxury of carving a couple of months out of our lives to play these 60 golf courses one after another. Each chapter finds us traveling onward to a new territory, which may have only one course that's on my list or could have five or six. We take them as they fall on the map, with little regard for their pedigree. In the end we will have seen much of this enchanting land, played her finest courses, learned a little about the men who laid them out, taken in some of the sights, stayed in attractive lodgings, and made the acquaintance of a number of interesting people.

It is a grand tour—a pilgrimage, if you will—that commences in the capital (Edinburgh) and concludes in the kingdom (Fife). Let us go and make our visit.

Chapter One

Edinburgh
and Points East

 It was a morning in August, the sun was fighting a losing battle with the thick cumulus clouds above the city, and I was playing alone. I had examined the line of my putt on the first green with some care—after all, how many 12-footers for birdie can I reasonably expect to have these days?—and now took my stance at the ball, striving to avoid a death grip on the putter. Just as I was about to draw the club back, a second ball crept silently into my peripheral vision. Startled, I straightened up and walked toward the offending sphere. Then I stopped. There was no one in sight as I looked back up the fairway. Of course there wasn't. I smiled at the realization that someone had just driven the green on this blind 325-yard opening hole, where the last 150 yards are steeply downhill and likely to be as fast as an Olympic bobsled chute.

I missed my putt and proceeded to the second tee, the sting of the blown birdie opportunity assuaged by the knowledge

that the happiest golfer in Edinburgh was playing right behind
me. He would be starting his day with a shot at an eagle. Golf
at Braid Hills is nothing if not exhilarating.

This is city golf (green fee less than $15, call ahead for a
starting time), on the south side of town and all of 10 minutes
from Princes Street, the sparkling main thoroughfare of the
capital, with its monuments and sunken gardens on one side
and its engaging hodgepodge of shops, banks, clubs, and hotels
on the other. Play began here on September 5, 1889, two years
before the Honourable Company of Edinburgh Golfers first
tested its links at Muirfield. In fact, the Honourable Company
was given the opportunity to acquire the land at Braid Hills for
its new course and politely declined. The rest of the world must
be eternally grateful, for the city then stepped in and promptly
built its first municipal course, Braids No. 1. Thirty years later,
Braids No. 2 opened for play.

A quick scan of the scorecard for Braids No. 1 may prove disappointing. How, you ask, can anyone take seriously a course
that, from the back of the tees, measures all of 5,731 yards
against a par of 70; where four of the two-shotters are under
300 yards and five more are between 300 and 350 yards; and
where, as we have seen, the opening hole—the blind fairway
beyond the crest is among the world's widest—is ludicrously
easy? But the 2nd, 134 yards, climbs almost vertically to a vast
level green with a steep falloff on its left flank. And now the
game is on: narrow plateau fairways to be hit and held; gorse-
covered hillsides (like those at Royal Dornoch, a blaze of gold
in spring) to be given a wide berth; frequent rock outcroppings
topped with gorse or long grasses or both; even more frequent
humps and hillocks and hollows; doglegs both sharp, as on the

8th, and gentle, as on the long sweeping downhill 11th; tees high and cruelly exposed to the winds (this is the "breezy Braids"); greens on perilous ledges or in lovely dell-like settings. And all of it roams across this splendid hillside, with its distractingly gorgeous views—which explain the presence of strollers, hikers, and joggers with whom we must share this common ground. To say nothing of the schoolboys, whose cries of success can be heard from time to time as they uncover yet another lost ball in the impenetrable gorse. They will soon be along to offer a bargain buy. It is all part of the rough and tumble of the game here.

Admittedly, there are four or five pedestrian holes. But there are many more that range from good to great. The memorable 202-yard 13th, for instance, rises gently on a lofty ridge, over broken ground to a tightly bunkered green where nothing less than a perfectly struck wood—often a driver—will suffice. Then we must be prepared to repeat that perfect driver swing immediately, for the 378-yard 14th calls for a long forced-carry from an elevated tee across a gorse-covered slope to the safety of a hidden landing area in the valley far below. That accomplished, we are now left with a medium iron over another expanse of the fearsome gorse to the haven of the green.

A word about the last hole. It is a par four of 261 yards. From a knob, we drive across a deep swale into a steep hillside pocked with mounds. If our drive is long, it is also blind, cresting the hill and disappearing. If our drive is short, then our second shot is blind. In either case, we arrive at the green to drink in one of the three or four most intoxicating panoramas in all of golf: Arthur's Seat; the city of Edinburgh, including the Castle on its crag; the Firth of Forth, with Fife on the far shore, Gullane and

North Berwick and Bass Rock a bit nearer out the East Lothian coast; the Pentland Hills and the Lammemuir Hills. It is the summation of all the splendid views that have accompanied us on our delightful round.

It is common in Scotland for golf clubs to grow up around municipal courses. The town—as, for instance, is the case with St. Andrews, Carnoustie, and Montrose, as well as Edinburgh—owns the courses, while the club owns only its clubhouse. Here at the Braids there are five golf clubs: Braids United, the Harrison, Edinburgh Western, Edinburgh Thistle, and Allermuir.

The first time I played Braids No. 1 it was in the company of Norman "Norrie" Robertson, Secretary of the Braids United Golf Club. An RAF pilot in World War II, he had received his flight training at Pensacola. He was 65 years old when we met and playing to an 8. He had been scratch in his prime.

"You may know that Tommy Armour developed his game here," he said. "He won the championship of Edinburgh Western. That was in 1919. And James Braid—no, no, Braid Hills is not named after him—was champion of the Thistle, Edinburgh Thistle, in 1892, which would not have been long after the course opened. Yes, they both played here when they were young men and it did their game no harm."

I asked Norrie whether he had ever won the championship of Braids United.

"As a matter of fact," he said, "I have—four times running, '59, '60, '61, '62. But I must confess," he laughed, "there is no name like Armour or Braid sharing the champions' plaque with me. I will tell you, however, that Ben Crenshaw is an honorary member of Braids United."

A little later he said that his brothers had also won the club championship. "Ed's name is up for '46 and '47, Albert's for '37, '41, and '42. They were both much older than I."

When we reached the 9th, a superb one-shotter of 175 yards where the green, on a knob, is slightly above the tee and there is a falloff front and left and gorse on the right, Norrie said, "Albert once hit the most remarkable shot on this hole. It was in the early forties. You cannot imagine how fast, how fiery fast, this course once played, the way the links courses all used to play in high summer—yes, I know this is not a links, but it is very like one, isn't it? Well, on this particular day a powerful wind was blowing, and Albert was playing right into the very teeth of it here on the 9th. Any ordinary shot would have gotten up in the air, then blown right back in his face. But the ground was like a motorway, so he took out his putter—Albert was very strong—and cracked his tee shot right onto the green, a 175-yard putt that never left the ground, just skimmed along on that burnt-out, frictionless surface and wound up traveling the full distance. They still talk about it."

Norrie also spoke of the No. 2 course, cocking his head back and looking heavenward. I followed his gaze and, to my astonishment, could make out golfers silhouetted against the sky. If Braids No.1 is on the heights, then Braids No. 2 is on the peaks. The notion of even climbing to that altitude, let alone playing golf shots on those vertiginous slopes, was beyond my grasp.

"It's much shorter," Norrie said, "only about 4,800 yards, but it's tighter and not to be thought of as a place fit only for women and children. Indeed not.

"It was up there that the 'mock city' was built at the start of

World War II. It was a decoy—not real houses, you understand, that people could actually live in. But from thousands of feet in the air, from German bombers, it was deceptive. So if they had attempted to bomb Edinburgh, they might have been fooled into dropping their bombs on Braid Hills instead of on the heart of the city.

"But it's this course, the No. 1, that is the marvel. In season it is always covered with golfers from dawn till dark. That's why I am also a member of the Bruntsfield Links Golfing Society, over in the Davidson's Mains section of the city. It's a private club that has its own eighteen. There's no trouble getting on the course there. But"—and now a note of confidentiality crept into his voice—"I could never leave the Braids. Ah, the Braids . . . to play here . . . the wonderful naturalness of it and the beauty and the thrill of the shots themselves . . . *this* is the game."

Norrie Robertson's "other" course, Bruntsfield Links, is short on thrills, and scenically it cannot approach his beloved Braids. Still, it is a perfectly pleasant layout. So is its next-door neighbor, Royal Burgess. As you would expect, Edinburgh has a number of good courses, most of them of the parkland variety. At Duddingston, for example, the sinuous Figgate Burn comes between player and target no fewer than 11 times in the course of the round. At Dalmahoy, a bona fide country club, there are two eighteens (the 6,700-yard East Course, on which the Solheim Cup was played in 1992, is the serious one), squash, horseback riding, loch trout fishing, clay pigeon shooting, archery, and a classically elegant clubhouse/hotel built in 1725 (with a flying external double staircase, no less!) for the 13th Earl of Morton. The Musselburgh Golf Club, at Monktonhall, forgives the less than accurate tee shot and offers a nice feeling of solitude. It is not to be confused with Royal Musselburgh, considerably tighter thanks mainly to trees, or with the historic Musselburgh Old Course, where, in the sixteenth century, Mary Queen of Scots is supposed to have whacked a ball, and where—this is not a matter of supposition—six Opens were contested, the last in 1889. Generally believed to be the oldest unchanged course in the world, it was once the home, concurrently, of the Honourable Company (they moved from here to Muirfield), Royal Musselburgh, and Royal Burgess. This nine-hole Old Course is located in the middle of a racetrack, and your first impression is of a dust bowl with, here and there, a flagstick. Nevertheless, this is hallowed ground, so you may want to park your car at the grandstand and have a look. Like the Braids, it gets plenty of play, and steps are now being taken to spruce it up. The trick will be to improve its condition without destroying its irreplaceable sense of times long past.

Edinburgh, it need scarcely be said, has a number of good hotels in the center of town (the Balmoral, the Caledonian, and the George, to name just three) and in its environs (Dalhousie Castle, Prestonfield House). There is one other accommodation, however, that I must mention, and it is not a hotel. It is Rosslyn Castle, in Roslin, no more than 20 minutes from downtown, yet isolated on a wooded and rocky promontory high above the river North Esk. Don't be put off by the name. A mere fragment of its fifteenth-century splendor, this dwelling sleeps just seven. There is no housekeeper, no cook, no help of any kind. Still, it is entirely manageable and, of course, wonderfully atmospheric, though perhaps it does not provide all the comforts of home; getting it warm enough in early October proved an insoluble problem, but stick to the summer and you won't have to worry about that. My wife and I occupied it for a week in 1986 while I was playing a number of the Edinburgh courses. You rent it from the Landmark Trust, which has its headquarters outside London.

Beyond Musselburgh, and sticking to the coast road (A198) along the southern shore of the Firth of Forth, we drive through Prestonpans and pretty Aberlady—the charming if unexceptional Kilspindie course is here and, not much farther on, Longniddry, which is partly links, partly parkland—and within minutes we arrive in Gullane.

Gullane is a village whose *raison d'être* is easy to discern: golf. Unless I'm mistaken, on any day in high summer there are likely to be more golfers here than inhabitants. That's because Gullane is the home of three golf clubs, one of which has three eighteens and a short nine. This place is a hotbed of the game.

I have yet to play the links of the Luffness New Golf Club, whose holes are laid out on relatively flat ground, whose steep-faced bunkers are to be avoided like the plague, and whose greens—this I can confirm from a recent inspection—are among the very finest in Scotland. (No wonder it is referred to as a junior version of Muirfield.) Playing Luffness New is, I suspect, a pleasure I have too long deferred.

It is Gullane Golf Club, founded in 1882, that offers three eighteens, not to mention the useful little children's nine, which is tucked away down a lane that also accommodates the Old Clubhouse pub, a convivial spot for drinking or dining. Gullane No. 1 has been the scene of the Scottish Amateur, the British Ladies', the Home Internationals, and final qualifying for the British Open when it is played at Muirfield. Today few visitors realize that it was here in 1947 that Babe Didrickson Zaharias became the first American to win the British Ladies' Championship. Some locals, however, still remember her triumph, and they speak in awe of the great Olympian's raw power. The 15th is a par five of 535 yards. The first 350 yards are level; the remainder of the hole climbs to a hillside green. In one of her matches, assisted by a moderate breeze, Babe reached the green in two, with a drive and a 4-iron.

At the start of the round, the sea is nowhere to be found. The culprit is Gullane Hill. This immense blockade stands squarely between the opening holes and the Firth of Forth. We must surmount it. The 1st hole on Gullane No. 1 is short and flat and gentle, a straightaway 300-yarder that should find us putting for a 3. The second hole is neither short nor flat nor gentle, though it is straightaway; it climbs straight up for the entire length of its 380 yards. There is a sheltered look to it, for it follows a natural cut in the hillside, but the prevailing wind, off the still hidden sea, comes whipping down against us, the cut functioning as a perfect funnel for it. The fairway is tauntingly narrow, with long bent grasses on both sides lurking to devour the shot that strays by so much as two paces. I have never known the hole to play less than 425 yards. It is merciless. Accept your 5, rationalize it as a par—you are not stretching the truth too much—and climb onto the 3rd tee.

Now indeed have we come up in the world, though we are not yet on top of it, for that must wait till the 7th. Nonetheless, a great deal of the vast golfing landscape stretches away before us, and the Firth itself is in view, its gray-blue waters stretching away toward the horizon.

Here begins the 14-hole stretch on the seaward side of Gullane Hill. And what delightful and challenging stuff it is, the holes running up and down, over, across and around this mini-mountain, constantly changing direction so that our joust with the wind calls for never-ending adjustments in alignment and strategy. Neither water nor boundaries bedevil us, and there are, of course, no trees. But the sand and slopes and gusts are more than enough to keep us off balance.

The 5th is the finest hole on the course—in all candor, it may be the only great hole on the eighteen, though many are very good. A 450-yard par four, it swings left around deep pits in the crook of the dogleg, then climbs vigorously to a vast green carved out of the hillside. If, somehow, we should couple two su-perlative wood shots and reach the putting surface in regulation, we may yet face more than we can cope with, for the green tilts sharply down from back to front. Ah, this is splendid golf!

The 6th also climbs, but at 324 yards and with a very gener-ous fairway, we catch our breath here. Its chief function is to lead us to the 7th tee, perched upon the pinnacle of Gullane Hill.

Yes, 7 is the summit, and one of the half-dozen most en-thralling spots in all the world of golf. The hole plunges 400 yards straight down, and though there is sand to imperil the approach shot, on the drive we are encouraged to swing from the heels. But *playing* the 7th is almost incidental, for the spec-tacle is mesmerizing. Colorfully dotting the landscape below are countless flagsticks on the three Gullane eighteens. A mile or two down the coast lie the pale green fairways of Muirfield and, beyond them, Bass Rock and the volcanic upthrust that is Berwick Law. Turn the opposite way and the elegant tracery of the great Forth Road Bridge transfixes the eye. And again, as from the final green at Braids No. 1, the capital itself is revealed and so is Arthur's Seat. Fourteen counties can be see from this tee on a clear day, including, some 15 miles across the water, that of Fife. As you stand there, with the sharp, clean sea breeze rushing into your lungs, you may be forgiven if, for a moment, you are overcome by this extraordinary combination of setting and sport.

At 3,500 yards, the inbound half is some 500 yards longer than the first nine. Early holes bring us close to the sea, with the tees at the par-five 12th and the par-three 13th set high above the strand. Here the huge gray concrete blocks, lodged in the thickets above the beach almost 60 years ago to stymie the German tanks that never came, serve as grim reminders of World War II.

The long run home, almost always with the breeze at our back, is full of satisfying golf, with the shot along the ridge to the narrow and beautifully bunkered green on the 186-yard 16th especially memorable. And at last, on the 17th, we gain our revenge on the 2nd, which parallels it. The 2nd went straight up, into the wind. The 17th—it is not called "Hilltop" for nothing—goes straight down, with the wind. That anemic 162-yard drive 15 holes ago is now miraculously metamorphosed into a Brobdingnagian blast of very like 315 yards. For most of us, it is the single longest tee shot we shall ever hit. And if the remaining 80-yard pitch over the fronting bunkers can be handled with restraint—who knows?—a birdie may await. If not here, perhaps on the equally hospitable home hole, a 355-yarder where a well-struck—and wind-assisted—drive will also leave us with dreams of glory.

To play on Gullane Hill is to experience simple, unalloyed

joy. Were someone to ask me to nominate the ideal course on which to be introduced to seaside golf, it might well be Gullane No. 1. And I would then urge the questioner to find time for a game on No. 2 and No. 3 (both somewhat less testing, but, routed over the same magnificent terrain, also grand) and time for a visit to the one-room museum next to the golf shop, itself adjacent to the first tee on the No. 1 course.

If the golf here is a thoroughgoing delight, so is Archie Baird's outstanding exhibit. Through a skillfully arranged selection of paintings, prints, postcards, and photographs, of balls and clubs and costumes, of antique medals of silver and antique buttons of brass, the story of the evolution of golf from its origin 500 years ago is presented. The owner and curator, Archie Baird, member of Gullane and the Honourable Company, and the foremost collector of golfing art in the world today, is also the presenter. Listening to him and examining his memorabilia is a once-in-a-lifetime experience. He somehow manages, nearly at a dead gallop, to be lucid, comprehensive, and engaging all at once. He is one of the two or three most irresistible expositors I've ever encountered. Understand, however, that Archie does not spend his days in the little museum; he is usually out on the links of Gullane or Muirfield, often enjoying 36 holes when the weather is pretty, so the door is generally locked and visits are by appointment only. Still, a telephone call—0875 870 277—is all that is needed to open this treasure chest.

Not too many years ago there used to be a tiny sign peeping out of the grass on the left side of the road at the far end of Gullane as we headed toward North Berwick. All it said was "H.C.E.G." Only the hawk-eyed were likely to spot it. It

marked the lane that leads to the home of the Honourable Company of Edinburgh Golfers, Muirfield. That sign is gone now, but there is a little one for Greywalls, the inn located near the 10th tee.

The course sits well above the sea and at a considerable remove from it. But the nobility and serenity of its location and the beauty of its distant views across this arm of the North Sea are enormously appealing.

The very first moment at Muirfield proclaims the specialness of the place: you park your car not in a lot but in a garage. Only one other golf club in my experience offers this amenity: Royal St. George's, Sandwich, another Open venue.

Fourteen British Opens have been contested at Muirfield. Nicklaus has won here. So have Player, Trevino, Watson, and Faldo, to say nothing of Harry Vardon, James Braid, Walter Hagen, and Henry Cotton. It is awash in lore. It was at Muirfield in 1901 that Braid won the first of his five Opens despite starting the championship by hooking his drive out of bounds, and finishing it with an aggressive swing from nearly 200 yards out that sent the clubhead flying off the shaft and the ball flying onto the home green.

Forty-seven years later, when Cotton won, there was an incident that strikes me as the quintessential Muirfield story. Winged Foot's Claude Harmon, having won the Masters in April, had come over to play in the British Open. Just as he was about to tee off he was advised by an R&A official that his playing partner had withdrawn. A hasty search of the clubhouse for a substitute uncovered only a retired army major, one W. H. Callender, who obligingly said he would "be delighted to give the fellow a game." Reporters subsequently observed something out of the ordinary taking place on the 3rd fairway. Hurrying over, they found Callender offering Harmon advice, complete with a demonstration. "Gripped down the shaft," the major was saying, "a short swing controls the ball more easily in the east wind." Muirfield is that kind of place.

Muirfield accommodates many hundreds of visitors annually (on Tuesdays and Thursdays, only, for those unaccompanied by members). But it does not seek this lucrative guest play, and tee time reservations must be made weeks—for safety's sake, months—in advance. Legion are the tales of those without reservations who have been turned away by the sometimes stiffnecked club secretaries. But these "defenders of the shrine" have an obligation to their members that cannot be ignored. Otherwise the course would be aswarm with outsiders.

Captain P.W.T. "Paddy" Hanmer, Secretary at Muirfield throughout the 1970s and much of the 1980s, once told me with considerable relish the story of the golfer who, with no prior communication, presented himself in the office and requested to play the links.

"Where is your home?" Hanmer inquired.

"New Zealand," the golfer replied. "Wellington."

"So you booked a flight to the U.K. and here you are," Hanmer said.

"Yes, been here about ten days now."

"Ah, you're touring Scotland in a rental car. You booked it before you left home, did you?" the Secretary added.

"Yes, that's right."

"And the same with your hotels, I don't doubt, booked them well in advance."

"Oh, yes, it's all working out just as I planned," said the golfer.

"Well," said Hanmer, "you obviously had not planned to play here, so you will not be upset if I tell you that it is impossible. You booked the plane, you booked the car, you booked the hotels, but you did not see fit to book Muirfield. Perhaps on your next trip you will think to advise us in advance, that is, if you still have an interest in playing this course."

Americans make up a large share of the visiting cadre at Muirfield. And they love it for a host of reasons (not least of which is the six-course lunch). The course is less foreign in feeling than other seaside layouts—there are few capricious humps and hollows to send the ball skittering off line. Its condition is generally excellent; probably, day in and day out, there is no Scottish links boasting finer fairways and greens. It puts little priority on local knowledge. Oh, the second shot on 10, over the cross bunkers, is blind, and so is the drive on 11, over what passes for a hill on this most gently rolling of courses. But otherwise, the problems are fully and frankly stated. The greens present clearly etched targets, each putting surface defended, usually on its flanks, occasionally in front, by bunkers that are at best punishing and at worst lethal. The other principal protector of par is the high and strangling rough. Muirfield is one of the most rigorous tests of driving in the world.

Some years ago I asked Jack Nicklaus whether there was anything in particular—a specific shot, an attitude, a strategic decision—to which he could attribute his victory there in the 1966 Open. "At Muirfield that year," he replied, "the fairways were the narrowest I'd ever seen, and the rough was a foot and a half high in some places so that it looked like wheat waving in the wind. . . . The whole secret was to keep the ball in play and not depart from that discipline. I actually used my driver only seventeen times in the entire tournament, four times in each of the first three rounds, five times in the last round."

At Muirfield there are no water hazards, no pulse-quickening forced-carries over gorse-infested swales. There are no "death or glory" holes. Unlike Pebble Beach, Muirfield is not thrilling. Unlike Ballybunion, Muirfield is not dramatic. Yet we never find ourselves wishing for a more adventurous landscape. No, there is a simple rightness about it all that serves us admirably as we play the round and makes a strong claim on our affections as we look back on the game later. Each hole is worthy. The good shot is consistently rewarded; the indifferent shot is just as consistently chastised.

Among the half-dozen great holes are three long two-shotters (par fours): the 6th, swinging left, a nest of gathering bunkers in the crook of the dogleg; the 8th, turning right, an even more alarming cluster of voracious pits in the angle; and the straightaway 18th, where the green, under the very windows of the clubhouse's principal room, is blockaded across the front and flanked on both sides by sand.

I recall an occasion many years ago when my second son and I—he was then 18—hit splendid shots to the last green, mine a suspenseful 3-wood that barely breathed over the fronting bunkers then skipped up to within six feet of the cup, his a high, soft 4-iron that homed in on the flagstick from the moment it left the clubface and rolled to a stop four feet from the hole. We strolled confidently toward the green, congratulatory—and self-congratulatory. Who had ever witnessed two shots in tandem of such princely sheen on this hallowed hole?

Five or six members sat behind the clubhouse glass, doubtless identifying us as the impudent American visitors we were. There were no borrows, subtle or otherwise, in my six-footer: it was string straight. "Knock it in, Dad," John murmured. I shoved it dead right.

Now it was his turn. I did not speak. Surely he would salvage our collective honor with this routine four-footer.

He yanked it dead left.

The faces in the window turned away, resuming their conversation, reassured that, indeed, God was in His heaven and all was right with the world. John and I slunk off miserably to our rental car in the garage.

Gullane possesses two outstanding places to stay and one equally outstanding place to eat. Greywalls, less than a hundred paces from the Honourable Company's clubhouse, is, for many experienced travelers, the ideal country-house hotel. Its traditional decor (antiques, chintzes, old dark paneling, abundant fresh flowers), its excellent food, and its distinctly clublike atmosphere invite a protracted (if costly) stay. But its real distinction may lie in its exterior. The celebrated Sir Edward Lutyens designed the house almost a century ago (golden beige Rattlebags stone from a local quarry and red roof tiles made especially for it in Holland), and the equally celebrated Gertrude Jekyll, so often his partner, laid out the ravishing formal gardens. Be sure to visit it, regardless of whether you are staying here. Incidentally, a reservation at Greywalls is no guarantee of a game at Muirfield—but it doesn't hurt your chances.

The other extraordinary accommodation in Gullane is called Seahouse. It is not a hotel. A stout brassie down the lane from that nonpareil 7th tee on Gullane No. 1, this is a handsome late nineteenth-century stone residence—gables, chimneys, high-ceilinged principal rooms with long windows, unobstructed views across the Firth toward Fife, rear garden sloping down toward the sea—that is offered for rent, generally by the week, from April through October. Unlike Rosslyn Castle, Seahouse comes fully staffed. It sleeps nine (eleven in a pinch), and the cooking is as fine as the house and the setting.

As for the restaurant, it is called La Potiniere, it is on the main street of Gullane, it is very small (capacity 26), and it is renowned for its French-inspired cuisine. Hillary Brown cooks, David Brown serves (and presides over the wine cellar, which, he once admitted to me, is larger than the dining room). The meal is complete and prix fixe and leisurely—the better part of three hours. There are no choices. You eat whatever Hillary is cooking—perhaps mousseline of sole and smoked salmon, pigeon breast with chanterelles and lentils, and a soufflé glace au

Praline with raspberry sauce. Don't be like Paddy Hanmer's New Zealander: book La Potiniere well in advance.

Four or five miles beyond Gullane lies North Berwick, with its two widely curving bays, its pretty protected harbor, and the rocky islands of Bass Rock, Fidra, the Lamb, and Craigleith distinctive features of its seascape. Developed during the nineteenth and early twentieth centuries as a golf and holiday resort—it was then that the substantial Victorian and Edwardian residences that give the town its air of dignity and permanence were built—North Berwick has never gone out of fashion, chiefly, one suspects, because the two courses, both seaside, have continued to attract golfers from all over the world.

The East (or Burgh) Links is the lesser of the two and should be thought of strictly as holiday golf. James Braid had a hand in expanding it from 9 to 18 holes in 1906, and Philip Mackenzie Ross revised it following World War II. Like Pebble Beach, it is a headlands course, stretched out high above the sea and affording uninterruptedly delightful views, which, on the way in, encompass the town. The overall length is less than 6,000 yards, the fairways are vast, and there is no rough to speak of. But the one-shotters—particularly the 4th (190 yards), the 9th (250 yards), and the 16th (200 yards)—are quite testing, and with the breeze out of the west so are a handful of the par fours. Few Americans of my acquaintance have ever played the East Links, but those who have think of it warmly and with a smile.

It is the West Links, home of the North Berwick Golf Club (A. J. Balfour, later Prime Minister of Great Britain, was captain in 1891 and 1892, and Burt Lancaster was a member in the 1970s), that gives North Berwick its fame. Golf, more or less as we know it, has been played on this stretch of linksland for at least 175 years.

Remarkably, for more than a hundred years the best holes have been changed very little. This is a course on which dunes, beach, burns, blind shots, and stone walls are the order of the day. It is, like the Old Course itself, a narrow out-and-in scheme—the 9th green is the farthest point from the clubhouse—but here the plan is a figure 8, albeit with a somewhat compressed look about it. We start along the sea for three holes, turn left at the short 4th and stay "inside" (though scarcely inland) through the 9th, return to the sea at the short 10th, following the strand through the 14th, then edge right to play the last four holes "inside." There is a charming unpredictability about this routing plan, but then, there is an element of surprise about much of the West Links. And it begins with the 1st hole.

Called "Point Garry Out" (the 17th is "Point Garry In") and measuring just 328 yards, the opener, with the beach tight along the right, is unusual and unnerving. A vast sandy area some 190 yards from the tee isolates the well-elevated green from the fairway, forcing us to lay up with our drive and then play a longer approach than we otherwise would to a target perched above on a spit of land. The green, partially hidden, is firm and fast and slopes wickedly right toward the rocks and the sea. Entirely natural, this hole also strikes me as wholly original. It is great fun, great sport—and potentially ruinous. Johnny Laidlay, one of North Berwick's most famous sons and winner of the British Amateur in 1889 and 1891, once got down among the rocks in a playoff for an important cup and took so many shots, all un-availing, that he finally picked up his ball.

The next two holes are long, wonderful two-shotters, and when the wind is out of the west they are more like three-shotters. On the 2nd, the view from the elevated tee will not re-assure the timid: the shoreline eats into the fairway on the right, and the slightest push sends us down onto the beach. The power hitter will, of course, bite off as much as he thinks he can chew, but it is a dicey business. On the 3rd, 460 yards, the sea again imperils the drive and a low stone wall must be carried on the second. Only with the wind at our back can we dream of a total of 8 on these two tartars. After playing them, we are not surprised that the course has, from time to time, served as a qualifying site for the Open.

There is a matchless trio of holes on the inbound nine. On the 355-yard 13th, the green is set in a small hollow between another of those North Berwick low stone walls and the sand-hills. It is one thing to have to clear the wall on our approach, but quite another to learn that this obstruction actually marks the collar of the green. It is thus possible to incur an unplayable lie on a putt! This is one of the North Berwick holes that has about it, to use Donald Steel's felicitous phrase, "a whiff of ec-centricity."

The 376-yard 14th, called "Perfection," may not live up to its name, but it is a dandy nonetheless. Here both shots are blind, the drive into wildly choppy terrain and the iron over a diagonal ridge and downhill to a bunkered low-plateau green not two strides from the beach. We are hitting straight out to sea on this second shot, trusting that somewhere down there is a safe harbor. Choosing the right club is as critical as swinging it smoothly.

Which brings us to 15, called "Redan." It is perhaps the most copied hole in the world. The green on this 190-yarder is hidden from the tee beyond a fearsomely bunkered ridge, though the flag itself can be seen. Angled away from the line of flight behind a deep bunker under its left front flank, the green also slopes off to the left and the rear. Complicated as that all sounds, the hole does reward the properly aimed and struck shot. Charles Blair Macdonald simulated it—perhaps even improved on it—at the National Golf Links of America, his incomparable layout at Southampton. Among the many superb holes on this, America's first great course, is the "Redan" 4th.

Speaking of Macdonald, we are again reminded of him at North Berwick's 16th, a 400-yarder where our drive clears first a wall and then, with any luck, a ditch about 200 yards out. The green here may be the only one of its kind in the British Isles, a long, narrow surface divided into three parts, from front to rear: plateau, hollow, plateau. It obviously inspired the similarly eye-popping 9th green at Macdonald's mighty Yale University course.

For sheer golfing pleasure—a pleasure bred of variety, unpredictability, challenge, and proximity to the sea—few courses surpass North Berwick's West Links. Admittedly, it is old-fashioned and, on occasion, even odd. But it is irresistibly old-fashioned and irresistibly odd.

A couple of miles west of the A198, the road linking North Berwick to Dunbar, there is a new course. Called Whitekirk, it opened in June 1995, and is a public course that welcomes everybody at all times. It was laid out by a young Scot,

Cameron Sinclair, whose previous design experience was confined to courses in the Far East. On the basis of this eighteen—6,420 yards, par 71—the future should find him in demand back home. On 160 acres of high, hilly, and treeless land, he has imaginatively routed a series of holes that are never less than good and, on at least one occasion, can claim greatness: this is the thrilling 420-yard 5th, which climbs, veers left in the tee shot landing area (a trio of bunkers here), and then plunges precipitously into a hollow only to rise even more precipitously to a shelf of green angled to the line of the long second shot.

Despite its location a good five miles from the sea, Whitekirk is distinctly linkslike in feeling, thanks to its openness, its undulating fairways (which are generally broad), its spirited greens (sometimes unaccountably narrow), and the marvelous naturalness that imbues it all. Blind and semiblind shots are not scarce. This is minimalist course design—very little earth was moved, and relatively few cavities were dug (the bunkering is light). There is gorse, but no heather. Water on the right imperils the drive on the 389-yard 11th and the second shot on the 13th, which, at 447 yards, is the longest of the two-shotters. The numerous lofty tees afford 360-degree views of the world of the East Lothian region, with rich farmland ringing the course, an occasional village catching our eye, Berwick Law and Bass Rock in the middle ground, and Fife itself on the horizon across the great Forth. On the grand 220-yard 17th we take dead aim on the Isle of May. And as we stand on the noble 18th tee, the ruins of Tantallon Castle lie far below on our left, Dunbar off in the distance to our right. It is all gorgeously distracting. Does Whitekirk, you may ask, deserve a place in the galaxy that includes Muirfield and Gullane No. 1

and North Berwick and Dunbar? It does. What's more, the green fee is about half what you will pay at those courses.

One final note about this newcomer: at the foot of the great hill over which many of the holes are laid out (and which does indeed call up Gullane Hill) is the endearing hamlet of Whitekirk, with its substantial fifteenth-century church and its two-story sixteenth-century barn, both built of what is now a deep rust-brown stone. Only a few steps from the old church is Whitekirk Mains, an attractive eighteenth-century farm-house of considerable character—on the exterior at any rate—which happens to be a B&B with all of three rooms, each of which has its own bath. Moreover, it is the property of George Huer, the canny developer/owner/operator of the golf course. My wife and I have not been inside it. Mrs. Huer runs it and Mr. Huer assured us that it is quite comfortable. I don't doubt it for a moment.

Continuing on to Dunbar, the easternmost of the East Lothian courses, we are no longer in the Firth of Forth, but out on the North Sea itself. If you wish to ingratiate yourself with the locals, you will put the emphasis on the second syllable, Dun-BAR. It took me only 20 years to catch onto this, and now that I have got it right, I find myself going out of my way to proclaim the word.

Like North Berwick, Dunbar is also a seaside resort, though the stateliness of the former is missing here. There are 20 hotels, miles of attractive beaches, two picturesque harbors, the Dunbar Winterfield Golf Course (about 5,000 yards long—I have not played it), and the Dunbar Golf Course, where the links served as a qualifying site for the 1992 Open, held at Muirfield.

The start of the round at Dunbar is unusual and unprepossessing: a couple of flattish and prosaic par fives run back and forth beside each other. They are inland in character. So is the 3rd, a falling one-shotter with its green squarely beside the clubhouse, but it plays straight toward the sea and holds out the promise that we are soon to taste the golf we have come for.

It is with the 4th that the real Dunbar commences. The next 14 holes are laid out—sometimes shoehorned—between the old deer-park's high and handsome fieldstone wall and the sea. This is no place for a slicer; the boundary wall nags all the way out and the rocky beach threatens all the way home (well, at least through the 17th, for the 18th is on the landward side of the wall, clustered there with the first three holes).

There is a pleasantly rolling quality to this long strip of land beside the crescent of bay. On the whole, the bunkering is light, but gorse rears its prickly head from time to time. The 7th, 386 yards long, is a particularly good hole, doglegging right and with a semiblind second shot over gently rising ground down to a green tucked between the great wall and a beautiful old barn called Mill Stone Den. On the rather easy par-four 8th, a steep ridge backdrops the green. Nine, the longest hole on the course at 512 yards, is inviting. A solid drive along the flat brings us within sight of the Barns Ness lighthouse and sets up a full-blooded 3-wood that, sailing high above the tumbling, sloping fairway, should put us within a very short pitch of the green far below.

The inbound half is played essentially along and above the

North Sea; and into a westerly it can be a beautiful but losing battle. Four of the two-shotters measure 414, 464, 436, and 441 yards. Not only are they long, but three of them are perilous, with the greens at 12, 14, and 15 sited above the rocky shore. Land is at a premium now, so much so that by the time we reach the 166-yard 16th the space between the stone wall and the beach is a scant 30 yards.

It is not easy to call up any stretch of holes with lovelier views than those at Dunbar. On a fine day, the blue of the sea is a cobalt reflection of the blue of the sky, the gannets chatter away as they dance from rock to rock, the fishing smacks net their catch not a mile offshore, and the Isle of May and Bass Rock and the distant outline of Fife all vie for our attention.

There is, of course, much to see and do out here in East Lothian, though a great deal of its natural glories can be appreciated without ever leaving the seaside golf courses. The town of Dirleton, on the road between Gullane and North Berwick, boasts two triangular village greens and a thirteenth-century castle, the substantial remains of which encompass a garden and a seventeenth-century bowling lawn. Half a dozen miles inland, Haddington is an ancient royal burgh of charm and substance, but its most beguiling moment lies well away from the town center, where the Church of St. Mary, dating from the thirteenth century, stands on the banks of the river Tyne. An arched sandstone bridge over the water provides a prospect that, both upstream and downstream, is idyllic.

Dirleton is also the home of a well-regarded inn, the Open Arms (a poor joke, but what can one do?). The guest rooms incline to be rather small, but the cooking—a "Taste of Scotland" menu is featured—is of a high standard. For those who wish to stay in North Berwick, the Marine is an imposing gray-stone turreted Victorian hotel adjacent to the 16th fairway of the West Links and affording splendid views to the Firth. Large sums have been spent in recent years to transform it from a once somewhat dreary hotel to a sparkling, comfortable, up-to-date place providing just about any service. Much closer to the 1st tee are Blenheim House and Point Garry, small hotels that also make a specialty of catering to golfers. Both are quiet, spic-and-span, professionally run. Neither makes any claim to luxury. But Blenheim House has, in Room #15, a spacious accommodation with a large bay window that commands the vast municipal putting green, the 1st tee of the wonderful old links, the strand, and the sea. Like all of East Lothian, it is all we could wish our seaside travels to be.

Two for the Road: Powfoot and Southerness

The drive from North Berwick down to Powfoot takes a little less than two and a half hours. We head first toward Edinburgh, picking up the A702 south of the capital and sticking with it, on a southwesterly heading, through West Linton and Dolphinton and Biggar. At Abington we take the A74 south, leaving this highway at Lockerbie and following the signs to Annan.

I don't know anyone who has played both Powfoot and Southerness. Tom Doak, the golf architect and a marvelous writer on the game, has been to Southerness and insists it is "not . . . worth a special pilgrimage." So, you may wonder, what—or who—prompted me to make the drive down to the Solway Firth to visit these two outposts? Well, it was Frank Pennink, like Doak a golf architect, but also English Amateur champion in 1937 and 1938 and a Walker Cupper in 1938. Exactly 20 years ago he published a book called *Frank Pennink's Choice of Golf Courses*. Not long after, I lucked across a copy of it in a Charing Cross Road bookshop, and ever since it has been my basic guide to the courses of the British Isles. The late Mr. Pennink liked both Powfoot and Southerness. A couple of summers ago, my wife and I made it a point to get there, and this report is the result of that overnight visit.

This section of Scotland, called Dumfries and Galloway, is relentlessly beautiful. You will not begrudge a moment you spend on the all but deserted roads that roam across close-cropped meadows or climb the lovely Galloway hills or coast through quiet villages or skirt the vast Solway Firth.

Powfoot Golf Club, which holds the distinction of being the first golf club in the south of Scotland to permit play on Sundays, is located four miles west of Annan, at Cummertrees (little more than a crossroads). The clubhouse, with its many-windowed main room, sits on rising ground and affords pretty views across the course to the Firth, which divides Scotland from England. It was James Braid who laid out the course, at the beginning of the century, over an undulating sand-based plain. Powfoot is compact—101 acres—yet there is space between holes and the cry of "Fore!" is rarely heard. Nor is this an out-and-in course. Indeed, holes from the two nines are often intermingled, and the routing plan is attractively unpredictable. No spot on the course is more than five minutes walk from the clubhouse, a happy circumstance should the weather take a turn for the worse.

The name of the club intrigued me. There seemed to me a curiously Native American ring to it: Powfoot. Nothing, as it turns out, could have been further from the truth. The fact is that the course occupies land at the foot of the Pow Burn.

Three longtime members invited me to join them for the

game. They took turns in pointing out the strategies and subtleties of a particular hole, and none of them was inclined to be-
labor the obvious. The two older men had worked most of their
lives at a nearby nuclear power plant, one of them as a safety
technician. "Aye, the stress was severe," he said in response to
my questions. "It never lets up. You knew you had done everything by the book, you had done everything right, you were
certain that nothing could go wrong. And still you worried all
the time. I was glad to retire."

His co-worker, a frail 68-year-old who had suffered a heart
attack seven months earlier and was still recuperating, had once
been club champion. There was an undeniable elegance to some
of his shots, particularly those from about 60 to 80 yards, but
the full hits were lacking in vigor and I had to believe that,
given his age, he was unlikely to regain much of his former
prowess. The third chap, also in his 60s, was a TV repairman
who had been employed by a company that rented television
sets. When the British switched from renting to buying, the
company went out of business and he lost his job.

There was nothing in the least bit melancholy about my
three playing companions. On the contrary—and thanks, I
daresay, to a happy combination of their beloved game (they
play four days a week), their affordable club (annual dues,
£180), and the close comradeship that exists among them—
they were cheerful and convivial, quick to take pleasure in each
other's good shots as well as their own. Golf at Powfoot more
than made up for the shortcomings in the cards they had been
dealt. I thoroughly enjoyed the round with them.

The opening hole here is poor. A 350-yarder from a modestly elevated tee, it plays straightaway, first to a broad fairway,

then to a broad green. Oh, there is a boundary off on the right and gorse off on the left and a couple of bunkers allegedly defending the flattish putting surface, but none of this really makes us stop to think twice before proceeding. Braid was a firm believer in the welcoming start, where a player need face no terrors while seeking to find his swing. This time, however, he was entirely too encouraging, and the result is a hole of blinding banality.

The 2nd makes amends. It is not great, but it is good and it has a true seaside feel to it. A par five of only 477 yards, it aims straight toward the Solway. The tee-shot landing area is constricted by sand on the left, a boundary on the right, gorse both right and left. There is a gentle rise and fall to the fairway, which also tumbles a bit, so that both stance and lie at some point along the way could be awkward. Backdropping the large and undulating green is the sea, the surface of which is punctuated by countless poles on which nets are strung to snare the salmon. Salmon fishing has long been an important source of revenue in these parts.

One of my companions pointed across the water. "England," he said. "You're looking at the Cumberland Hills, with the Lake District not far beyond. There's a very good golf course along the Firth right there, Silloth-on-Solway. You can't make it out from here, but the distance is not that much on a direct line. Still, to get there, you have to drive forever. It's been years since I've played it."

The nine concludes with an excellent three-hole sequence. Eight bunkers surround a somewhat triangular green at the 154-yard 7th, and for good measure high mounds at the front on both the left and right sides make it impossible to see the putting surface, though the flag itself beckons. There is no margin for error: only a sound stroke gets the job done here.

The 8th, 360 yards long, is the best hole at Powfoot. Gorse-clad low dunes frame it much of the way, and there is a lovely cloistered feeling as we move along this sheltered allée. The narrow fairway first edges right, then swings softly left. The constricted landing area, with rough grass on both sides, slopes just enough from left to right that it is difficult to hold. The second shot—probably a 7-iron if wind is not a factor—rises gently to a medium-sized green framed in gorse. You get the impression that not a thimble of earth was ever moved to shape this hole. It is a completely natural gem.

The 9th, on the other hand, was the scene of considerable earth moving, though not by Braid and company. No, indeed, it happened some 40 years later, in the middle of World War II.

A 402-yarder that drifts a little uphill, the hole culminates in a spectacular punchbowl green that gathers and ultimately deposits at its center a variety of second (or third) shots. Still, this green is not the hole's legendary feature. That distinction belongs to a great deep hollow some 80 yards short of the putting surface and eating well into the right side of the fairway.

"This," the former club champion explained as I stood looking down in astonishment, "is a bomb crater. And 'Crater' is now the name of the hole. It was done by a German bomber. We think the target was a munitions plant not too far from here. The bomb blew such a big hole that the club decided to put some sand in the bottom and use it as a hazard. It's something to steer well clear of, and on a day when the wind is against you and blowing from left to right, that isn't always easy."

There are no reminders of the Luftwaffe on the second nine at Powfoot, which, on the whole, is more parkland in feeling than seaside. But there is a lot of enjoyable golf, and I recall with pleasure the par-four 11th, a worthy cousin of the memorable 8th and, like it, sequestered in gorse-covered dunes; and the 15th, a brawny wide-open one-shotter of 200 yards across a swale to a green full of tricky slopes.

Powfoot does not provide great golf, and at 6,226 yards from the back tees against a par of 71, it needs a breeze to be challenging. But the turf is very good, the holes are attractively varied, and the setting on the shores of the Solway Firth is delightful.

My three friends were curious about my next stop. I said I would be playing at Southerness tomorrow morning.

"Ah," said the erstwhile TV repairman, "Southerness, yes, yes, that's been built since the War."

"So it's not as old as our 'Crater,' " said the nuclear safety technician. "I'm not sure you'll like it, not if you enjoyed your game here. It's plain, very plain. Oh, there's a lot of hitting to be done—the two-shotters all seem so long, too long—but it's not Powfoot. No, no, it is not Powfoot."

We spent the night at the Balcary Bay Hotel. It is not down the road from Powfoot. In fact, it is more than an hour's drive, first through Dumfries, then out the coast road signposted for Stranraer. Its formal address is "Auchencairn, Nr. Castle Douglas, Dumfries & Galloway." I suspected that it might be inconvenient, but I allowed myself, as the designated tour guide, to be seduced by the romantic promotional copy: "Dating back to 1625, this Country House Hotel is located in one of the most secluded and enchanting situations on the edge of Balcary Bay, standing in three acres of garden. . . . Heston Isle, the famous smugglers' haunt, serves as the foreground to a delightful panorama of the lovely Solway coast with the Cumbrian Hills in the background. . . ."

It is true, every enticing word of it. Our room—there are 17 guest rooms—beheld this very scene in its entirety. Smartly decorated in traditional English country fashion (which must include chintz and, at the very least, pseudo-antiques), this accommodation was also small to the point of being cramped, a room for one night and one night only despite the scenic charms immediately beyond the broad double window.

I should point out that if you come down to the Solway to play Powfoot and Southerness, the logical place to stay is the town of Dumfries, which straddles the river Nith (picturesque waterfront, fifteenth-century bridge). Dumfries has, I'm told, several very comfortable small hotels, and it is about midway between the two golf clubs.

As my friends at Powfoot warned me, Southerness is plain. But I don't hold that against it, and neither, I believe, will most people who love honest seaside golf. In fact, despite the absence, within its own capacious boundaries, of much in the way of visual charm, despite the merely minimal changes in elevation, and despite the paucity of genuinely unforgettable holes, put me down as a fervent fan of this serious and exacting layout.

Southerness is the most contemporary of Scottish seaside courses, having been laid out in the late 1940s by Philip Mackenzie Ross at much the same time that he was resuscitating the Ailsa Course, at Turnberry, some 70 miles away. Interestingly, the same Mackenzie Ross who used the bulldozer to such wondrous effect at Turnberry moved earth very sparingly here on the Solway, so much so that this links was built for £2,000, including the turfing—not seeding—of it.

This day there were three of us playing, the other two being Bill Remage, the club's secretary, and Mike Williamson, a principal in a management consulting firm specializing in golf-centered leisure facilities. Mr. Williamson was spending a week in the south on holiday with his family. He hit four splendid shots on the first two holes, and I was sure we were to be treated to a round of very like level fours. In fact, he did not strike the ball so squarely over the next 16 holes; in the end, all that we could congratulate him on was his unfailing good humor in the face of adversity.

Mr. Remage, a retired bank manager who had held the secretary's office here for several years, took great pleasure in life (he and his wife had just come back from a most enjoyable trip to Baltimore which found them flying to the States but returning on the *QE II*), in golf (his attack on the ball had a certain rambunctious freedom to it), and in his club (he believes that no man needs better golf than Southerness provides). It was a delight to have him pointing the way.

The ground over which Mackenzie Ross routed the eighteen was once grazing land, and his aim was to make the golf holes as natural looking as possible. He succeeded admirably; one gets the distinct impression that the links simply evolved from the pasture. There is nothing in the least contrived or jarring. Indeed, for some, perhaps a little more spirit, a bit more surprise, might have been welcome, but I did not miss these attributes here. The setting of stern Southerness is sublime: a vast golden beach strikingly backdropped by tall cliffs in the western distance; the embrace of the wooded Galloway Hills in the middle ground; on the far side of the great Firth the rumpled outline of the English coast. How dare the workaday world ever intrude on this peaceful spot?

Peaceful, of course, is not meant to imply calm. A calm day on the links at Southerness is virtually unknown. The members tend to take the blasts in stride. "We don't consider it windy," Bill Remage said, "until the seagulls are walking—and telling the rabbits to move over so they can crawl down their holes, too."

Off the competition, or medal, tees, this is actually a very long golf course. Total yardage is 6,566, but par is only 69. There are just two par fives and neither is quite up to the 500-yard mark, but of the five one-shotters, two—the 215-yard 7th and the 217-yard 15th—may, depending on the wind, require drivers. And of the eleven par fours, eight range from 408 to 467 yards. All your woods get a workout on this straightforward stalwart of a course.

So merely keeping the ball in play will not suffice. You've got to give it a whack just about every time up. However, there is a problem with such aggressiveness: the driving is, if not intimidating, certainly demanding. The fairways are not ungenerous, but miss them and either heather or gorse or bracken will extract a terrible toll. This is particularly true of the heather. On no other course in my experience is that pretty little violet strangler so consistently close to the fairway.

The first seven holes work their way around a large expanse of grazing land, with the heavily bunkered double-tiered green on the short 4th and the elevated "vaulting horse" green on the long 5th (no sand at all here) especially noteworthy. The 8th—here the lighthouse is our target—begins a stretch of holes along the shore that culminate with the altogether splendid

12th, an emphatic dogleg right of 421 yards that plays into the prevailing wind and, once we have turned in the landing area, straight out to sea. The drive must avoid bunkers in the crook of the bend. Now follows a long shot to a semiblind green on what appears to be a small shelf set amidst some decidedly repellent bunkers and humps. Just beyond the green, the ground tumbles down to the beach. There are those who regard the 12th at Southerness to be the finest two-shotter in Scotland.

The 13th, its tee all but cantilevered over the strand, is, at 467 yards, a brute of a par four (we can only pray that the wind this time is at our back), and the final holes now carry us home at a considerable remove from the Solway. By this time we have become used to the extraordinary advertising medium at Southerness: Printed on the bottom of each cup was a product promotion message which, as we bent over to retrieve the ball, was difficult to ignore. An amusingly ironic touch was the advertisement that stared up from the cups on 15, 16, and 17; it read: "BACKACHE? Tiger Balm Liniment."

The excellent 17th perhaps epitomizes the naturalness of the entire course, which has only 65 bunkers. On this 175-yarder, Ross has seen fit to dig no sand holes whatsoever, relying solely on the cunning slopes and hummocks around the long, narrow green to serve as its defense. The round closes with a 495-yard par five on which a necklace of four bunkers strung across the line of flight some 70 yards from the green endangers the long second shot that is not quite long enough.

Championships are held here from time to time—the Scottish Amateur in 1985 and 1995, the British Youths' in 1990—but even these events have not gained for Southerness a large following. I'm inclined to give Bill Remage the last word: "Its remoteness is the source of its greatest strength and its greatest weakness—its greatest strength because it is not overrun by the traveling golfers of the world, its greatest weakness, if you will, because the world does not appreciate what a splendid course this is."

Chapter Three

Ayrshire:
Three Shrines
and Western Gailes

The drive from Southerness up to Turnberry requires about two hours. The first leg of it is by way of Castle Douglas (nearby Threave Garden, open throughout the year, presents almost 200 varieties of daffodil blooming in the spring) and Creetown, on the A75 to Newton Stewart. Here we take the A714 north. The appeal of this particular leg of the trip lies in the immediate accessibility, shortly beyond Newton Stewart, of Galloway Forest Park, some 150,000 acres of forest, moor, bog, burn, loch, and mountain (ten mountains higher than 2,000 feet). At the heart of the park is Loch Trool, with its steeply wooded banks. The road climbs high above the lake to reveal striking panoramas of truly wild and remote country.

Back on the A714 after this brief diversion, we carry on through tiny Barrhill and perhaps even tinier Pinwherry to gain the sea at the pleasant holiday town of Girvan. Some four miles up the coast is Turnberry.

If Mackenzie Ross's superb links at Southerness have yet to catch the world's fancy, the same can scarcely be said of his masterpiece, the Ailsa, at Turnberry. One of the eight courses on the British Open rota (the other seven are the Old Course, Muirfield, Carnoustie, Royal Troon, Royal Birkdale, Royal Lytham and St. Annes, and Royal St. George's), it is guaranteed the spotlight at least once a decade. And in between, the Turnberry Hotel itself is a veritable magnet for people of means.

Stretched out along the crest of a hill, the graceful white Edwardian structure overlooks the links and the sea. The public rooms are bright, elegant, supremely comfortable. So are the guest accommodations, where we find a nice attention to detail (heated towel racks in the bathrooms, terrycloth slippers to match the robes). The cuisine is of the highest order: classical Scottish and French dishes in the main dining room, with its glorious views toward Ailsa Craig; a lighter style of cooking with the emphasis on natural ingredients in The Bay Restaurant; and over at the golf clubhouse, an extensive buffet.

The centerpiece of the spa, which is linked directly to the hotel and which opened in 1991, is a large indoor swimming pool. As you would expect, there are also steam rooms, sauna, a plunge pool, the latest fitness equipment, and a trained staff to provide such cosseting as hydrotherapy, aromatherapy, massage, mud wrap, body polish, and more. What it all adds up to is a five-star golf resort—sophisticated, luxurious, impeccably run—that is without peer at the sea not simply in Scotland but anywhere in the British Isles.

Both of the eighteens at Turnberry, the Ailsa and the Arran, date back to the early years of the twentieth century, and both were victims of the two World Wars. In 1915 and again in 1940 they were transformed into a Royal Naval Air station, complete with miles of concrete runway. Many of the features and contours of the golf holes were flattened beyond recognition. However, not long after the end of World War II, Mackenzie Ross was brought in to undertake the restoration. Using modern implements like the bulldozer, itself a wartime invention, he not only resurrected the links but, in the case of the Ailsa, rerouted a number of holes and endowed the course with a nobility and challenge it had never possessed. The Ailsa that we play today, owing little to its earlier existence, is truly the creation of Mackenzie Ross.

I have two memories of Turnberry that go back well over 20 years. I met a Scot there—his home was Dundee—more obsessed with the game than I. As a boy he had regularly played 72 holes a day. Now he was reduced to a mere 36. He told me that for many years, so enslaved was he by his determination to conquer golf that, when playing alone, if he hit a poor shot at any point during the first three holes he would promptly walk back to the first tee and start all over again. (Is this what is meant by a "traveling mulligan"?) He also revealed to me the secret of the game: "To play golf well, you need big feet, good wrists, and no goddamn brains." My personal inventory was not reassuring.

I also recall the occasion in the early 1970s when, immediately following the overnight flight from New York to Prestwick, I set out on the Ailsa shortly after we had checked into the hotel. My wife chose to walk along. Actually, we did very little walking. This was late March, the sky was leaden, the temperature hovered just below the 40-degree mark, the balmy zephyrs from the much overrated Gulf Stream had surrendered to the frigid gusts by way of Nome, and not a soul was abroad on the links.

We had dressed bulkily for the occasion, which meant that in my case anything even remotely resembling a golf swing was now out of the question. By the 5th hole we were operating in a survival mode, running from one bunker to the next, pitching ourselves face down in the bottom of these sandy pits in a desperate effort to evade the chilling blasts that rampaged overhead. Bunkers in the lee of the great sandhills were more to be coveted than those on open ground, and singling them out became my principal responsibility. Having caught my breath and spotted our next haven, I would climb out, lunge at the ball—golf shots as such, you may be sure, were utterly incidental to our progress—signal to my wife to follow, and race furiously to the next sandy refuge. Thus did we tack our way around this great course.

Yes, the Ailsa will do that to you. Its lure is inescapable. What is more, the case for its appeal can be simply put: golf holes to equal the scenery. Lore is distinctly tertiary, despite the fact that its three Opens have been won by Watson (1977), Norman (1986), and Price (1994).

Consider the visual splendor first. Gazing out from the hotel or from most points on the Ailsa, the eye is ravished. Across the water, with the Firth of Clyde at long last giving way to the Irish Sea, lie the imposing mass of Arran's mountains, the long curves of the Mull of Kintyre, and, nearer still, lonely Ailsa Craig, that striking turtle-backed mound of granitic rock which, rearing out of the depths, is the plug of a long extinct volcano. When the day is truly crystalline, even Northern Ireland's Antrim coast, by the Giant's Causeway, hoves into view. It is all of such grandeur and enchantment that in the entire world of golf no scene surpasses it.

Hand in hand with these distracting seascapes goes a procession of outstanding golf holes, laid out on a stretch of coast that carries us gently up from the 4th tee, only a few steps from a sliver of beach, to the headland heights of the 8th, 9th, and 10th, with the sea now thrashing wildly over the great rocks far below. Inevitably, the same three holes at Pebble Beach, also two-shotters of more than 400 yards each, come to mind as we make the turn on the Ailsa. On the Carmel Bay course the sea awaits on the right; at Turnberry it is on the left.

You must make it a point to walk out to the championship tee on the 9th, unless you are subject to vertigo. Alarmingly isolated on a scrap of turf high above the rocky shore and fearfully exposed to the wind, it calls for a 200-yard carry across the abyss and past the white lighthouse that is the Ailsa's landmark. The hole itself, measuring 460 yards, has come in for considerable criticism, because both fairway and green incline to shunt the ball away. The criticism seems to me to be warranted, but I dearly love this hole.

The inbound half—and again we are reminded of Pebble Beach—is made up of holes that, once we have left the 11th green, are well removed from the sea, but they are testing nonetheless and have been the scene of high drama in the Open. Who is likely to forget the 55-foot putt that Nick Price rolled down the sloping 17th green in 1994 for an eagle to snatch the old claret jug out of Jasper Parnevik's hands? Or the even more miraculous shot executed by Tom Watson on the 15th, a long par three with a chasm to the right, in his epic victory over Jack Nicklaus in 1977? Nicklaus held a one-stroke lead as the two, playing head to head, teed off on the 69th hole. His 3-iron finished not 30 feet from the cup. Watson just missed the green to the left, and now elected to rap the ball with his putter. Rap it he did—off the hardpan, over the apron, tight to the putting surface and true to the unattended flagstick some 60 feet distant, a straight-on contact with the pole, then gone, down, an astonishing 2 where he had been in danger of taking 4.

"Was it," I once asked Nicklaus, "the most unexpected shot ever hit against you at a critical moment in a major championship?"

"Well," he answered, "that one was a big surprise. I thought there was a chance I would add to my lead, and suddenly we were even. But I got an awful lot out of my short game that week. I'm not sure I hit the ball all that well. Watson obviously played fantastically, and he played one stroke better than I did." Clearly, the memory did not rankle.

Just how great a course is the Ailsa? At the least it is one of Scotland's four finest (the Old Course, Muirfield, and Royal

Dornoch being the other three, in my opinion). And the most? There are those who believe it to be the best.

Small wonder, then, that its sister eighteen, the Arran, is often overlooked. Yet this course, a par 69 layout measuring 6,310 yards, has plenty of spunk. Four of its two-shotters are in the 440-yard range, and two of its short holes—the 230-yard 7th and the 215-yard 17th—often demand a driver. Unlike the Ailsa, the Arran does not skirt the sea and offers little in the way of elevation changes. What it does have in abundance, however, is gorse, so much gorse, in fact, that the holes are generally isolated from each other and we play much of the round in private, believing that there must be no more than a handful of golfers on the links this day.

The late and much-loved Henry Longhurst, in an essay published nearly 40 years ago, wrote: "In those long periods inseparable from wartime service when there is nothing to do but sit and think, I used to find myself sitting and thinking of the time when once again we might be playing golf at Turnberry." Visit it just once and you will understand his longing.

Some 20 miles up the Ayrshire coast—we are heading due north now from Turnberry, toward Glasgow—lies Prestwick, where the British Open was born in 1860, where it stayed put till 1873 (the year of St. Andrews' first Open), and where it was staged a grand total of 25 times, serving as the championship's venue for the last time in 1925, when Jim Barnes, a Cornishman who had become an American citizen, won. By then Prestwick was judged too short, too gimmicky, too old-fashioned, too confined for the thousands of spectators.

The club was founded in 1851 with a course of 12 holes (six more were added in 1883). Old Tom Morris, whom one instinctively thinks of in connection with St. Andrews, came to Prestwick when it opened to serve as custodian of the links, or greenkeeper. It was here that he won his four Opens (1861, 1862, 1864, 1867) and here that his son, Young Tom, succeeding him as champion, won three of his four (1868, 1869, 1870). Over the years that followed, the roll call of Open winners at Prestwick would include one amateur, Hoylake's immortal John Ball, Harry Vardon (three times triumphant on this links—1898, 1903,1914), and James Braid.

Worth singling out is Braid's victory in 1908, particularly when speculation arises as to how good those early champions actually were. His total for four rounds was 291, a mere three strokes over level fours, and this despite an eight in the third round. Mind you, that was almost 90 years ago. Picture for a moment the equipment Braid was using, the assorted—ill-assorted!—wooden-shafted clubs, the primitive balls. Then think of what the condition of the course must have been—you didn't carry a "rut-iron" just for the fun of it (there is no free lift from a rut)—rather a far cry from today's exquisitely groomed turf. As recently as 1985 Sandy Lyle won at Sandwich with 282. Two years earlier Watson took the title at Troon with 284. Those scores are not all that different from Braid's 291 at Prestwick in 1908.

Well, it is time to get to the first tee—and, having arrived there, perhaps to turn right around and head back to the clubhouse. Here is a truly demoralizing opener. Its name is "Railway."

The hole is only 346 yards long, it is level, it is straight. Yet it is boldly confrontational. There is a high stone wall hard against the right side from tee to green, and edging in scarily from the left as the fairway narrows is scruffy low duneland dense with gorse, heather, and sand. The green itself is smack up against the wall (shades of North Berwick's 13th!). There is no safety here, not on the drive, not on the approach. The slightest fade on either shot, very possible if the breeze is off the sea, puts us over the wall and on the railroad tracks, bouncing briskly along toward Glasgow. A pull or hook will not result in penalty strokes, merely in penalizing rough or penalizing sand. It is a memorable beginning and a fair harbinger of much that is to come.

Prestwick has it all: towering sandhills, fairways straight out of a moonscape, hidden greens cunningly defended by humps and hollows, two of the world's most storied blind holes, one of the world's three or four most spectacular sand bunkers, fairways and greens of true seaside turf, and, withal, a handful of golf holes that, by any standard, are superlative. Like North Berwick, Prestwick, so little changed over more than a century, may indeed be a monument to the era of the gutta percha ball. But it is no tombstone. The golf here continues to be gloriously vital.

Once past the fearsome 1st, we have only to wait till the 3rd for another dose of danger. It is provided on this 490-yard par five by the fabled "Cardinal" bunker. This vast excavation—10 to 12 feet deep, its sheer ramparts faced with great timbers standing on end and stretching from one side of the fairway to the other—imperils either the drive or the second shot, depending on the wind. It was here that Braid took the 8 in 1908, as Bernard Darwin has described it, "playing a game of rackets

against those ominous black boards." Pete Dye visited Prest-
wick for the first time in 1963, and the result is plain to see at
Crooked Stick, PGA West, and the TPC Stadium Course at
Sawgrass.

The 4th, bending from left to right and with the burn bordering the right side of the fairway, is generally believed to
have introduced the principle of the dogleg and is thus historic,
but it may strike today's golfer as unexceptional. This is not the
case with the 5th. Emphatically not. It is not only exceptional,
it is very nearly irrational. Called "Himalayas," it is also terrific
fun. A one-shotter of 206 yards, this is a blind hole. Rising between tee and green is the implacable bulk of a 25-foot-high
sandhill covered with wild grasses. We take aim at the small
white stone marker in the face of this massive hump and let fly,
trusting that our 3-wood will come to rest somewhere on the
invisible putting surface beyond. Our trust is often misplaced,
for the green is also defended by five pot bunkers, one on the
right, one at the front left, three on the left. If nothing else, the
5th at Prestwick keeps us on tenterhooks.

Now come five consecutive two-shotters, four of them quite
long, all of them worthy (and testing in a more orthodox fashion), with the 454-yard 10th a marvelous hole. Our drive from
the "Himalayas" ridge of sandhills must first clear the burn, as
we strike out toward the sea. There are ravenous bunkers on
both sides of the uphill landing area, and the hole now climbs
into the prevailing wind, with pits corseting the fairway on
both sides as we struggle in vain to reach an elevated green that
itself is appropriately free of sand. It is too much to ask that we
should get home in two, but what an altogether splendid hole!

The 11th, a 190-yarder over broken ground to a green

ringed by six deep pots, calls for nothing less than a perfect shot. I recall hitting just such a shot with a 2-wood into the teeth of the wind the first time I played the hole. The ball finished some 25 feet from the cup. Standing behind the green when I came up was a man wearing a sleeveless sweater over a shirt and tie. I wondered what he might be doing out here— looking for lost balls, taking a walk, observing the play? "Well done," he said as I approached my ball. "Very well done." I smiled and nodded modestly. I then proceeded to charge the 25-footer 6 feet past the cup and leave the return 3 inches short. He now said, "Rather buggered that one up, didn't you?" I did not smile and nod. I would cheerfully have buried my putter in his skull.

The 12th is a straightaway and heavily bunkered 500-yarder (10 pits, 9 of them marching along on the left from the tee-shot landing area all the way to the green) that plays along a protected valley shaped by low sandhills. A good chance for a birdie. The par-four 13th is a good chance for neither a birdie nor a par. Except for an invisible pot bunker in the middle of the fairway about 240 yards from the tee, there is no sand. What there is is length (460 yards), another channel-type fairway, this one with more than its share of uneven ground, and a small (only 15 paces deep) convoluted green that is not receptive to even the shortest pitch let alone to a fairway wood. In its own quirky way, a hole of great style and distinction and, for many observers, the very best on the course.

The 17th is the most famous hole at Prestwick, and for more than a hundred years it has been one of the most famous holes in the world. In 1912, when the reigning U.S. Open champion, Philadelphia's Johnny McDermott, made his first visit to

Britain, he wrote home to fellow Philadelphian A. J. Tilling-
hast, boasting of having made a birdie three on the "Alps."

The hole is 383 yards long. From the slightly elevated tee,
the fairway stretches away flat and straight and ample along a
valley between two sandhills. There is a rather steep mound in
it at about 220 yards, after which it flattens out for a bit, then
climbs precipitously and, in the process, narrows absurdly. At
its crest, the fairway is not a dozen paces wide, little more than
a path now, or, more functionally, a line on what one trusts is
the direction to the green. Before attempting your second shot,
you must walk forward, ascend the hill, and reconnoiter. At the
pinnacle, "like stout Cortez on a peak in Darien," look down,
straight down; your gaze will not encompass the vast blue Pa-
cific, but, in fact, a vast deep bunker with the green on the far
side of it. Say what you will, it is one of the indelible moments
in golf.

Which, I am afraid, is rather more than one can say about the
home hole, a 284-yard par four where we aim on the clubhouse
clock and, if we manage to steer clear of the sand that threatens
only the drive, might well come away with a 3. The danger
here, such as it is, is an indifferently struck little pitch that
wanders far from the hole—the green is 141 feet deep. It may
well be a good match-play hole, with birdies and bogeys as
common as pars.

"So ends Prestwick," wrote Darwin in *The Golf Courses of the
British Isles,* "and what a jolly course it is, to be sure!" As ever,
his adjective is apt, and appears to apply equally to the club.
That was certainly the impression I got from a conversation
with Walter Hagen, Jr., a longtime overseas member.

"It's been a wonderful thing, membership at Prestwick," he

told me, "and it goes back to the strong feelings I've always had for Britain because of my father's success in the British Open [Walter Hagen won four times]. I don't think there's any other club like Prestwick. They put together these matches where you play seven holes out and seven holes back and you have as many players on each side as want to play. The sporting aspect of the game is so important there; it always has been. Sport and tradition. You wear your coat and tie to the club, you have a kummel, you eat lunch, then go out for the game, come in and put your coat and tie back on and have another kummel. Wonderful club!"

Very nearly next door is Royal Troon, which managed to get along for exactly one hundred years without that exalted appellation. It was in 1978, on the occasion of its centenary, that Troon became the newest of the "royals." No golf club has been so honored since.

The very word itself, *Troon,* has a Robbie Burns Scottishness to it that we take pleasure in articulating. There is an inclination to linger on this single syllable, to retain it on the tongue an instant longer than the letters themselves might merit. Would that the course itself was equally inviting, equally appealing. Alas, the magic is often missing here.

This cannot be blamed on the setting. I recall the first time I saw the course, many years ago and in company with my two sons, then 16 and 17. We had slipped out of the Marine Hotel shortly before seven one morning and now we stood there on the 1st tee. There was no one else about. And there was no denying the utter tranquility of the moment, with the links gray-green, severe and shaggy, pockmarked with bunkers, stretching away without interruption down the coast as far as the eye could see; the blue of the water hard on the right all the way, waveless and gentle as it lapped the stone-strewn strand; the peaks of Arran and the Heads of Ayr and, in the far distance, Ailsa Craig, all contending for a share of our attention. It looked as though the links of Troon had been there forever.

Nor does Troon lack in lore. The club has hosted countless important competitions over the years, including six Opens, the last four having been captured by Arnold Palmer (1962), Tom Weiskopf (1973), Tom Watson (1983), and Mark Calcavecchia (1989, in a playoff with Greg Norman and Wayne Grady). Weiskopf, with his characteristic honesty, told the press after the first round of the 1973 Open that he did not like the golf course.

"That's O.K.," a friend said. "Ben Hogan never liked a golf course either."

"Then what do I do?" asked Weiskopf. "Just go out and kill it, right?" He promptly did, his 276 (68-67-71-70) tying the Open record set there 11 years earlier by Palmer.

Like Prestwick, Troon, which James Braid extensively revamped in 1923, offers rumpled fairways, grass-covered sandhills, strangling rough, and ferocious bunkers. But it is altogether more linear and less whimsical than its neighbor. It is a pure links, not only laid out along the sea but at sea level as well. It is a pure out-and-in design. The 9th green is as far as we can get from the clubhouse and still stay on the property, then we turn around and head home.

Almost 7,100 yards from the championship tees, the course is some 900 yards shorter from the members'—and visitors'—

markers. Somewhere in between would probably be ideal, but I doubt that any arrangement of markers would alter the basic fact about Troon: it is, on balance, dull. The first six holes, essentially level, march straight out. The last six holes, also essentially level, march straight in. They are all too much of a piece. There is a sameness that verges on monotony.

As for the "middle six," ah, here is a handful of holes that possess originality, character, and drama. They are fascinating and, in one or two instances, nerve-wracking just to look at. More to the point, they are a joy to play.

At the 355-yard 7th, after six holes paralleling the shore (including the par-five 6th, 577 yards from the tips, the longest hole on an Open course), we turn our back to the sea and drive inland from the first elevated tee. A rampart of sandhill and bunkers in the crook of the right-hand dogleg dares us to cut the corner. Our approach must carry a deep swale and a dune to reach the raised, tightly bunkered green, where only the flag is visible.

The 8th, called "Postage Stamp," is world-renowned. It measures 126 yards from the back (114 yards otherwise) and is the shortest hole on any Open course. Isolated and tranquil in the dunes, it is a pulpit-to-pulpit jewel that gives players of all abilities a chance to make a birdie. The rather narrow tabletop green is guarded by five bottomless pits—one across the front, two at each side. We are hitting straight out to sea and, depending on the wind, may be called upon to play any club from a 4-wood to a pitching wedge. Among the hole's particular admirers is Gene Sarazen. At the age of 71, Sarazen came back to Troon for the 1973 Open—precisely 50 years after he had made his bow in the championship, also at Troon—and proceeded in the opening round, using a 5-iron, to hole the "Postage Stamp" in one! What is less well known is that in 1989, Greg Norman, who would lose in the playoff, bogeyed only one hole, this one, in his dazzling final round 64. Among numerous "Postage Stamp" anecdotes is the one about the woman who hit her driver into the bunker short of the green, then shrilly denounced her caddie: "You underclubbed me!"

The 9th and 10th both measure about 370 yards and both have been subject to revision over recent years in an effort to eliminate the blind second shot on the former and the blind drive on the latter. They are doubtless now more acceptable to contemporary purists and have lost little of their bite, though perhaps a bit of their uncertainty. In the third round of his Open, Weiskopf was tickled pink to get out of the 9th with a double-bogey after he hooked his drive fully 100 yards off line into the chest-high gorse. Forced to take an unplayable lie penalty, he chose to drop the ball some 125 yards behind the spot where he had been fortunate (or unfortunate) to find it. He would later laughingly refer to this strategic decision as "one of the longest drops in history."

The second shot on 10 remains a tester: slightly uphill over some modest ripples and swales to a shelflike green with an embankment of gorse on the left, a nasty falloff on the right. The greens at Troon, which tend to be on the small side, putt reliably and are often quite fast. Dramatic undulations are uncommon, and so, for that matter, are deceptive little borrows.

I have played the 11th as a two-shotter (at both 357 and 421 yards) and a three-shotter (at 481 yards). The last is the Open setup. I urge you to play from the Open tee—and by so doing experience one of the thrilling holes in golf. This despite the fact that it is a short par five, not at all devious, and the level green, a mere extension of the fairway, is defended by one lonely little bunker at the left front. When Palmer won here in 1962, he played the 11th four under par: one eagle, two birdies, one par. Yet he called it "the most dangerous hole I have ever seen." Come now, Arnold, how dangerous can it be? Maybe we should ask Jack Nicklaus. He took a 10 on it that year. And he was not alone.

Like just about any hole you can think of, this one is no problem whatsoever as long as you hit the ball straight, very straight, and solidly. The railway that makes the 1st at Prestwick such a diabolical starting hole is back to haunt us again, running ominously close along the right side and serving as a none-too-gentle reminder that a gentle slice will incur a two-stroke penalty. But some would insist that's not the half of it.

The drive, from a tiny and elevated tee, must carry some 200 yards over a sea of long grasses, heather, and gorse to an angled fairway no more than 30 yards wide. And standing expectantly there, to devour the "steered" tee shot that somehow manages to hang left when it should slide right, is indisputably the most robust, the densest, the man-eatingest jungle of shoulder-high gorse in all of Scotland. If ever there were a time when a player must trust his swing—and when that swing must be worthy of this trust—surely the 11th at Troon is that time. Let the tiniest seed of self-doubt take root and the outcome will be calamitous.

As for the long second shot, it too is a tiptoe on a tightrope between gorse and railroad, only now the railroad's encroach-

ment has grown even more disturbing, for the green nestles in
the very shadow of the low stone wall separating it from the
tracks.

The last of Troon's wonderful "middle six" is the 12th, a
380-yarder that, into the prevailing wind, plays more like 425.
Not a patch on the 11th for pure drama—I doubt we could sur-
vive two such holes in a row—it doglegs ever so slightly right,
the fairway characteristically pitching and heaving. There is
throttling rough every foot of the way, and the slightly raised
green is guarded by a bunker on the right and a sharp little
falloff on the opposite side, where a second bunker awaits.

Now we head home, rather consistently on the straight,
rather consistently on the flat, and, sad to say, rather consistently on the dull. The holes are not easy. There is yardage
enough, and there is sand more than enough. It is interest, variety, and flair that we miss.

One word of caution as you play to the 18th green: do not
overclub. The attractive stone clubhouse, its broad facade a
many-windowed thing, looms all of seven paces behind the
green.

Troon is an honest links, sturdy, four-square, rigorous. The
sea, the wind, the sandhills—all are there. So are the penalizing
bunkers and the punishing rough. But if you tee off without
anticipating the pleasurable excitement of a truly great seaside
course, you will enjoy your round a lot more.

Only a few miles farther up the Strathclyde coast lies Western
Gailes Golf Club. Going back a couple of decades, Western
Gailes was, at least from an American viewpoint, little known,

a so-called hidden gem. Never host to the Open, it did not possess the celebrity of its neighbors. But it has become so well appreciated in recent years that it even pops up on the offerings of golf tour packagers. You will want to contact the secretary well in advance of your proposed visit.

As this book goes to press, Western Gailes is in its 100th year, having been founded in 1897 by four Glaswegians who had been playing on parkland courses in the city but were eager to enjoy the game at the sea. In order to make the new club attractive to golfers who, like themselves, were already members of other clubs, they set the annual subscription at only 10 shillings and sixpence, almost as wonderful a value as the lifetime membership dues: £5. I have enjoyed my share of bargains in Scottish golf—after all, in 1971 in high season I paid 75 pence to play a round on the Old Course—but I am still inclined to view the lifetime subscription to Western Gailes as the best there ever was. In those very early days the members shared the greenkeeper's small wooden shed to change and to consume whatever food or drink they had brought down on the train that stopped beside the 1st tee.

Western Gailes looks and feels like one's ideal of a first-rate Scottish golf club at the sea: old paneling (the lockers themselves are millwork to prize!), old leather, old silver, plus magnificent views across the links and, as at Troon, Prestwick, and Turnberry, across the water to the hills of Arran and the bold outline of Ailsa Craig. The clubhouse is actually on a little rise, enough to guarantee the glory of the vista from any of its many windows.

It was a father-and-son team, Willie Park, Sr. and Jr., from Musselburgh (together they won six Opens, four, including the

inaugural, by Willie, Sr.) who designed Western Gailes. Fred
W. Hawtree revised several holes in 1975. Over the years it has
been the scene of a number of important competitions, including the Scottish Amateur, the British PGA, and the 1972 Curtis Cup (this last despite the absence of lady members and
ladies' tees). From the medal tees, it measures 6,639 yards
against a par of 71 (2 par fives, 3 par threes, 13 par fours).

The holes are laid out on a long, narrow strip of land between—you will have already guessed it—the sea and that railway line. You can slice into both. There are dunes and heather
and gorse, and long, spiky marram grass. On terrain that offers
very little in the way of elevation changes, there are gently
raised tees (essential to appreciate the lovely scenery as we gaze
over the top of the sandhills) and greens in dune-framed dells
(the exquisite one-shot 7th, for example) and on exposed
plateaus (the classic long par-four 11th). On seven holes burns
make us think twice, particularly at the 8th and the 10th,
where they front the green. By careful count, there are 100
bunkers, some of them deep pots where a stroke is irretrievably
lost. There is very little—perhaps just enough for visitors—in
the way of blind or partially blind shots. The doglegs are never
excessive, providing shots to angled fairways and greens that
add to the interest without being in the least contrived.

Finally, beginning at the 1st and running without interruption through the 11th, there are golf holes—natural and challenging, fair and fascinating—that we not only take the most
intense pleasure in playing but that actually articulate why true
links golf is the best golf there is. These holes are routed over
the perfect terrain: undulating, mildly hummocky, rising here,
tumbling there, the greens sited exactly where—indeed, *only*

where—the greens should be, the fairways marvelously defined by the low dunes and the wild grasses and the heather. For the longest time—through 11 holes—we suspect that this just may be the perfect seaside course. The greenkeeping itself—excellent turf, silken putting surfaces, precisely cut cups, perfectly maintained bunkers—is a model.

And then, a hundred or so yards down the 12th fairway, we notice, with apprehension, that the ground we are now walking on has none of the character of what we have delighted in from the start. The rippling and heaving are gone; the low, rough-covered duneland that framed the holes has wandered away; and, to all intents and purposes, we play home over terrain that has neither sport nor spirit, though it does have rather more sand (50 bunkers on these 7, the same number as on the first 11, a sure indication that the holes' natural defenses are weak or nonexistent). Is there no saving moment? Yes, the 17th, a 443-yarder that swings left away from the railway after following it for more than half the hole's length. A long ridge, some six or seven feet high in the left half of the fairway, is the critical element. If we manage to place our drive atop it, we have a clear view of the flag tucked away in a nest of hillocks and hollows. But, forced to play from the base of the ridge, we not only have a blind shot to contend with but must get this wood or long iron up very quickly. I know no hole quite like it. It is superb.

Permit me to insist, along with thousands of others, that Western Gailes is a grand place to be and to play, for it is surely no less. But permit me also to suggest that a realistic attitude toward the latter holes may help to make your day here more satisfying—and your memory more pleasurable—than both might otherwise have been.

Ayrshire is not always at the top of a nongolfer's travel agenda, but it has many moments of more than passing interest. Next door to Turnberry and high above the sea on tree-clad cliffs is Culzean Castle, a magnificent late-eighteenth-century house designed by Robert Adam. Eisenhower occupied it as his headquarters for a time during World War II, and a flat in it was later presented to him for his lifetime use. That flat has been converted by the National Trust for Scotland into six beautifully appointed guest apartments, principal among them being the Eisenhower Suite, which consists of two bedrooms, bathroom, and dressing room. Guests in all six accommodations share the round drawing room, the dining room, and the study. We have not stayed at Culzean Castle, but friends who have done so say it was a memorable experience.

For sheer fun, and also within minutes of Turnberry, is a section of the road to Danure which is famous for an optical illusion known as the "Electric Brae." You would swear your car is traveling uphill, when in fact it is going downhill. A few miles north are Crossraguel Abbey, whose evocative ruins provide some sense of monastic life centuries ago, and, in Ayr, the Tam O' Shanter Museum, which commemorates the life and work of Robert Burns.

In addition to the Turnberry Hotel and the Culzean Castle Apartments, there is a wealth of accommodations of all types and tariffs in Ayrshire. Much favored by golfers for many decades is the Marine Highland, a four-star hotel overlooking the 18th fairway of Royal Troon. An elegant and stylish newcomer is the four-star Westpoint Hotel, in East Kilbride, 20 minutes from Glasgow International Airport, 25 minutes from the first tee at Western Gailes, Prestwick, and Royal Troon.

Golfers looking for more than a firm mattress are finding the Westpoint's leisure club (swimming, sauna, squash, fitness equipment, etc.) and Simpsons Restaurant (cooking to rival Turnberry's) attractive indeed. Still, it is the classic seaside courses that draw the golfing visitor to Ayrshire today, and that will continue to exert this pull as long as the game is played.

Chapter Four

On the Bonnie, Bonnie Banks

 Time to leave the golf-rich Ayrshire coast (all told, there may be a dozen links courses here, to say nothing of the parkland layouts) and head north, taking the A736 toward Paisley as we head for Loch Lomond. I would mention in passing—and that is to be taken literally—the Greenock Golf Club, some dozen miles or so down the Firth of Clyde from Glasgow. I am not suggesting that you go out of your way for a game on this old James Braid course, but I do have a soft spot in my heart for it. In 1952, by invitation of the Greenock Golf Club, those of us on the aircraft carrier *USS Wasp* (anchored at the time there in the Firth) who claimed to play the game were invited to compete against the club. The club trounced us, then treated us to an excellent dinner.

I returned some 20 years later to find the course little changed, still a par 68 of 5,850 yards. There are a couple of strong 200-yard-plus one-shotters, with the 7th particularly good—knob to knob along a ridge high on the great hill crowned by the course—and genuinely memorable, but not because of the demand on our swing, though this can be considerable in a fresh breeze. The hole is called "Cross of Lorraine." During World War II, Greenock served as the chief Free French naval base in Britain. Beside the tee, an imposing granite Cross of Lorraine and an anchor were erected by the French as a memorial to their men who died in the Battle of the Atlantic. The townsfolk regularly hike up to this point on a Saturday or Sunday afternoon. To stand on the heights above this shipbuilding center and look down on spires and chimneys and farther down yet to the mammoth oceangoing vessels steaming slowly up the Clyde, and then gaze away to the distant mountains in the north—this is no mean thrill.

Having crossed the Erskine Bridge over the Clyde, just outside Glasgow, we now head up the A82 to Loch Lomond, the southern reaches of which are not 30 minutes from downtown Glasgow. The contrast between the Loch Lomond Golf Club and the Greenock Golf Club could scarcely be sharper. At Greenock the design and construction of the entire course may well have cost less than the excavation and shaping and filling of a single bunker here.

Just before turning off the highway, we spot through the trees a couple of holes on the second nine. The entrance drive itself meanders for nearly two miles across the 600-acre property—mostly wooded, with occasional glimpses of the fabled loch—skirting the 17th green, then carrying along past the 9th hole and the old walled garden up to the columned portico of the great manor house, Rossdhu, which has been converted into the clubhouse. Just getting there from the A82 is a deliciously tantalizing business. Can the golf, one wonders, possibly live up to it?

My first visit, in late July of 1993, was an unusual experience: the club was not in existence and the course was closed. Still, I was expected.

The situation was what might fairly be called *transitional*. David Brench, the original developer—the man with a dream of golf on Loch Lomond—had acquired a lease on the property from the Colquohon family (Rossdhu is their ancestral home) in the mid-1980s and had retained Tom Weiskopf and Jay Morrish to design and build the first eighteen. There would be a second eighteen and a hotel if all went according to plan. But the subsequent economic downturn, which carried into the early nineties, pulled the rug out from under Mr. Brench. The course was finally completed, perhaps six or eight weeks before I arrived, but the property was now "in administration," having been taken over by the Bank of Scotland, the chief creditor. The bank was looking for a buyer.

The scene that greeted me as I entered the great manor house at about 8:45 that morning was not one to inspire a sense of well-being. Restoration work had been halted. The vast and nobly proportioned room was barren—no furniture or furnishings of any kind. Seated against the far wall on a simple wooden chair behind a plank that rested on two "horses" was a man by the name of Donald MacDonald. Mr. MacDonald was an employee of the Bank of Scotland, functioning as a kind of caretaker/overseer/public relations practitioner. It was the PR job that kept him busy. Resting on his makeshift desk was a telephone, and it rang repeatedly. No sooner would he hang it up than it would peal again. The conversation was unfailingly the same, and he was unfailingly pleasant: "No, no, I'm afraid that will not be possible. You see, the course is not open. . . . Well, yes, it is true that from time to time there are those who are permitted to play, but the bank is not encouraging it, no, no, quite the opposite at this time. . . . Do you have an account with the Bank of Scotland? . . . Ah, yes, I understand, I understand. . . . Well, if you were a customer it might be possible to discuss it with your local bank manager and perhaps . . . We are hoping to sort this out fairly soon and be in a better position to respond to requests. Thank you for your interest and your understanding."

In between these ongoing and remarkably consistent displays of courtesy, Mr. MacDonald was somehow able to inform me, piecemeal, that the existence of the course had been widely publicized, that the failure of the developer had been widely publicized, and that the enthusiastic comments of those prominent in the game who had had the opportunity to play here had been widely publicized. Every Scottish golfer worthy of the name knew that a jewel of a golf course lay there on the very banks of Loch Lomond, and half of them, it seemed, were avid to have a go at it. The Bank of Scotland, on the other hand, was not in the golf business and earnestly hoped that someone would come along to take the property off its hands. For the time being—he pointed up to the graceful crown molding, where I could see that the stripping of the old paint had come to an abrupt halt—there would not be another farthing spent in transforming this grand house into an equally grand clubhouse. However, he added, the course was being maintained as though the Open were to begin tomorrow. It would not do to have a prospective purchaser see it gone to seed. I should feel free to tee off—I would be the only one on the course.

Though it was now after 9 o'clock, the mist on the loch had not yet fully lifted. Nor was the sun ever to break through and dry up the heavy dew. But the day was calm, so there would be no battling the breeze on this resplendent parkland course. Trees and flowering shrubs such as rhododendron—this is virtually an arboretum—give it its beauty, its richness and much of its character. A single hole may well display oak, copper beech, silver birch, maple, chestnut, larch, holly, Scotch pine, and Douglas fir. And these are mature specimens, some even hundreds of years old. On more than one occasion it is a tree that dictates the line of a specific shot, as, for instance, on the par-four 15th, where the green is defended on the left by a huge silver birch.

There is good reason why Loch Lomond is singled out in that sentimental ballad. Twenty-four miles long and varying in width between five miles in the south, where the golf club is, and less than a mile at its northern end, it is the largest stretch of inland water in Britain as well as one of the most varied and beautiful. In the north the loch becomes a narrow finger piercing into the Highlands. By contrast, in the south its waters are broad and dotted by many islands, its shores washing pastoral scenery backed by wooded hills.

The course measures just over 7,000 yards from the championship tees, some 6,300 yards from the regular markers. Par is 71. The first nine has few elevation changes. The second nine is far more rolling. There is not a poor or mediocre hole on either side.

The round begins with attractive par fours of 377 and 398 yards, the 1st hole straightaway over ground that very gently rises and falls, the 2nd doglegging smoothly left and requiring that our approach shot clear a low stone wall (not the first time we've encountered such a hazard, though usually it is accounted for by the antiquity of both wall and course) some 60 yards short of what turns out to be a double green shared with the 4th. There is room to swing away on both drives—this is characteristic of much of the course—and the approach shots must avoid sand only on the left.

The 3rd and 4th parallel each other in opposite directions and are separated by fierce high rough that spells lost balls or unplayable lies. At 453 yards, the 3rd is an extremely difficult par four (the solution to this problem is to play it the way the professionals do, as a 506-yard par five) that angles left in the landing area. The gently falling nature of the second shot and the sand-free green are not enough to make up for the distance we have to travel on ground that provides very little roll. On the 4th hole, a hundred yards shorter, the raised green makes an inviting target.

This brings us to the great loch itself, or will after we have struck our iron on the 152-yard 5th, where the deep and narrow green, adroitly bunkered, is sited against a backdrop of the shimmering water. It is a lovely moment, made even lovelier by the anticipation that we now will play some holes—two, as it turns out—along the shore. Indeed, the next hole, in an amusing pun, is called "Long Loch Lomond." In both senses of the word is this true, for the hole, a 500-yarder (626 from the competition tees!) is long and does play 'long the loch, but not, it should be pointed out, smack beside it. A bona fide slice may find the water, but a mere fade will not. There is a saving strip of rough between the fairway and the bank.

As I walked this fairway in splendid solitude, the huge bulk of Ben Lomond on the far side of the water looming above the low-hanging clouds, I thought I heard voices, perhaps members of the greenkeeping crew, but there was no one in sight. For some few moments there was no recurrence of the sound. Then, shortly after I hit my second shot, I heard voices again, this time closer and accompanied by the low, steady throb of an engine. I turned now toward the water. Coming up the loch behind me through the mist, not 25 yards offshore, was a boat—it might once have been a rowboat, but now had an outboard motor—with two men in it. It knifed neatly through the glassy calm of the water's surface. I could make out fishing rods, and as the men chugged past, quite oblivious to my presence, I heard one say, "Farther up, a bit farther up, about a mile on would be the spot." The other said, "Aye," and then they were gone. It was their loch and it was my golf course.

If the 6th is called "Long Loch Lomond," I suppose we should not be surprised to find the outstanding 7th, a 409-yarder that also skirts the great loch, labeled "Yon Bonnie Banks." Here a solitary tree on the left, 90 yards from the green, forces our second shot to flirt with a large bunker just short of the green on the right. This sand, however, often serves to keep a slice from drowning, something Weiskopf and Morrish must have had in mind when they placed the hazard there.

The 8th, a short one-shotter where the green is an island in a sea of sand, turns inland from the loch and carries us past the clubhouse. The drive at the 313-yard 9th is menaced by a bunker in the very center of the fairway; the green is small, intricately shaped, and tightly bunkered. The bunkering throughout is elegant, even artistic, often with peninsulas of turf breaking up the expanses of sand. None of these hazards is harshly penal. Long shots can be played from the bunkers that snare drives. As for those at greenside, they are never pots, where a combination of depth and steep banks renders a stroke-saving recovery unlikely. Weiskopf and Morrish clearly believe in giving the golfer a chance.

It is claimed that these are the first bent-grass greens in Scotland. They are superb creations—endlessly varied in size, shape, and contouring, spacious when the shot to them is long, less generous when it is short. And how true and nicely paced they are. No pains were spared in making these green complexes—the putting surface and environs—as fine as talent, taste, and money can produce.

The 10th signals new territory to be explored, almost all of it quite rolling and much of it with water, not on its periphery, but squarely in the center of things—a stream here, a pond there, wetlands here and there. In truth, the second nine may possess a little more pepper, a little more flair and surprise and zing, than the undeniably excellent but somewhat more passive outward half. The great loch is now at a considerable remove, but great golf is very much at hand, almost as though the architects, no longer sustained (constrained?) by the legendary beauty of the loch, have now unleashed their full powers to make up for any perceived deficiency in this admittedly less romantic setting.

Hole after hole, almost without exception, sparkles, beginning with the dramatic downhill 10th (403 yards, a pond men-

acing the second shot at the left of the green) and culminating
with the classic 392-yard 18th, a cape hole bending left around
Rossdhu Bay, where we aim our second shot on the ruins of the
ancient twelfth-century castle behind the green. And in between are many other wonderful moments, not the least of
which is the aptly named "Tom's Chance," only 307 yards long,
where the big basher who believes he can carry his drive an
honest 255 yards will be tempted to go boldly for the flag
across wetlands that will swallow the shot hit even a fraction off
center. The rest of us will play meekly left and still be faced
with a ticklish little pitch to an elevated green on the far side of
a stream.

Tom Weiskopf has said, "Jay Morrish and I firmly believe
that Loch Lomond Golf Club has the best 18 holes of golf that
we have ever created—or quite possibly may ever create. Each
hole, both aesthetically and strategically, has something special
to offer."

It would be difficult to quarrel with either of these state-
ments. This is an undeniably wonderful course—indeed, a
great course in the opinion of a number of qualified observers.
The holes fall with perfect naturalness on the terrain, a particularly remarkable achievement when you keep in mind that they
were obviously charted right down to the last square inch.
Nothing is forced or gimmicky here. The demands on the
swing are fair and the shot values of a very high order. What is
more, the holes themselves are attractively varied—the only
time I found myself sensing a similarity was on 10 and 13, both
downhill and in the same general direction and both with water menacing the second shot, but since 10 is a par four and 13

a par five and since these are two of the grandest, and best, holes on the entire eighteen, I welcomed the kinship.

I would point out one aspect of the course, not as a cavil, but as something that can scarcely be ignored: it is very much an American beauty. It is lushly, gorgeously green, it is lovingly manicured, and it is the epitome of pristine parkland golf. As such, it comes as a bit of a surprise here on the banks of Loch Lomond. Surely there is nothing else in Scotland quite like it.

About the time of my first visit, another American was taking a close look at Loch Lomond Golf Club and, as I learned much later, he soon decided to acquire it. Lyle Anderson, the developer of Desert Mountain and Desert Highlands, in Scottsdale, Arizona, heads the partnership that now owns the facility and is marketing memberships in the club, mainly to people not resident in the United Kingdom. A limited number of Scots will be able to join. Construction of a second eighteen, this one designed by Jack Nicklaus, is expected to get underway in 1996. The magnificent clubhouse (the eighteenth-century manor fully restored) will provide several suites for members. On the drawing board are cottage-style accommodations for members and their guests.

On my visit I stayed at nearby Cameron House, which, like the Loch Lomond course, comes close to perfection. Set on the southern shores of the loch, it is a traditionally decorated nineteenth-century country house of notable grandeur, charm, and warmth. Three specifics about it stand out: First, I enjoyed here the single finest meal of my life, dinner in the Georgian Room: terrine of highland game accompanied by a compote of quince and cherry vinegar dressing; champagne and melon soup; roast mignon of pork sliced on croustillant and with a grape-and-thyme-flavored sauce; squash mousse, baby asparagus in a filo pastry, tiny new potatoes; and, for dessert, "Blackcurrant Mousse enhanced by an Elderflower Anglaise and a bouquet of Highland Berries." Second, the hotel has, among many other diversions, its own golf course, called the Wee Demon, a nine-holer of 2,266 yards (six par threes, two par fives, one par four) that offers water holes, tree holes, hard holes, easy holes, and, from its heights above the loch, a couple of enchanting vistas. Third, the hotel envisions the day when it will transport its guests by high-speed motor launch directly to the boat landing beside the 18th green at Loch Lomond, a prelude to a round of golf that just may be as marvelous as the round itself.

Chapter Five

Two Big Macs
To Go

Perhaps 20 minutes due north of the Loch Lomond Golf Club you have an opportunity to leave the A82 at Tarbet, and, on the A83, head briefly west, then lengthily south. I urge you to do so. Awaiting you as a reward for your venturesomeness, to say nothing of perseverance, are two of the most wonderful links in all of Scotland: Machrihanish and Machrie. Since Machrie is farther off the beaten track—indeed, since we must take a ferry to get there!—let us head for it first.

The drive south through Argyll is so gloriously beautiful—the great fiord Loch Fyne, the mountains and the glens, the welcoming lochside villages of Inverary, Fornace, and Lochgilphead—that we are almost reluctant to see it end. At Kennecraig we board a Caledonian Mac Brayne ferry (reserve the space for your car well in advance during high season for the nonstop two-hour cruise to the Isle of Islay, pronounced *Eye*-la). This is a big, comfortable ship with a bar, a cafeteria, and a gift shop. On a clear day land is always in sight as we cross the Sound of Jura, to dock at either Port Ascaig or Port Ellen. The latter is only a couple of miles from the Machrie Hotel and its golf course.

Nothing in my years of seeking out remote golf courses prepared my wife and me for the Machrie Hotel. The entrance drive in late August of 1994 was a potholed madness that threatened to rip off not simply a wheel but both axles. Once in, we dared not drive out. The hotel itself—there are 23 guest rooms, plus 15 self-catering cottages, the latter, I suspect, much more habitable than the former—was a disaster of faded or torn or grease-spotted fabrics, chipped and discolored paint, peeling wallpaper, stained and threadbare carpets, severed window sash ropes, you name it. Our own accommodation, quite possibly the best in the house, was a corner room with bath, with a broken lock on the door, scarcely enough floor space to tiptoe sideways around the old-fashioned (read: *small*) double bed, and with two tiny windows and a view of the sea only if you were standing and could bring a vivid imagination to bear as you peered out in search of a patch of water. Ah, you say, but surely the bathroom was a cut above the bedroom. In truth, it was. Not in the least cramped, it had contemporary fixtures, and the piping for the shower was actually encased within the wall, as at home. Relatively, the bathroom was palatial, and well it might have been. I shall not soon forget the telephone conversation I had with the then manager, the excellent Mr. Anthony Chick, in making our reservation.

I asked about the rates.

"At the time you plan to be here," he replied, "the room with breakfast would be seventeen pounds fifty per person per night, which would be thirty-five pounds for two."

"That's thirty-five pounds for room and bath?" I asked.

"Oh, no, no, that rate is *without* bath. *With* bath, it would be eighty pounds per night."

"What?" I screeched. "Forty-five pounds a night just for the bathroom? That's seventy-two dollars—there must be a mistake."

"No," he said. "I realize that it's a considerable difference, but we have very few en suite bathrooms here at the hotel, very few. Most of our bathrooms are on the hall."

Plumbing, which is to say your own private plumbing, comes dear at Machrie. Golf, on the other hand, comes cheap, ten pounds per day—not per round, per day. Nor was dining expensive. The table d'hote dinner, three courses and coffee, was £12.50 per person (just under $20), inclusive of service and VAT. And it was very good, as was the cooked breakfast.

The game has been played here at Machrie for more than a hundred years. It was in 1891 that Willie Campbell, another member of the Musselburgh school, laid out the course. Donald Steel, brought in to revise it in the early 1980s, worked out some of the kinkier kinks, but it is still unique among the first-rate courses of the world: par is 71, and of the 35 full shots thus to be played by a low-handicap golfer, 19 are likely to be blind!

Just how did this come about? From what I was able to observe during the two rounds I played, three factors converged to create this astonishing circumstance: the natural contours of the terrain, the selection of green sites, and the inability—or reluctance—to move ground.

To begin with, this is magnificent golfing country, dominated by grass-cloaked sandhills of all shapes and sizes, some of them very imposing. Within this magical landscape are numerous natural green sites—amphitheatres, punchbowls, plateaus, ridgetops, ridge bottoms. An architect might well commence his task by identifying the 18 best green sites; in each instance he would then work out the route—short, medium, long—back to where a tee might reasonably—sometimes unreasonably!—be spotted. And always he would avoid, like the plague, even the thought of shifting the earth around. The result of this approach to laying out golf holes, given ground of this exuberance, could well turn out to be Machrie. Here the sandhills, modest or mighty, intervene with unprecedented frequency between tee and green to create a game that is, above all else, marked by the thrill of the unknown.

It begins with the 1st hole on this 6,226-yard course. The opener is only 308 yards, but because of the rising ground in front of the tee, and the hollow, at the foot of a ridge, which harbors the green, both drive and pitch are blind. Only the drive is blind on the 2nd, a 508-yarder that doglegs sharply left as it skirts the bank of a fast-flowing stream, also on the left, from tee to green. The uphill 3rd, 319 yards, culminates in a blind and outlandishly terraced green just over a ridge. Four, at 390 yards, plays from an elevated tee with our back to the sea down to a splendidly billowing fairway that blocks the landing area from sight, then up and out of this secluded spot to a blind green beyond yet another ridge. It is a thoroughgoing and suspense-filled delight. The 5th, from a pulpit tee across broken ground, is, I am happy to report, in full view, all 163 yards of it. The green is defended by a large bunker some 12 to 15 yards short of it and a tiny one that eats into the right edge.

This would be the appropriate time to comment on the bunkering at Machrie: it is very nearly nonexistent. There is a grand total of six sandpits, two spent profligately right here on the short 5th, one each reserved for the 1st, 11th, 13th, and 17th. A reluctance to dig holes is abetted by a reliance on the natural contours of the greens themselves—often wildly sloping and/or undulating—and of the green surrounds, which almost always contain cunning little folds and creases, hillocks and hollows.

Now begins a stretch of four exceptional two-shotters that round out the nine. The best is the 6th, a 344-yarder played straight toward the sea from an elevated tee into a dune-framed valley. The drive must be slotted into the left side of the fairway to reveal the green in its lovely dell.

The 7th is unforgettable. Surely this 395-yarder is the blind hole of the world, eclipsing both the 5th and 17th at Prestwick. It goes beyond the merely theatrical into the realm of grand opera, though some would insist it is opéra bouffe. The tee is tucked away in a tiny hollow on low ground. The fairway is— well, yes, just where is the fairway? There is no hint of it or the direction of it, unless your perplexed gaze happens to pick out an overgrown footpath stepping up the immense dune that towers some 40 to 50 feet above you, a good 150 yards out from the tee. Could the fairway possibly lie somewhere on the far side of this shaggy peak? It could and it does. In the calm, your sound swing will get the job done—the forced carry has a value of not less than 185 yards. Into the wind, either cry out for help or locate the forward tee, for you will not surmount this pinnacle otherwise. And to fail is to find yourself—if you can find the ball—in deep and clinging grass somewhere on a slope so precipitous as to rule out both a sensible stance and an acceptable stroke.

The drive that clears this "Alps," this "Himalayas," this "Andes"—in fact, the hole is called "Scot's Maiden," whose meaning I am ignorant of—now plunges down into a vast uneven fairway along and above the sea. Miles of golden sand sweep away endlessly on Laggan Bay. Beyond the Rhinns of Islay, on their promontory some half-dozen miles across the bay to the west, lies the open Atlantic. To the northeast the striking Paps of Jura soar 2,500 feet above the water. No mere golfer deserves it, this extraordinary combination of beauty and solitude and freedom.

What he or she does deserve, having conquered the great sandhill, is a clear shot at the green. It is not there. The green is concealed just over a low ridge, though a high dune behind the broad putting surface helps provide some sense of distance and the shot is thus not the purest guesswork.

The final two holes on the outbound nine also parallel the strand and are, if considerably less eye-popping than the incomparable 7th, excellent in their own right. Both require stout drives over very rough country, and the 9th, 392 yards, turns out to possess a bilevel fairway. We would prefer to land our drive on the left hand, or lower, part, but a boundary is uncomfortably close here. The safe drive to the right, however, incurs a 175-yard approach to a green largely obscured by the shoulder of a hill bulging in from that side.

We play the other two short holes—there are three par threes, two par fives, and 13 par fours at Machrie—early on the inbound nine. The 10th is a 156-yard charmer from a modestly raised tee in the dunes beside the beach down to a green protected by wetlands on the right and the broad Machrie Burn on the left. The 12th could not be less like it. There is a starkness about this exposed and windswept 174-yarder. It rises ever so gently on a suggestion of ridge to a green more than a hundred feet deep that falls off to the left. Beyond the slope is a vast peat moor—the malt whiskies distilled on Islay are celebrated for their distinctive peaty quality—that stretches away to a horizon bounded by dark low hills. Again, the sense of remoteness, of isolation, is palpable.

Now we head back toward the sea, relishing a marvelous assortment of holes routed over characteristically heaving linksland, a patch of bracken here, of heather there, in the fierce rough flanking the essentially generous fairways. High tees continue to provide surpassing views. Blind shots—the second on the par-five 13th, the approaches on 14, 15, and 16—continue to intrigue even as they befuddle.

Which brings us to the 17th. If you have even a hazy recollection of what I said about the 17th at Prestwick, in an earlier chapter, there is no need for me to describe the 17th at Machrie. Suffice it to say that the blind second shot on this 352-yarder— up and over a high sandhill, then vertically down to a green defended in front by sand—is the closest thing you will ever encounter to Prestwick's "Alps." Nor is it in any sense put in the shade by that fabled hole.

Home now, spiritedly, on a 374-yarder that, to the surprise

of absolutely no one, culminates with a totally blind approach shot, this one to a green in the lee of a broad ridge, a green that, though invisible, inclines to welcome our shot.

Yes, it *is* excessive, this astounding eighteen at Machrie. But I insist that the excess is justified, first on the grounds of sheer golfing fun (to say nothing of the challenge to both our psyche and our swing!) and second on historical grounds. The course is a bona fide relic, not so old as North Berwick or Prestwick, but, like them both, a priceless example of the way golf courses were once brought into being.

I make no claim for greatness here; there is entirely too much of the unknowable, the unpredictable, the chancy. What I do guarantee is a full measure of pleasurable excitement in a setting of uncommon beauty.

And one thing more, something I'd been saving till the end to mention as a clincher for those who may be on the fence about spending the time or the money getting to Machrie. If you do go, you will not find it thronged. On the contrary, under ordinary circumstances you will find it all but deserted, even in high season. When we visited this outpost in late August of 1994, there were six others who played the course the day we arrived—four locals and a somewhat elderly couple who have been making the long trip from well south of London, in Kent, twice a year for a dozen years. On the second day of our overnight stay there had been, by the time we departed at 2 P.M., a total of 10 teeing off. On a pretty weekday, in the heart of the summer, the average play is less than 30; on a weekend, when the residents of Islay—there is an Islay Golf Club, which plays over the links at Machrie—are able to get out, there may be as many as 60 on the course during a span of some 15 hours of daylight. Here you find the rarest luxury in the world of out-standing courses that welcome all comers: a 1st tee that, for all practical purposes, is always open.

The hotel being the dodgy business that it is and the links being the eccentric business that it is, Machrie is not everyone's cup of tea. But for those who do not object to simple accommodations and defiantly old-fashioned golf, Machrie can well be, in its own way, a paradise. Nor is it necessary to spend the biggest part of a day getting here. We drove, but you would not have to; Loganair flies back and forth regularly out of Glasgow, landing next door to the links and even offering a one-day package that includes golf, lunch, and round-trip airfare. Still, you should spend the night and play the course at least twice. The second time around not only will you know where you're going, but you will be able to focus on the shots themselves rather than on the mystifying marvels of Machrie.

Well, we are scarcely around the corner from Machrihanish, but once we have debarked from the ferry back on the mainland at Kennecraig we are less than an hour from it, and that run down the lower half of the Kintyre peninsula—hills and sea, sea and hills—is another treat.

The Machrihanish Golf Club was founded in 1876. It was—and so it remains—a classic example of the simple, democratic approach to the game characteristic of most Scots. When in the mid-1960s the present clubhouse, a modest white stucco one-story structure with plenty of big windows, was acquired (it had been the holiday home of a member), no contractor was called in. The stripping of the old clubhouse and the transformation of the new one from private dwelling into an appropriate home for golfers was carried out by the members in their spare time. The bar itself was the handiwork of one member, Ian Wardrop, who, in addition to his obvious skill as a joiner, was also the club's finest player. One can easily imagine the bond that must be forged among members who have actually worked side by side in the fashioning of their own clubhouse.

The Machrihanish Ladies Golf Club occupies its own clubhouse, right across the car park, and has its own nine holes, right beside the regular eighteen. I recall a conversation I had with Duncan MacFarlane, secretary of the club when I first visited it, in 1978.

When he spoke of the ladies' course, I asked whether the women did not also play on the main course.

"Oh, they do, indeed they do. But they must pay for the privilege," he replied with a small smile.

"How much is it?"

"Ah, just over one pound fifty. One pound fifty-four, as a matter of fact."

"So," I said, "every time a woman wants to play on the regular eighteen she must pay about a pound and a half. That seems reasonable enough."

"No, no, no," he said. "Not every time. Just one time is all she pays it. Once a year. That pound and fifty-four is the *annual* fee."

That was in 1978. As for today, in this era of equal rights—and equal obligations—it is probably many times more. But I don't really want to know.

Duncan MacFarlane, who struck me as a man not often called upon to present a gift to a visiting golfer, was waiting for me that same day as I came out of the spartan locker room, having put on my golf shoes.

"I want you to have this," he said, handing me a maroon necktie. "It's our club tie. The bird on it, that's an oystercatcher, the same as on our club flag. You'll probably spot quite a few oystercatchers as you play the round. Especially going out, when you'll be nearer the shore."

Machrihanish measures 6,228 yards from the medal tees against a par of 70.

The first shot here is my favorite first shot in all the world, and the debt is owed to Old Tom Morris, who put his imprint on the course in 1879. From a tee hard by the golden strand and elevated some 10 feet above it, we play this 423-yarder on the diagonal across the Atlantic's frothing combers to a gently rolling fairway tight along the shoreline. The problem is clearly stated: how much of Machrihanish Bay—the beach is in play—dare we bite off on this, our initial stroke of the round? Well, if we are not overly greedy and if the swing be sound, we are away in high spirits for what, we whisper to ourselves, might well be the game of a lifetime.

The 2nd hole is another stirring two-shotter, 395 yards long, where the uphill approach first clears the Machrihanish Water, a little river entering the sea at this point, then sails over a bluff gashed with a pair of large bunkers, coming to rest out of sight on a vast and spectacularly contoured putting surface. Judged on whatever merits you choose—originality, beauty, daring, texture, trueness, pace—the greens at Machrihanish are among the greatest in the British Isles.

At the 3rd hole, a par four called "Islay," dead in our sights is the island we've just visited. Our second shot on this 376-

yarder targets a very deep—144 feet—and swooping green in a dell framed by dunes. The green on the 4th, a beguiling 123-yarder in the dunes, is much too spacious for such a short shot.

Now comes a four-hole sequence that surpasses the 6th through the 9th at Machrie and ranks right alongside 7 through 10 on the great Ailsa. It is all there in this rough-and-tumble stretch of picturesque duneland: elevated tees with breathtaking views across high shaggy sandhills; half-glimpsed fairways pitching and tossing at every imaginable cant or dog-legging gently around sentinel dunes; now a blind green in a hollow, now an exposed green atop a breezy shelf. And the lengths of these two-shotters are so varied—385, 315, 432, 337—that we find ourselves playing to the green with a long iron, a pitching wedge, a full-blooded wood, and a 7- or 8-iron. This is seaside golf at its purest and most compelling, and re-markably, though a worthy test for the scratch player, it is not in any sense discouraging to the 22-handicapper.

The 9th, with its tee tucked up in the dunes beside the beach, brings us alongside the airfield. Over the years this facil-ity has been shared by commercial operations and the RAF. Lo-ganair, as is the case at Islay, offers daily flights to and from Glasgow, just 25 minutes away. In 1978, the first time we vis-ited Machrihanish, our second son, John, took advantage of this service to join us. He was working as a volunteer counselor with underprivileged children in the ghettos of Belfast at that time, and this respite was well earned.

The inbound half at Machrihanish lacks the thrilling duneland that characterizes virtually every hole going out, but it does not lack excellent golf holes, and the movement of the undulating land gives hole after hole real character. Par is again 35, but where the first nine was made up of nothing but two-shotters except for the short 4th, the second nine has an appealing mixture of four par fours, three par threes, and two par fives. Adding to the challenge is the fact that almost every stroke is played either into or across the prevailing wind. Two holes are particularly outstanding, the 505-yard 12th, where a pair of deep sandpits lurk unseen in a swale just short of the green to snare the overly ambitious second shot, and the 233-yard 16th, a murderously long one-shotter over rough country, with par winning the hole eight times out of ten.

Lamentably, as at Prestwick and North Berwick, the home hole is a disappointment. A 315-yarder, it limps along on flat and featureless ground to a slightly raised green with some token bunkering at the left front. Still, on a course that is not rife with birdie opportunities, here at any rate is a chance to improve our score.

In a fairly recent ranking of the best courses in the British Isles, Machrihanish placed 78th. Are there really 77 courses in Scotland, England, Wales, and Ireland superior to this diamond? I sincerely doubt it. For me, it belongs much higher on the list. And as a place to be, taken all in all—course and club and remote, entrancing Kintyre—it has earned a singular niche in my affections.

Returning for a moment to that nonpareil 1st tee perched above the beach, look beyond the green and farther up the coast to the land just past the links, the tilled land. For some years the second farm belonged—and it may still belong—to former Beatle Paul McCartney, who fell in love with this corner of

Scotland, the sea, the green hills of Kintyre, the islands of Islay, Gigha, and Jura. In 1977 he composed a song called "Mull of Kintyre," which he recorded with the Campbeltown Pipe Band (Campbeltown is 10 minutes due east of Machrihanish) and which, with its wistful evocation of this idyllic spot, has had considerable worldwide success. There is no doubt about it: Kintyre—Machrihanish—will indeed bring out the song in your soul. No wonder Michael Bamberger, in his admirable— and enormously enjoyable—*To the Linksland*, said, "If I were allowed to play only one course for the rest of my life, Machrihanish would be the place."

Not 15 minutes below Machrihanish is the fittingly named Southend, a holiday village at the Mull of Kintyre, which is the name given to the peninsula's southwestern tip. The coast of Northern Ireland is a mere 12 miles away across the North Channel of the Irish Sea.

Here at Southend is a golf course, Dunaverty, that measures all of 4,597 yards and plays to a par of 64. It is, in literal truth, a cow pasture. The first time I played it two sturdy Ayrshires were chewing their cud squarely between the markers on the first tee. One of them edged over to permit me room to swing. For the record, this cow pasture is also a sheep meadow. Low wire fences are generally in place around the small squarish greens to deter the wandering livestock.

The local rules conveniently suggest the nature of golf at Dunaverty: "1. SUNKEN LIES. A ball lying in a rabbit scrape, rabbit hole, sheep path, hoofmark, or cart road [the reference is *not* to a golf cart] may be dropped without penalty. If lifted in a bunker, the ball must be dropped in the bunker. The shore is a bunker. 2. When a ball lies in or touching DUNG, or if dung interferes with a Player's stroke or stance, the ball may be lifted and dropped without penalty. The ball may be cleaned. . . . 4. HAZARDS. The Shore and the River are HAZARDS. . . ."

In addition to "the Shore and the River," there are elevation changes, long rough grasses, occasional blind shots, and infrequent patches of gorse, all of which help to give the links spine. And the splendid views—of Dunaverty's Rock and the island of Sanda and the Ulster coast—give it charm. True, we cannot take seriously a course that has only three holes over 350 yards and none so long as 400, but there are four or five very good holes here, including the 240-yard 6th, a heroic one-shotter if ever there was one, and the 387-yard 17th, where the 50-foot-wide Conie Glen Water (referred to in the local rules as "the River") fronts the green, rendering the second shot, if played into a stiff breeze, daunting.

Before I played for the second time at Dunaverty, I visited Angus MacVicar, then 73, at his house, "Achnamar," a simple white cottage at the sea with a front lawn that could have doubled as a putting green. Angus MacVicar was the patriarch of the Dunaverty Golf Club. A tall, slim man, though slightly stooped now, with a full head of silver hair parted in the middle matinee-idol style, he had long enjoyed a considerable reputation throughout the British Isles as an author of adult fiction and of adventure stories for children (the "Lost Planet" series was especially successful) and as a radio and TV personality. His son, Jock MacVicar, was, Mrs. MacVicar proudly informed me, "the golf correspondent for the Glasgow *Daily Express*. He has a piece in the paper this very day." Later, when we were sitting by the fire in the living room, she said with a tinge of regret, "Of course, when there's no golf to write about, then he writes about soccer."

Angus, as warm and easygoing a man as you will ever hope to talk golf with, was the soul of modesty, but I managed to learn that he had been a member of Dunaverty longer than anyone else (47 years), that he was a former captain of the club and many times champion, and that his handicap had crept up to 5. "I'm nae getting the length now," he explained simply and with a rueful smile.

He spoke of the Reverend George Walter Strang of Campbeltown, a force behind the founding of Dunaverty as well as Machrihanish: "He was hauled up before the presbytery on two counts, for playing golf with the local priest and for the excessive time he devoted to the game. Said he to the elders, 'I play with the priest for ecumenical reasons, and I play so regularly for reasons of my health.' "

Because of the power of the kirk (church), there was no Sunday golf at Dunaverty till 1981.

"The annual dues are twenty-five pounds," Angus nodded, "with those of us over seventy now paying just five pounds. The trouble is, people here live so long that the club will surely go bankrupt." We laughed with him.

He told me that James Braid had once had a hand in revising the links, that there used to be a number of bunkers but the winds and the rains had eroded them to the point where they no longer exist as such, that the club employed just one greenkeeper to take care of the course, and that the greens are mowed twice a week, the fairways about ten times a year. Electricity, he said, came to Southend in 1950, only a couple of years before television.

He also spoke affectionately of Belle Robertson, who was born at Southend, learned the game at Dunaverty, and went on to become the leading Scottish amateur in the 1960s and early 1970s (four-time Scottish Amateur champion, three-time runner-up in the British Ladies', four-time Curtis Cupper). He recalled an alternate-stroke match when he was partnered with Belle. "I drove over the dunes and down on the beach and the ball came to rest in a great sandcastle. First we couldn't get it out of the sandcastle, then we couldn't get it back on the hole and we ended up taking—now I'm not sure what it was, but it was well into double figures and certainly a record."

His day was a fairly—and, for him, pleasantly—structured one: writing in the morning, golf in the afternoon. He genuinely regretted that he would be unable to accompany me around Dunaverty that particular afternoon. "A couple of chaps from the BBC are due here from Aberdeen any minute, and I'm afraid I'll be tied up with them for hours. The next time you come this way we'll be sure to have a game."

I can speak from experience about two places to stay in Kintyre. The first is Oatfield House, equidistant from Southend and Machrihanish. An attractive B&B with beautiful gardens and, of all things, a swimming pool, it offers both comfort and style. The big high-ceilinged bedroom at the top of the stairs has a four-poster bed, a fireplace just awaiting your match, a large carpeted bathroom, and a pretty view over the countryside. For dinner, try Machrihanish. The club's food is good, the price is right, and the atmosphere convivial.

The other place is a Landmark Trust property, Shore Cottage, over on the far side of Campbeltown, in the hamlet of Saddell. Turning off the main road, you drive down an embowered lane to Saddell Castle, continue through the low archway in the garden wall, and there, dead ahead, perhaps 150 yards away and precisely at the water's edge, sits Shore Cottage. The surrounding trees and rocks combine somehow to give the white, slate-roofed dwelling a sheltered look, even though it is sited on a spit of land where Saddell Bay meets Kilbrannon Sound, with the Isle of Arran not six miles away across the water.

For me there can be no finer day in golf than the morning round and the afternoon round at Machrihanish followed by a good meal in front of the fireplace at Shore Cottage. I recall taking down Alisdair Carmichael's *Kintyre* from the bookshelf after dinner one evening and reading as long as the embers continued to glow. Then I closed the book and went outside. A few steps and I was standing on the rocks at the water's edge. The night was overcast and calm. Tiny rivulets ran silently between the rocks. I looked across to pastoral Arran. No sign of life there, but I could make out its peaks if nothing else. I went back into the cottage, optimistic that the next day would be equally satisfying.

Machrihanish and Shore Cottage—together they surpass our most immoderate dreams.

Chapter Six

"North to the Links of Dornoch"

 The chapter heading above is pure plagiarism. These same words were chosen by Herbert Warren Wind for his account of a Scottish golf trip that appeared in the June 6, 1964, issue of *The New Yorker*. At that time I had never heard of Dornoch (dubbed "Royal" in 1906 by grace of King Edward VII). But if Wind, the best golf writer this country has yet produced, could say of Dornoch, "It is the most natural course in the world" and ". . . no golfer has completed his education until he has played and studied Royal Dornoch," then I had to get there.

The only time we ever drove from Machrihanish to Dornoch, the trip took six and a quarter hours. On the map—the route runs from the southwestern corner of the country to the northeastern—it looks as though it might take even longer. In fact, today it's probably an hour less, thanks to a couple of bridges at the northern end. It's an unlikely drive, but a rewarding one.

The direct route is up the Kintyre Peninsula on the A83

through Kennecraig, Tarbert, Ardrishaig to Lochgilphead. Here we pick up the A816 for Oban, a picturesque port with ferry service to some of the western islands (Mull, Colonsay, Lismore, and others). The A828 carries us from just north of Oban through Portnacroish to Ballachulish. Quite nearby, at Kentallen of Appin (too small to be on most maps), is Ardsheal House, a handsome and rambling eighteenth-century manor on a hill above Lough Linnhe. In every respect—comfort, serenity, natural beauty (the water-and-mountain views are enchanting), old world charm, and cooking—it is one of the outstanding country-house hotels of Scotland. Bob and Jane Taylor, New Yorkers who stumbled upon this jewel a good 15 years ago and turned their backs on successful business careers in Manhattan in order to acquire and run it, have realized the dream that many of us, at one time or another, have surely toyed with. For anyone contemplating this long drive, Ardsheal House makes a lovely dividing point.

At Ballachulish the A828 runs into the A82, which takes us north through Fort William, along Loch Lochy, the Caledonian Canal, and Loch Ness, to Inverness. Here we join the A9 for the final leg of the long drive to Dornoch.

This is a 200-mile trip on two-lane roads, but since it is unfailingly scenic, we do not mind. The stretch between Lochgilphead and Oban, on the A816, with its arresting views of sea and islands, of lochs and mountains, is one of the two or three most hauntingly beautiful in all of Scotland.

My first trip to Dornoch came seven years after Wind's seminal piece. I was accompanied by my wife, our six-year-old daughter and two teenage sons and the older boy's high-school sweetheart. The two boys were keen golfers already; the three ladies did not play. But everyone loved Dornoch—the royal burgh, the links, the beach, the gloriously beautiful sea and mountain surroundings.

Seven more years passed before I returned, this time with only my wife, and I mention it here because of a brief exchange I had prior to that visit in 1978. I had just finished a game at Royal Birkdale and was introduced to the secretary of the nearby Formby Golf Club, Alan Thirlwell, who asked about the next stop on our itinerary.

"Dornoch," I answered. "We're driving up to Dornoch."

"I've never been there," he said. Then he added, smiling, "It's simply too far north."

Alan Thirlwell, I learned later, was one of the finest British amateurs for some 20 years: English Amateur champion in 1954 and 1955; Walker Cup player in 1957; runner-up in the British Amateur in 1958 and 1972. Yet here it was, 1978, and he had yet to play Dornoch.

For years—indeed, it sometimes seemed, forever—that had been the story as far as Dornoch was concerned. Many knew, generally by hearsay, that the golf was wonderful, but few took the trouble to go up there, on the same latitude as Juneau (which translates into more than 20 hours of daylight at the summer solstice). I remember learning in the late 1960s that Bing Crosby had chartered a small plane and flown in from St. Andrews for a round. I also recall learning, years after the fact, that Billy Joe Patton had made a point to get to Dornoch after the 1963 Walker Cup Match at Turnberry, and that Pete Dye had also played it the same year on the trip that was to have such a powerful influence on his work. But through the 1970s and into the early 1980s it was rarely a priority for most golfers.

Then three things happened: the game exploded around the world; the British Amateur was staged at Royal Dornoch in 1985; and the two bridges mentioned above were built, one spanning the Cromarty Firth, the newer one over the Dornoch Firth. The journey from St. Andrews is now down to 3½ hours, and as a result, from May through October, there are starting times all day long every day of the week. And though it is not overrun by Americans and Japanese, the days of simply breezing in from somewhere south and teeing off are a thing of the past. Dornoch may not be on the British Open rota, but it certainly has taken its place on the touring golfer's preferred list.

The game—or some very rudimentary form of it, as we must continually remind ourselves—has been played here for more than 350 years. Only at Leith (Edinburgh), St. Andrews, and Montrose has it been played longer. The club itself dates to 1877. Some ten years later John Sutherland, who would serve as its secretary for more than 50 years and who would extend the course to 18 holes, invited Old Tom Morris to come up from St. Andrews to lay out "nine proper golf holes."

Five years before the Dornoch Golf Club was founded, Dornoch's most famous son, Donald Ross, was born in the modest row house that still stands at Three St. Gilbert Street, just off the town square. He learned the game on the Dornoch links. (So did his younger brother, Alec, who would win the U.S. Open in 1907.) After a short stint in St. Andrews acquiring the fine points of the game and of golf course design and turf maintenance from Old Tom Morris, followed by six years at Dornoch as greenkeeper and professional, Ross immigrated to the United States and began the nearly 50 years in golf course design and construction in which he would create or remodel more than 500 courses here, including such celebrated eighteens as Pinehurst No. 2, Seminole, Oak Hill, Inverness, and Oakland Hills. During the first half of the twentieth century he was undoubtedly the best-known golf architect in America. In his work—at least in those very rare instances when it is essentially the same today as he left it (Pinehurst No. 2 is now such an example)—we see crown greens, subtle slopes and falloffs around the putting surfaces, and an overall naturalness and adherence to the original topography, all so characteristic of Dornoch.

Like so many links, the course runs out and back, although in this case it is the 8th green that signals the most distant point and the 9th tee on which we head for home. The first eight are played on the higher ground, much of this stretch along the slopes of a great gorse-covered bluff (blindingly orange-gold in late spring). The next eight are routed beside the gently curving shore of the Dornoch Firth, and the final two holes lead us into the middle ground and back to the clubhouse.

From the friendly opener (only 332 yards, but the pitch must beware the deep pots) to the strong finisher, a 461-yard par four over humpy ground, it is all marvelous stuff, in a setting where the sea is always in sight. One of the arresting moments in golf comes when, following a brief walk on a footpath through a dense tract of gorse behind the second green, we break into the clear: From the high 3rd tee there is a glorious vista stretching away hole after hole, seemingly without end, sea and hills and linksland. The world has been left far behind, and as we play on, there is this strong sensation of being outward bound, of heading toward land's end. Indeed, we feel that we may outrun the district of Sutherland and penetrate to the very wilds of Caithness on this journey over an ancient landscape where so little seems owed to the hand of man.

Every hole is either a challenge or a delight; many are both. Even in a dead calm—there's not been such a day in the memory of man—the movement of the ground, the siting of the greens, and the menace of the bunkers see to it. From the medal tees the course measures 6,576 yards against a par of 70. And since neither the two par fives (497 and 516 yards) nor the four one-shotters (182, 164, 150, and 168) are stretchers, that leaves a lot of mileage for the dozen par fours to spend. In fact, nine of them range from 400 (the steeply uphill 16th) to 463 yards (the level and straightaway and isolated 7th). More times than not, the long approach called for is to a plateau green, often crowned and with steep and sometimes shaven falloffs on one side or the other or both. The 3rd, 4th (the giant statue of the Duke of Sutherland on the distant hill above Golspie is our target from this tee), and 5th (two of them from high tees, one from almost fairway level) constitute a particularly fine sequence of two-shotters, where there is room to let fly on the drive, but unless it finds the right spot in the landing area the second shot to the plateau green will be very exacting. Blind shots are rare at Dornoch—the uphill approach on 16 and the blind drives on 8 and 17 are the only three that come to mind.

Of all the excellent holes coming in—including the two par threes, both mercilessly bunkered, the 10th out in the open beside the beach, the 13th secluded in the dunes—the most celebrated is the 14th, called "Foxy." Totally natural (there is not a bunker anywhere in its 445 yards), the hole breaks sharply left in the landing area, then, after proceeding straight ahead for the biggest part of 200 yards, jogs right, the fairway soon to rise sharply some five feet to a wide but not deep plateau green. Prompting both changes of direction is a long, formidable upthrust of dune on the right covered with bushes and rough grasses. To reach the green in two requires a strong and perfectly drawn drive followed by a softly faded 4- or 5-wood. Harry Vardon called it "the finest natural hole I've ever played." That was 80 years ago. He would still be of the same mind today. The 14th at Dornoch is surely one of the greatest par fours in the world. Just as inarguably, Royal Dornoch is among the greatest courses in the world.

In recent years some of the game's outstanding players have found their way to Dornoch, determined to see for themselves what all the lyrical outpourings have been about. Ben Crenshaw has played it ("I nearly did not come back," he would say later), Greg Norman has played it, Tom Watson has played it. Watson was made an honorary member of the club. He remained in Dornoch overnight and a few weeks later wrote to the secretary describing the *three* rounds during his 24-hour stay as "the most fun I have ever had playing golf."

The championship course is not all the golf to be had in this part of Sutherland. Royal Dornoch itself provides a "relief" eighteen that, while not nearly as demanding as its sister, is more than merely pleasant and offers many of the same views. Up the coast road, the A9, are two other seaside courses, one good, the other superb. It was Willy Skinner who advised me to play them both, and you must take seriously the advice of a man who was Royal Dornoch's club champion before becoming its professional some 25 years ago, whose father succeeded the redoubtable John Sutherland as secretary of the club, and whose mother, more than once the ladies' champion, fashioned the flags for the holes out of flour sacks during the pinched times of World War II.

The Golspie Golf Club, 11 miles above Dornoch, was founded in 1889, though golf has been played on that strip of land between the stone wall and the sea (shades of Dunbar) for much longer. The course, largely seaside in feeling, is a delight. Quite short—there is only one par five in its 5,836 yards, and par is 68—it is nonetheless blessed with some very good holes, particularly the 530-yard 4th, which rolls along right beside the beach over rippling ground, and a pair of par fours of just over 400 yards, the 8th and 9th, where heather constricts the shots. Both play into the prevailing wind, and the 9th, drifting uphill as it turns left, cautions us with a steep heather-covered falloff at the left of the green. It is a hole that would not be out of place on any highly regarded seaside course.

Coming home, where the holes are at a remove from the sea, we encounter back-to-back par threes toward the end that we hope to capitalize on for the sake of our card. The splendid 16th, at 176 yards, plays out to sea from a lofty tee over a valley to a double-terrace green. The 17th, less striking, is more difficult: 210 yards long and only the flag can be seen.

The views at Golspie—mountains and meadows and sea—are never less than captivating. This is not a course that must be played, but it is one that we remember with affection.

Seven or eight miles farther up the coast lies a course that *must* be played. Its name is Brora, it is 6,110 yards long from all the way back, par is 70, and it is among my dozen favorite seaside courses in Scotland. Too short to qualify as great, it is still no less than superlative. There is not a prosaic moment. We relish every hole—indeed, every shot. From the standpoint of playing characteristics, as opposed to visual enticement, this eighteen is routed over as wonderful a tract of golfing duneland—from modestly wrinkling to fantastically billowing, with every conceivable variation in between—as any golfer could wish for. I am not talking about the towering sandhills of Machrie or Machrihanish or Cruden Bay—no, those are absent here—but rather the less flamboyant but still immensely active topography of North Berwick or Nairn or the Old Course. At Brora both stances and lies are often awkward, and flexibility in setup and swing is sometimes called for. It is a shotmaker's course.

The club was founded in 1891, with the course to have nine holes and the membership subscription set at two shillings and sixpence. The first "Golf House" was a tin hut that measured 5 feet 4 inches across. One year later, plans for a new and more commodious one were put before the membership. A proposal that it be 12 feet by 10 feet was amended to 15 feet by 11 feet, and the expansionists had their way—as they did several years later when John Sutherland came up from Dornoch to enlarge the links to 18 holes. But it was not until the 1920s that the course and the holes took the shape they possess today. This occurred under the widely practiced hand of James Braid, who surely never traveled so far compiling his splendid record in golf championships as he did in covering the face of Scotland with golf courses.

In the case of Brora he arrived by train one day in January, 1924, walked the course with a member of the green committee, spelled out his recommendations as they proceeded over the links, and returned south by the next train. His fee was £25 plus expenses. Even these frugal Scots believed they had gotten their money's worth. At the end of that year he paid his second and final visit to Brora, when he suggested certain refinements.

Brora is as fine—and as pure—an example of Braid's work at the sea as we are likely to find today. In keeping with his fundamental precepts, the round opens with a pleasant and encouraging two-shotter; the four shot holes each face a different cardinal point of the compass so that the wind must be variously contended with; there is at least one hole out of reach in two long shots; the natural attributes of the land are taken full advantage of, thus minimizing the need for bunkering; and the game ends under the clubhouse windows.

The holes on this classic out-and-back links range from good to great, with water in the form of sinuous burns (the 125-yard 13th is called "Snake" for that very reason) intruding on five holes. Going out, the 3rd, 447 yards, and 5th, 428 yards, are both extremely demanding and not simply because of their length. The second shot on the 3rd hole, over a ridge and over hummocky ground, must be held skillfully up to the left because the ground slopes away toward the sea on the right, where a remorselessly gathering bunker also lurks. At the 5th, surely the best hole on the nine, the Clynelich Burn must be crossed on the second shot; the green, partially hidden, is defended at the right front by a big sandhill covered with long rough grasses; a ravine behind the green discourages an aggressive stroke.

Waves crashing on the rocks beyond the 162-yard 9th call up Masefield's "blown spume and flung spray," and now we head home, one first-class hole after another, with the final four offering no help to the player who must make up ground. Finding the fairway on the 430-yard 15th with a blind drive over a high ridge—farmland beyond a boundary fence edges in unseen on the right, and a thicket of gorse precludes bailing out left—is part one of this two-part examination. Finding the green, defended by sand and mounding, on our long second is part two. This is an original and terrific hole.

At 16, which measures 345 yards and plays 385 yards, we are uneasily conscious of the boundary on the right all the way, but it is the need to get up on the fiercely climbing second shot that should engage us. The rough hollow on the left, far below green level, that swallows the underhit second shot is cruel.

The 17th, 438 yards, is named "Tarbatness," for the lighthouse down the coast that signals the line of play. Braid—this is believed to have been his favorite at Brora—designed the hole for two drawn shots, the drive from a moderately elevated tee over rough ground into the neck of the fairway, the second, also from right to left, to an adroitly bunkered green in a little hollow on the far hillside. It is all there before us and it is all splendid, another indisputably great hole requiring two excellent swings.

The final hole is, in a sense, unusual: it is a par three. Tending uphill all the way, it is tight—three greenside bunkers—and, at 201 yards, long. The depression in the forepart of the green, doubtless meant to call up the Valley of Sin on the 18th of the Old Course, may be overkill, especially with the clubhouse all but cantilevered above the green, so that any shortcoming is exposed to a highly critical audience.

This is as far north as I've ever played, and now we must return to Dornoch, to "suburban Dornoch," if you will, some two or three miles southwest of the royal burgh. Here, in 1994, a new golf course opened for play. It is called the Carnegie Course, it was designed by Donald Steel, and it is the principal sporting attraction of the Carnegie Club at Skibo Castle. Among the other diversions on the 7,000-acre estate are salmon and trout fishing, deer stalking, grouse and pheasant shooting, sailing, swimming, tennis, and archery.

The Carnegie Club is defined by Peter de Savary, the English businessman who owns Skibo Castle, as "a private residential golf and sporting club, with an international membership limited by invitation." You cannot simply knock on the front door at Skibo and declare your interest in playing the golf course. On the other hand, given the right auspices, a game can sometimes be arranged, and perhaps even a night or two in the great Scottish-style baronial castle itself, which Andrew Carnegie built almost exactly a hundred years ago. (It might not hurt to mention this book as having prompted your interest.) Such a visit could engender a desire to join the Carnegie Club (the castle

serves as its principal accommodation), which could be an attractive proposition if you see yourself spending a week there every year.

Andrew Carnegie had a nine-hole course laid out here at the turn of the century for himself and his guests. No, James Braid did not design it. In fact, it was Dornoch's John Sutherland who did. And it was the legendary J. H. Taylor, like Braid a five-time winner of the Open, whom Carnegie invited to stay at the castle and teach him and his wife, Louise, to play golf. Though the steel king was at best only average, he played every match as if his life depended on winning. The staff used to warn guests that if they beat Mr. Carnegie they risked not being invited back.

The Sutherland nine was allowed to go to seed decades ago, and there is little or no suggestion of any of those holes in the Donald Steel layout, though it is routed over much of the same ground as the original course. The setting is sublime, with the waters of the Dornoch Firth, the river Evelix, and Loch Evelix providing a lovely surround for the eighteen, itself on a peninsula, and the great forests and hills of this corner of the Highlands stretching away as far as the eye can see. Carnegie and his wife and their only child, Margaret, routinely referred to Skibo as "heaven on earth," and a game on the new course will reveal why. It will also reveal that this is very good golf, perhaps half a rung below Dornoch.

The early holes range from first-rate to outstanding, and the late holes have, by and large, both strength and style, but through the middle there are several unexceptional though admittedly traditional links-type holes that I know Donald Steel is looking at closely with a view toward improvement. There are five sets of tees, permitting the course to be played at lengths ranging from 5,436 yards to 6,671 yards. Par is 71 in each case.

A couple of top-notch two-shotters doglegging right get us away from the clubhouse (brand new and, with its enclosed courtyard, its fireplaces, and its long views over the water, one of the best in the country). On the 2nd, both drive and approach are semiblind, and the kidney-shaped green is protected by a little hollow on the left and sand on the right. The links-type bunkers—generally pot-shaped and with steep, perfectly revetted faces in the tradition of Muirfield and the Old Course—are themselves works of art at Skibo. They are also rare—all of 12 going out, 24 coming in.

The 150-yard 3rd is a great hole and a beautifully natural one. We play from the top of one dune across a forbidding hollow to the top of another dune. The sandpit short is an abysmal place, the steep drop down and away to the right demands a miraculous recovery, and the slopes and rough grass on the left are merely punishing. There is, effectively, no margin for error.

The same can be said of the angled drive on the delightful 311-yard 4th, where the humpy fairway tends to shunt the ball off into the thick long grasses and gorse on the right. The short pitch, uphill over a ridge to a long, narrow, and sloping green, will be blind for all but the long hitter.

The lofty 5th tee offers panoramic views over the Dornoch Firth to the surrounding hills together with the single most exacting drive on the course. The narrow fairway on this 355-yarder, lying well below, is flanked on the left by heathland, on the right by the sea. Nor is the rising approach to a plateau green any picnic, for here, too, the beach awaits the pushed shot.

There is seclusion in the dunes on the 6th. A lone bunker, deep and large and unnerving, at the left front of the green must be carried on this exacting 183-yarder (215 from the back), where the green is sited in a little dell.

Well, it has been a marvelous skein, these first six holes—balanced, testing, exhilarating. Now, out on a broad and meadowy plain, we soon face three par fives very nearly in a row—9, 10, 12. They are worthy holes, and they are honestly testing, but they are not routed over terrain that has much in the way of feature or intrinsic interest.

The 11th, a 153-yarder, provides a break from the long straightaway hitting. My caddie for this game in mid-August of 1994 was Alan, a 28-year-old who had studied textile design in London but who now lives in Dornoch on a farm that he and his brother own. Alan handles the renting of their six holiday cottages, while his brother tills the soil. To supplement his income, Alan would occasionally carry a bag at the Carnegie Club.

"I'm surprised you don't caddie at Royal Dornoch," I said. "There must be more opportunity."

"Oh, there is, and I could get a bag. But I don't caddie that often, and I'm a member there."

From the outset he had struck me as highly knowledgeable and companionable, and as we moved farther into the round I concluded that he was one of the two best caddies I'd ever known (Pine Valley's Jim Blaylock is the other one). Standing on the tee of the short 11th, I expressed surprise that there were

no bunkers. "I think you will find, sir," he said almost diffi-
dently, "that the convolutions of the ground will provide all the
defense the hole needs." He sounded exactly like Jeeves ad-
dressing Wooster. And quite right he was.

There is an attractive variety to the finishing holes. The
green is angled on the superb 15th, 186 yards, so that the right
side of it sits no more than a step or two from a steep drop to a
tidal inlet. At the 421-yard 16th, the brave drive out to the
right, menaced by a falloff down to the 18th fairway, is rewarded with an open shot to a green set among low dunes.

The 17th is one of those newly fashionable very short par
fours (the 10th at the Belfry, where so many Ryder Cuppers
have come to grief in the water fronting the green, is another)
that tempt the tiger into believing that he can drive the green.
With only 267 yards to go from a tee perched high above the
Firth, he can do just that, providing he is willing to flirt with
the sea that runs along below on the left, and providing he can
carry the large and deep bunkers in the heart of the fairway
some 30 yards short of the green. It is great fun and, in match
play, an obvious "swing" hole. It is also an extraordinarily beautiful spot, with the mighty Struie Hill to the west, Skibo Castle itself to the north, the rest of the golf course south and east,
and the gray-blue water shimmering all around us.

A patch of that water, perhaps more marshy than shimmering this time, must be carried on the drive at 18, an uncompromising 545 yards long. The fairway sweeps dramatically left
as it skirts the bay shore en route to a large raised green on a
spit of land with water just left and beyond and a concealed pot
bunker at the right to snare the too-safe approach. A splendid

finish in every sense, where the tiger can again gamble, this time on both shots, in the hope of getting home in two.

Donald Steel has captured in a contemporary links the true feel and challenge and spirit of traditional seaside golf. The result at Skibo Castle is an enormous welcome addition to the game in the Dornoch area. Andrew Carnegie once said, "Golf is an indispensable adjunct to high civilization." I sincerely doubt it, but the statement is so deliciously pompous that I've found it unforgettable.

For your spare time, I have two suggestions and one command. It will be very easy to obey the command: see Dornoch. The old royal burgh, with a permanent population of about a thousand, is quite small. It centers on the town square. Clustered here are the cathedral, dating to about 1225, a surviving tower of the Castle of the Bishops (now a part of the Dornoch Castle Hotel), and the old jail, which houses the Dornoch Craft Centre. By daylight or moonlight, this is an irresistible place—neither picturesque nor quaint, but dignified, quiet, and fine.

A first suggestion is the nearby fishing village of Embo, with its traditional stone cottages and attendant tiny gardens. The second suggestion is Dunrobin Castle, at Golspie. The most northerly of Scotland's great houses, it is the ancestral home of the dukes of Sutherland. It dates in part from the early fourteenth century, contains an opulent collection of furniture and furnishings, and boasts magnificent formal gardens and a setting high above the sea that is an integral element in all this grandeur.

If you're of a mind simply to get in the car and roam, you are within two hours of John O'Groats, the village at the top of the England/Scotland/Wales land mass. Such a drive would also provide the opportunity to see Wick and Thurso, two pleasant market towns, the latter with a pretty promenade along the strand.

As for accommodations, this is holiday country and there is thus something for everybody. In 1971, on that family pilgrimage I mentioned earlier, we stopped at the Dornoch Hotel. My log of that trip reveals that the total bill for our overnight stay—there were six of us—came to £29 and 50 pence (just under $74 then). This included a 10 percent service charge and covered everything: three twin-bedded rooms (two with bath; the one without got the sea view), full breakfast, tea, the table d'hôte dinner with wine, and sandwiches for the boys when we arrived. It's a wonder I ever leave home today.

If you stay at the Royal Golf Hotel in Dornoch, your room may be within 50 paces of the 1st tee. It may also offer grand views over the Firth. The Dornoch Castle Hotel, on the square, is rather more atmospheric, with lovely gardens and a dining room in what was once the dungeon. Speaking of lovely gardens, just across the square is a charming B&B called Trevose Guest House. We've never stayed there, but we have inspected it and it looks quite nice. The "in" place is Burghfield House, formerly the home of Lord Rothermere. It is not nearly so luxe as its provenance might suggest, but it is very comfortable and its cooking is generally held to be the best in town.

Two out-of-town places are worth mentioning. The Links Hotel at Brora lives up to its name. It abuts Braid's wonderful course, commanding both it and the sea from its public rooms and many of its guest rooms. The other spot is Skibo Castle. My two 24-hour stays there have been the most enjoyable experiences in a lifetime of overnighting. A sampler of the highlights would include the bagpiper on the lawn at 7:30 in the morning rousing us all for breakfast (yes, that is the way Andrew Carnegie did it a century ago and that is the way Peter de Savary is doing it today); accommodations in which the bath/dressing room was a shade larger than the bedroom and the two rooms had matching and working fireplaces; a tranquil hour poring over the beautifully bound old books (an occasional one with pages yet uncut!) in Carnegie's library; dinner in the state dining room with the blaze from the great hearth and the flames from the great candelabra casting a glow upon the massive dark-stained oak furniture; the after-dinner coffee and brandy in the drawing room that has scarcely changed since Carnegie's death in 1919. Among the castle's guests have been Kipling, Paderewski (you can play the old Bechstein grand piano that he played), King Edward VII, Lloyd George, assorted Rockefellers, Booker T. Washington, and Helen Keller. Mr. de Savary may not attract such world-renowned figures as his steely predecessor, but those who get there will find distinctly improved plumbing and, in their urbane host, one of the world's great raconteurs.

Chapter Seven

Tain and
Nairn

We are leaving one ancient royal burgh, Dornoch, and heading straight to another, Tain, to play a links with the same paternity as that of its illustrious neighbor on the opposite shore of the Dornoch Firth. It was Old Tom Morris who, in 1890, first laid out golf holes at Tain, and it was John Sutherland, not too many years later, who extensively revised the St. Andrean's design. This time, however, the tract of land was essentially flat—there are no hills, not even gentle ones, at Tain—and unremarkable. From the medal tees, the course measures 6,207 yards; par is 70. The course is an honest test of links golf, and the game here, though admittedly in a minor key, is a satisfying one.

Since there are only two par fours over 400 yards, sound iron play is at a premium; the greens are moderate in size and pleasantly undulating. Bunkering is not heavy, but the pits themselves are penal.

On the whole, the rumpled fairways are generous, but it is

essential to hold them, for they are often corseted by dense growths of gorse, magnificent in full bloom and, in my experience, a magnet to swarms of flies. Forced-carries over heather are also a feature of the driving here.

There are clear views of the sea at 11, 12, and 13, and, on a pretty day, glimpses of the links at Dornoch. The unassuming Tain River makes its first appearance quite early, on the 394-yard 2nd, where it meanders across in front of the green to claim the underhit approach, but then it is gone until the final three holes. On the 213-yard 17th (as at Golspie, 16 and 17 are both one-shotters), we must carry the broad and snaking stream twice with our wood and, having done so, also stay clear of it as it edges back toward the right side of the green. The 17th is the hole most likely to linger in our memory of Tain.

About an hour's drive southeast, on the shores of the Moray Firth, lies Nairn, a family seaside resort of substance (9,000 permanent residents) and style. In late Victorian times successful Empire builders retired here to erect the imposing houses in large wooded gardens that contribute to the town's charm and to an air of prosperity and well-being reminiscent of North Berwick. With its vast stretches of sand that form the East and West Beaches, its two-mile-long seafront promenade, its low dunes, its snug harbor, and its two golf courses, Nairn has been attracting vacationers and golfers for well over a century.

Though I have visited Nairn on four separate occasions over a number of years, I have never played the Nairn Dunbar course, which lies toward the eastern end of the town, where it is laid out on a compact plot of ground beside the sea and appears to be full of good sport. Measuring 6,431 yards against a par of 71, this is no pitch 'n' putt course.

Still, it is the links of the Nairn Golf Club, routed over bouncy, rippling, hummocky ground smack beside the West Beach, that today attracts golfers from all over the world, more often than not on the way to Dornoch.

I viewed myself as a pioneer, a trailblazer, when I came here for the first time, 25 years ago, a long way by Scottish standards from such tourist attractions as St. Andrews and Carnoustie and Gleneagles. During the brief wait while a twosome ahead of me was teeing off, I said to the professional, "I don't imagine you get too many Americans all the way up here."

"You're right," he replied. "Not too many, but some. Americans are not all that scarce."

I was surprised. "Then you . . . you've had some here recently?"

"We have, the day before yesterday. Julius Boros."

"Julius Boros? Here in Nairn?" Of all the outstanding American players at that time, Boros struck me as the least likely to be roaming around Nairnshire. Maybe he had come for the fishing, something I believe he enjoyed even more than golf.

"What do you think could have brought him to Nairn?" I asked, brainlessly pursuing the subject.

"Why, the links," said the professional, looking at me askance. "What other reason would the man have? After all, this is Nairn. It's an old course and it's a fine course. A Julius Boros would surely want to play here at least once in his lifetime."

With that he handed me a scorecard, admonishing me in a fashion that might not have been necessary in the case of a person less dull-witted, "Keep to the sea."

In truth, few courses skirt the sea more closely or more persistently, at least on the outward half, than Nairn. It is entirely possible to slice onto the beach, which is not out of bounds, six times on the first seven holes.

Both the club and the links date to 1887, when Archie Simpson, then professional at Royal Aberdeen, laid out the course. Old Tom Morris came along a couple of years later to put his imprint on the links Many years passed before James Braid was called in, and at first he was the soul of restraint, suggesting only a mound here and a bunker there. But in the late 1930s he advanced rather more ambitious revisions, and it is the resulting links that we so much enjoy today.

Nairn has long been the scene at regular intervals of the major Scottish championships—the men's, the women's, and the professionals'—but it was only in 1994 that for the first time it played host to the British Amateur. In 1999 the Walker Cup will be played here. The course can be stretched as long as 6,722 yards against a par of 72, though you are more likely to tackle it at about 6,400 yards.

A round at Nairn can be a deceptive business. It is an easy and lovely walk—the only hill takes us up to the 13th green, then down to the 14th—and the waters of the Moray Firth are always in full view, with the dappling effect of sunlight and shadow on Black Isle and the beauty of the distant peaks about Strath Conan delighting us at every step. Then, too, the firm and sometimes even fast fairways often bring even the longest two-shotters—there are five over 400 yards—within range. This course, we say to ourselves, should be manageable. But then we realize, along about the 7th or 8th, that getting our figures has been elusive. Why? Above all, because Nairn is a serious examination in driving, with the narrow fairways hemmed in by heather and gorse and the mildly undulating nature of the ground not conducive to reliable bounces. What's more, the approach shots to greens that are intriguingly angled, or concealed behind a dune (as on the wonderful 4th, a 145-yarder played out to sea), or on tricky plateaus, or beyond seemingly innocent little ridges, are difficult to judge and to hold. This is traditional duneland golf, with as much of the game played along the ground as in the air. The demands on our creativity and our patience are unceasing.

We remember a number of holes warmly: the 374-yard 5th, where the drive is over the edge of the beach and a pesky Braid bunker awaits precisely where we would choose to land in order to make certain of staying dry; the clever 325-yard 8th, where the crowned green seems to shed all but the most precisely struck pitch; the long par-four 12th, where the confining gorse on both sides of the fairway dares us to swing away as aggressively as we know the 445-yarder requires; the 206-yard 14th, like the 6th played out to sea, but this time from a lofty tee to a green with a deep cleft in it; and 16, 418 yards, where a teasing burn just short of the green makes us grateful for the breeze at our back.

The round closes with a straightaway 516-yard par five. That same helpful breeze gives us a reasonable expectation of getting close enough in two to make birdie a possibility. You may be as surprised as I was by the impressive new clubhouse, which cost something in the neighborhood of £2,000,000 and which proclaims the club's confidence in considerably more green fee revenue today than there was when I made my initial visit in 1971.

Two tidbits, not totally unrelated, about Nairn may be worth mentioning. In 1899 it became the first Scottish club to charge admission to a golf match. And in the 1950s a prominent member who had made his fortune importing coffee gained a reputation for frugality by anchoring his tee on a string to a penny and thus managing never to lose the little wooden peg. After 14 years, worn to a shadow of its former self, the tee finally broke.

There is much to see and do in the environs of Nairn. Inverness, popularly dubbed the "Capital of the Highlands," is split by the river Ness (the mysterious loch of the same name is barely 20 minutes outside this city of 40,000) and makes for an enjoyable half-day visit. Cawdor Castle, legendary scene of Duncan's murder in *Macbeth,* is a medieval fortress in very good repair and boasting notably beautiful gardens. And Culloden Battlefield, of strong appeal to history buffs, was, in 1746, the site of the last land battle to be fought in Britain, marking the end of the Jacobite uprising led by Bonnie Prince Charlie.

In a holiday town offering a nearly limitless variety of accommodations, two hotels within a few hundred yards of the Nairn Golf Club are almost certain to satisfy. At the Golf View Hotel the gardens run down to the beach, the outdoor swimming pool is heated, and the special gourmet dinners scheduled half a dozen times a year showcase the hotel's good wine cellar as well as its cooking. The Newton, a handsome castellated and turreted, gabled gray stone house set in 27 acres of secluded grounds, also offers splendid views over the Moray Firth. Available here are a sauna, solarium, tennis court, fitness equipment, and, not three minutes walk from the front door, the short nine-hole Newton course.

Chapter Eight

A Grand
and Glorious
Fivesome

I don't know how many golf courses there are in what might loosely be termed the "Aberdeen orbit"—40 to 50, I should think—but there are five in particular that exemplify the most appealing aspects of seaside golf, and two of them might fairly be called great. Let's examine the five on a north-to-south axis, beginning at Peterhead, which is a little less than two hours due east of Nairn. It is an easy and unremarkable drive, following the A96 through Forres to Elgin, the A98 through Banff to New Pitsligo, and the A950 through Mintlaw to Peterhead. Except at Cullen and Banff, the sea is not in view.

Peterhead was a busy whaling port in the first part of the nineteenth century and a busy herring fishing center in the latter part of it and well into the twentieth century. Today it is at the heart of the North Sea oil operations. The attendant prosperity and bustle are unmistakable, and perhaps nowhere more apparent than at the golf club. Tranquility is not its long suit.

Day in and day out—and, one suspects, out of season as well as in season—given weather that is even remotely bearable, the eighteen and the relief nine are thronged with members, green fee payers, visiting societies, youngsters learning the game, oldsters forgetting the game, everybody. The flat-roofed contemporary clubhouse (built in 1969, when the erosion of sand threatened to engulf the old one) is at least as lively a scene as the links, the activity centering on a very large and open space that functions as bar, dining room, lounge, and pool hall. No one would mistake it for the R&A.

For several years prior to my first visit to the Peterhead Golf Club, in 1994, I had heard two diametrically opposed views of the course. Graeme Lennie, professional at the Crail Golfing Society, just south of St. Andrews, is an enthusiastic admirer of it. "You must play it," he insisted. "It's wonderful, absolutely first-rate, the dunes, the sea, the undulating fairways. It's just the sort of course you're always on the lookout for. There's a river there, too, but it has almost nothing to do with the game. You park your car on one side of it and cross quite a nice high bridge to get to the clubhouse. I don't know of anything quite like that. But you've got to play this golf course."

The naysayer is another good friend of mine, who shall remain nameless. For years he played his golf in this part of Aberdeenshire. "No," he said to me on a couple of occasions, "no, I don't think you'd like it that much. A few good holes, of course." He was no more forthcoming. I was surprised that two people, both of whom knew and loved the game and had played widely, could hold such contradictory views of Peterhead. It was imperative that I play it.

At the time Peterhead was founded, in 1841, there were not

25 golf clubs in existence, and virtually all of them were on the east coast of Scotland. Even venerable Prestwick, one of the two or three earliest of the west coast clubs, is 10 years younger than Peterhead. For 50 years the Peterhead Club played over a cramped piece of linksland (just six holes, with a couple of crisscrosses) in another part of town, moving to its present site, at Craigewan Links, in 1892. During the next 35 years, Willie Park, Jr., St. Andrews' Laurie Auchterlonie, and the ever-available James Braid all figured importantly in fashioning golf holes here, which at one time numbered 36. During World War II the newer of the two eighteens was neglected owing to a shortage of greens staff, to be reopened later as a nine-hole relief course. The regular eighteen today is in large measure a reflection of Braid's skill. It is a short course, not quite 6,200 yards from the medal tees, with only three par fours over 400 yards in its par of 70.

The first three holes, which were laid out some 25 years ago, when the present clubhouse was built, have come in for considerable criticism. They admittedly possess an inland feeling and strike some as contrived. Still, the opening shot, over the river Ugie and then tight along it, can be disquieting if we haven't spent 10 minutes warming up on the practice tee; the 140-yard 2nd hole climbs almost vertically to a plateau green bunkered right and left; and there is sand to catch the wayward drive or approach on the 375-yard 3rd.

The ditch about 60 yards short of the green on the 380-yard 4th should not matter unless the hole is playing dead into a strong northeasterly breeze, as has happened more than once in the history of the course. The uphill 5th, on the same heading and 15 yards longer, plays 40 yards longer and brings us to the start of the wholly splendid middle stretch of the links. Now, for six or seven consecutive holes, we have it all: greens fearfully exposed to the wind on the one hand, neatly sheltered on the other; towering sandhills, secluded valleys, restless, heaving fairways framed by long rough grasses; and, again and again, the sea popping into full view each time we ascend to one of the lofty tees. On the 133-yard 10th the pulpit tee is shielded on three sides by a corrugated steel "windscreen"—otherwise it would often be impossible to fashion anything resembling a golf swing.

Beginning with the 180-yard 6th, a superb one-shotter along a ridge to a narrow, sand-squeezed green, and ending with the steeply climbing 12th, where a large mound blockades the left front of the green, my card shows this string of adjectives: *great, terrific, grand, great, delightful, fine, excellent.*

The views grow more and more entrancing from the 5th green onward, and the 13th tee, the highest point of the links, commands the entire world of Peterhead—links and hills and town and, it must be conceded, not too many miles off, flame-tipped oil towers soaring out of the sea.

The 423-yard 13th sweeps expansively downhill; the 14th, the other long two-shotter, is endangered by a burn on the left its entire length; the rumpled ground in front of the 15th green introduces an element of chance.

For me—and this may be an indefensible personal preference—the 174-yard 16th, ironically labeled "Target," is the most memorable hole at Peterhead. The true target, which is to say the green, is invisible, tucked just over a ridge at the bottom of a steep, short slope. The shot is played over broken and tumbling ground toward a flag that beckons, but from precisely where? What we have is a very peculiar piece of work, one in which the green site simply proved irresistible to either Auchterlonie or Braid. Thank heaven!

The last two holes, both routed along the headlands high above a ruddy golden curve of sandy beach, are an ideal climax to the round. The concealed green on 17, in its little dell, is defended across the front by a "double cartgate" of hillocks. The last hole, 500 yards long, offers room to fire away from a high tee and, if we should connect, a good opportunity to finish with a birdie.

Peterhead is not filled with great holes—the one-shotter 6th and the 460-yard par-four 9th, along a dune-framed valley, certainly are, and maybe, just maybe, the whimsical 16th is, too—but it is filled with good golf and great fun.

I remember reading some time ago that Pete Dye had singled out five courses as his particular favorites, making no claim that they were the greatest or the best or the toughest, just that they were the five that he liked most of all. It was not difficult to remember them, because three begin with a "P" and have long been famous—Pine Valley, Pinehurst #2, and Portrush—and two begin with a "C" and, on the contrary, are scarcely household names: Camargo and Cruden Bay. I have never played Camargo, a Cincinnati course that Seth Raynor laid out in 1921, but I have played Cruden Bay on a number of occasions, the first time in 1978.

There is no gradual revelation of the glory of Cruden Bay. You climb out of the car, walk over to the clubhouse on the heights, and look down. Below you, in all its turbulent splendor, lies one of the most awe-inspiring stretches of linksland in Scotland, indeed, in all of the British Isles. Against a backdrop of the gray-blue waters of the North Sea, the sandhills rise 40, 50, even 60 feet, their shaggy slopes covered with the long and strangling grasses that spell disaster to the off-target stroke. This is heroic ground, and if it is thrilling to contemplate, it is markedly more thrilling to play. From the medal tees the course measures 6,370 yards against a par of 70.

The first three holes are par fours—a very testing opener of 416 yards played from an elevated tee and calling for a gorse-skirting drive down the right to open up the angled green for the long approach; a 339-yarder, with the purest tabletop green waiting high above for a very carefully judged short pitch; and a blind 286-yarder over broken ground that, in high summer, the smiter just may reach with his drive. It is marvelous—and marvelously varied—but it scarcely prepares you for what is about to unfold: four consecutive *great* holes.

The 4th is simplicity itself, a 193-yarder played straight toward the sea (and often straight into the wind) from an elevated tee carved out of one imposing sandhill across a deep grassy hollow to an elevated green carved out of the facing hill. A bunker at the left front in the slope and a steep falloff on the right dictate the need for a perfect stroke. No other will suffice.

At the 5th, a daunting 454 yards, we begin with a blind drive from high and deep in the dunes, sighting on the wispy top of some vague hillock. This is followed by a full-blooded wood along the valley floor to a large but ill-defined green in a pleasant little dell. There is a cloistered quality to much of Cruden Bay, a feeling prompted by the high dunes that we have the course to ourselves.

The 6th—not for nothing is it called "Bluidy Burn"—is a dogleg left par five of 524 yards. Again the tee is cocked up in the sandhills, but this time the green, dramatically undulating, is tucked away beyond a dune and protected from the birdie-seeker's wood by a little burn, itself invisible, some 50 yards in front.

One final hole in this sequence. The 390-yard 7th commences from another exquisitely sited tee high in the sandhills and, as at the mighty 5th, offers not a glimpse of the fairway. If we find it with our drive, we turn smartly left and face uphill, where the flag beckons from beyond two sandhills that guard the narrow green like the Pillars of Hercules.

Four great and unforgettable holes in succession—par 3, 4, 5, 4.

To whom are we indebted for this feast? Not, you may be surprised to learn, James Braid. At no point in Cruden Bay's near-hundred-year history did Braid have a hand in shaping it. No, it is the Englishman Tom Simpson, in partnership with Herbert Fowler, who deserves the hosannas for the 27 holes (there is a third, shorter and thoroughly delightful nine called St. Olaf's here as well). A rudimentary eighteen was built at the turn of the century for a resort hotel complex that later fell victim to the Depression and World War II and was demolished in 1952. Simpson was brought in during the great hotel's heyday, in the mid-1920s.

Educated in the law at Cambridge, Thomas G. Simpson chose never to practice it but rather to concentrate his energies on golf, which he played at scratch. Rich, eccentric, and talented, he traveled from site to site in a silver chauffeur-driven Rolls-Royce, emerging from its soothing interiors to supervise construction dressed in an embroidered cloak and beret, with either a shooting stick or riding crop in hand. He is said to have hired Philip Mackenzie Ross (Turnberry, Southerness, *et al.*) as a construction boss because of Ross's advice on how to mount a license plate most becomingly on the Rolls-Royce.

Not a man to hide his light under a bushel, Simpson chose the 1st, 8th, and 18th at Cruden Bay among his selection of the best 18 holes in Britain and Ireland. He described the 258-yard par-four 8th as an "outstanding jewel of a hole, mischievous, subtle, and provocative, the element of luck with the tee shot being very high." The hole is set in a confluence of sandhills, a confined territory of hilly, broken ground. Both tee and green are moderately elevated, but the green confounds us. It is a roughly triangular upthrust, with the ground sloping away steeply on the sides. Even if our drive should uncover a level lie, the little pitch calls for uncommon deftness. It is easier to make five than three. John Glennie, whom I came to know rather well over the last 10 years of his life, once scored a hole-in-one here, using a 1-iron off the tee.

A solicitor whose home and offices were in Peterhead, John Glennie was one of the outstanding amateurs in northeastern Scotland between 1920 and 1960. Perhaps more important, however, it was he who put Scotland's handicapping system on a realistic, workable basis. And stepping in to acquire the golf course after the resort hotel was demolished, he founded the Cruden Bay Golf Club. Over the years he would serve as captain and, later in life, be named honorary captain. He loved the game as few men do and understood it as do even fewer. My wife and I visited the Glennies—Edda was the ladies' captain for several years—at both their house in Peterhead and their

tiny, picture-windowed chalet on the heights above the 1st hole
at Cruden Bay. The Glennies occupied the chalet from June
through September.

"It's a prefab," John told us. "It cost four hundred ninety-five
pounds back in 1965 and it was put up in a day. We've been using it now for twenty years. If my mathematics is correct, that
comes to about twenty-five pounds a year—not at all bad for a
long summer's holiday."

When prompted, John could be counted on to unfold a story
or two—more often than not about a celebrated figure—from
what I suspected must have been an inexhaustible fund.

At Mougins, in the south of France, he found himself one
winter playing a round with Henry Cotton, whom he had
known long before this chance encounter. He asked Cotton
what kind of a match they might make.

"We'll play even," Cotton said.

"Even it is, then," John Glennie replied, "despite the fact
that you've won three Opens and I haven't struck a ball in four
months."

John continued, "Cotton and I were playing what you call a
Nassau. Going out he beat me 1 down, but I had him by a hole
on the inward half as we came to the 18th. Then he hooked his
tee shot out of bounds and that was the match. As a matter of
fact, he never did play the hole. He simply walked straight to
the clubhouse."

Twice the Glennies visited the United States, in 1971 and
1975, for the Ryder Cup Matches.

"The first time," John recalled, "the match was played in St.
Louis, at the Old Warson Country Club. We went over because
of our professional—you met Harry Bannerman today, but he

had not yet taken the job here when he was selected for the
1971 Ryder Cup team, though I had known him for some time
and had followed his career closely. Well, Harry played wonderfully against your fellows at St. Louis. He and Bernard Gal-
lacher beat Billy Casper and Miller Barber in the foursomes.
And in the singles Harry beat Gardner Dickinson and halved
with Arnold Palmer. If the rest of our team had done as well, we
would have brought the cup home. That was when I met
Palmer. Then, four years later, when the match returned to the
States—it was played at Laurel Valley, you remember—Edda
and I went over again. And this time I played with Palmer at
Latrobe, that course of his not far from Laurel Valley. Oh, I
must show you something."

He now drew out his wallet and took from it one of his business cards. On the back in ink was Arnold Palmer's signature
with the characteristically large and graceful "A" and "P." Immediately above the signature, in John's own hand, were four
words: "John Glennie beat me." We all laughed at the little
joke and John carefully returned the card to his wallet. It surely
got additional exposure on occasions like this one.

The inbound nine at Cruden Bay begins at the highest point
of the course. Bram Stoker, of *Dracula* fame—there is no evidence that he ever played golf, but during his holidays here he
regularly roamed the links—was standing on the 10th tee
when he envisioned the bay itself, with its great rocky promon-
tories jutting into the North Sea, as the jaws of a wicked monster luring ships to destruction on the rocks. He saw the perfect
golden beach, "smooth as a cathedral floor," as the monster's
tongue. I confess that this flight of sinister fancy was lost on
me, perhaps because I was focusing fiercely on the need to put

my drive, sailing away into the wind off this splendid peak, into play on the fairway so far below.

The next three holes—a par three, a par four, and a par five—are all first-rate, with an air of uncertainty on the 550-yarder created by a high bank that hides the green.

Fourteen, 15, and 16 are quintessential Cruden Bay, the first two played from tees high above the beach into a very narrow neck of land pinched by a great gorse-clad hillside on the left and the dunes buttressing the course from the North Sea on the right. The hillocky landing area on the 372-yard 14th is scandalously narrow, and the approach vanishes over a direction marker into a dell, where the long, level green, suggestive of a sunken garden, gathers the shot.

There are those who consider the 15th bizarre. Heaven knows it is out of the ordinary! This is a very long one-shotter, 239 yards, more often than not played with the wind. We stand on a tee elevated above the strand and gaze over broken ground down a dune-framed chute. Nothing beckons. Both green and flagstick are invisible. We must take it on faith that they await. The green inclines to fall away toward the back and the well-struck shot to creep inexorably over it into the rough. It is all very much in a class with the mad 5th, the "Himalayas," at Prestwick. Do not forget to ring the bell once you have cleared the green.

Well, after this adventure, the 182-yard 16th strikes us as almost routine. We play from a hillside tee over a valley to a green set high in the dunes. The putting surface and its protective bunkers and hollows are hidden, but at least the flag is in sight.

On the strong 17th, a 428-yarder, there is an astonishing

mound—a sugarloaf really—perhaps a dozen feet high and rearing up in the middle of the fairway just where a solid drive should come to rest. Some believe that this mound was a burial ground for Danish invaders almost a thousand years ago. In 1011 the Danes were finally driven out of Scotland when they were defeated right here on the linksland of Cruden Bay. But no bones or fragments of weapons have ever been unearthed. Still, if it is not a monument of any kind to the Danes, it is certainly a monumental problem to the golfer whose ball skips up it or winds up dead behind it.

The home hole is both excellent and orthodox—a broad fairway on two levels, boundary on the left, a burn to snare the pushed drive, undulating ground ending in a diagonal ridge just short of the spacious green. All this and 416 yards.

Bernard Darwin wrote of Cruden Bay that "there are burns to cross, hills to carry, and hidden nooks to drop into. Some of the shots are blind—willfully blind if you like to call it so . . . but there are also some truly fine golfing holes, on the grand scale." Donald Steel says, "The course is a perpetual battle of wits, but it is unmistakably fun" and "Majestic is almost too weak a word to describe it all." As for Pete Dye, it occupies a very special place in his affections. I would add only that Cruden Bay—outsized, nonconformist, unpredictable, flamboyant—is certainly among the 10 or 12 courses in Scotland that on no account should be missed.

Some 14 or 15 miles due south, and only 5 miles north of Aberdeen, lies a trailblazer of a golf club. Its name is Murcar and it is boldly leading the clubs of Scotland into the twenty-first century with one of the significant golfing innovations of our time: 150-yard markers. No need for the practiced eyeball here—just check the handy marker and let fly. Murcar is, in my experience, the only club in Scotland to provide this American crutch.

But perhaps we should not be surprised at such enterprise here. After all, Murcar was also the first private club in the north of Scotland to permit golf on Sunday, which it did shortly after its founding in 1909. And it is also the only club to have owned a railway, the Strabathie Light Railway, by which members in the early days were transported from the Bridge of Don to the clubhouse for a penny.

The architect of Murcar, however, had no need of such a convenience. Archie Thompson was given the assignment, and all he had to do was walk over from next door, where he was the professional at Royal Aberdeen. Let the record also show that the "great revisionist" entered the picture some years later, and that the course we play today may well owe more to Braid than to Simpson. One thing is certain: together they made a wonderful job of it.

The land at Murcar is very close to ideal: tumbling, linksland, great sandhills, gorse, heather, the spiky marram grass, even a couple of burns for good measure. An unusual feature of the terrain is the way the sandhills rise above one another in successive ridges from the beach, providing a terraced effect and revealing the sea from almost every hole—the broad curve of the bay and of Aberdeen's harbor down to Girdleness lighthouse in the south, eastward over the North Sea to the horizon (the oil drilling much in evidence), and northward to the farmlands and the long and regular line of coast stretching away toward Cruden Bay and Peterhead.

From the back tees, Murcar measures just under 6,240 yards and plays to a par of 71. From the regular markers, the length is just over 5,800 but the par is 69 (no three-shotters to help our relationship with par here).

The first couple of holes, shortish par fours running back and forth over pleasantly rolling ground, let us get warmed up before facing the rigors that begin on the 3rd, a 400-yarder where we drive over very hummocky country to a shelf, the fairway then plunging violently to a gully where the ball inclines to bounce left into heavy rough. The green lies in a veritable punchbowl at the far end of the gully in the very lee of the elevated 10th tee at Royal Aberdeen. For the uninitiated, nothing would be more natural than to putt out, climb up onto that teeing ground, and hit away on the wrong golf course! It has happened.

Instead, we locate the 4th tee at Murcar, high in the sandhills above the beach (on land that belongs to Royal Aberdeen), and begin a run of six splendid holes north along the coast. We seem to be forever driving from elevated tees in the dunes—and this driving had better be accurate, for these are not broad fairways—down into mogul-strewn valleys, then firing uphill to a green, sometimes exposed, sometimes sheltered, that is large enough if only we can get there.

Each hole in this skein, which includes a superlative knob-to-knob one-shotter and a very long up-hill-down-dale two-shotter where a par feels like a birdie, is outstanding, but it is the 7th, called "Serpentine," that is preeminent. Tom Doak calls it "all world."

From a hilltop tee on this 423-yarder we must carry not only the burn that gives the hole its name but, at about 190 yards, a second branch of the same stream as it cuts across the fairway in the valley far below. A fade will disappear into a ravine, a pull into heavy rough. It is a moment that calls for our soundest swing and, having produced it, then a long second up this rising dune-framed valley to a green sited in a sort of saddle at the crest and bunkered right and left. This is a hole—and not the only such at Murcar, by any means—that proclaims the superiority of seaside golf: natural and thrilling and mighty.

The inbound half, which sees us leaving the coastal sandhills and now enjoying somewhat easier stances and lies, is also very spirited. For much of the way the changes in elevation are quite pronounced, with the hills, as on 10 and 11, prompting a blind shot here and there to lend a certain piquancy to the proceedings.

Fifteen and 16 are particularly noteworthy. From a tee atop a sandhill ridge, we set off on the 357-yard 15th downhill over a tributary of the burn into the valley. The second shot, sharply climbing an escarpment with the principal flow of the stream at its base, seeks a green on the plateau above. This, into a stiff wind, can be a real "death or glory" undertaking, for the shot that is the least bit anemic is likely to plunk into the face of the cliff and retreat, as we watch in horror, slowly back down into the burn.

The 16th, a 160-yarder, offers a shade less drama, but it is unusual. First of all, it crosses in front of the 15th green—courtesy and alertness are called for here. Both tee and green are set on the plateau, but intervening is an immense falloff brought on by a curve of the cliff. We should clear it without a second thought, but if that second thought somehow arises, so might a too-quick takeaway.

Seventeen, a pretty 360-yarder doglegging left, presents a blind drive. And the home hole, 329 yards, is regrettably rather ordinary, routed over uninteresting level ground and decorated by a total of ten bunkers, six along the way and four serving sentinel duty at the green. A southeast wind, not uncommon, does impart some bite, but neither Simpson nor Braid managed to solve the problem of getting back to the clubhouse in style. Still, 17 out of 18—and I want to go on record as liking every hole on this golf course except the finisher—is an extremely high batting average in any league.

I asked Bob Matthews, the very cordial secretary of Murcar, whether the course gets much play during the winter.

"More than any course I can think of," he replied. "We have so many members who are keen golfers—a lot of them retired now—and the days are so short—actually no more than seven hours of daylight in the depths of winter—that there aren't enough tee times for all who want to play. So we have what is called a Winter League. And the important thing is to get your name on the league list. What happens is that a Saturday in October is set aside for making up the list, which opens for signatures at eight that morning. Since the policy is to accept no more than one hundred names all told, players begin to queue up at midnight Friday, out in the car park, so that they will be at the head of the line that Saturday morning at eight o'clock to sign up for the Winter League."

I was surprised at this club policy, but not at all surprised at the members' response. To be shut out at Murcar, even in the dead of winter, would be intolerable. Access to the very good relief nine, 2,850 yards long and laid out over rolling duneland, would not make up for it.

Well, now it is time to go next door and play Balgownie, as the links of the Royal Aberdeen Golf Club is familiarly known. Here we find a great and historic club and a great and historic links. The world is not overrun with this combination.

Royal Aberdeen is the sixth-oldest golf club in the world (Royal Blackheath, Royal Burgess, the Honourable Company, the R&A, and Bruntsfield Links Golfing Society are older), dating to 1780, when the Society of Golfers at Aberdeen was founded. In 1815 the Society became the Aberdeen Golf Club, and in 1903, by grace of King Edward VII, the Royal Aberdeen Golf Club.

For the first century the club—which, incidentally, introduced in 1783 the five-minute limit on searching for golf balls—played over a public links, a common ground, within the city. When that course became impossibly crowded, a lease was negotiated on ground to the north of the river Don, at Balgownie. Over the years, one Park (Willie, Sr.) and three Simpsons (Robert, celebrated Carnoustie clubmaker; Archie, Royal Aberdeen's professional; and Tom, he of the embroidered cloak and beret and the chauffeur-driven Rolls-Royce) took turns in shaping the golf holes here. So sketchy are the records that it is difficult to ascribe the lion's share of the credit to any one individual. Let them all take a bow, for from the splendid start to the equally splendid finish, this is seaside golf of the highest order.

Now it is one thing to end the round under the clubhouse windows and the skeptical gaze of one's fellows, but to commence it, in a state of typical uncertainty, on a swatch of turf tucked conveniently between two vast bay windows of the clubhouse's principal rooms is the very definition of mental cruelty. At Balgownie, that is the way the game begins. Still, the fairway that lies below is broad, the sea that lies beyond is sparkling, and the prospect of a grand day on the links will never be brighter than it is at this very moment. So we swing, not too lustily, perhaps, and with any luck find ourself in a position to swing again on this 410-yarder where the green, boldly undulating, 'sits on a rise just beyond a deep, concealed dip and silhouetted against the sky and the sea. Can the course—indeed, can any course—possibly live up to such an overture?

We quickly get the answer. The next eight holes, beginning from a lofty perch above the beach, weave their way—beautifully, naturally, hauntingly—through a landscape of towering sandhills and over terrain that ranges from rippling to tumbling to billowing. All the ingredients are here: gorse, heather, long bents (sometimes laced with bluebells!), punishing sandpits, an occasional burn, an occasional blind shot, an occasional bad bounce, tees atop dunes, greens in hollows, greens on plateaus, forced-carries over wild and forbidding country, and ribbons of fairway tracing their lonely paths along dune-framed valleys. We play this first nine at Balgownie in seclusion. We also play it in wonder and delight. The 4th (423 yards) and 9th

(453 yards) are an extremely testing pair of two-shotters, with the latter—falling tee shot from high in the dunes to an angled fairway that doglegs smoothly right, followed by a wood up the hill to a well-bunkered bilevel green—a fitting finale to the outward half and, in my judgment, the finest hole on the course. From the medal tees, this nine, against a par of 36, measures 3,372 yards.

The inbound half—this is a pure out-and-in design—measures only 3,000 yards, and it is played over much less captivating ground. The great dunes are gone now, and with them some of the magic, but none of the test. Into the prevailing breeze, the second nine actually plays harder than the first. On neither half, it should be noted, is putting likely to be a serious problem (unless the surfaces are burnished), for the greens, taken as a whole, are not as festive as we might wish.

Boundaries on the right give the slicer something to fret about on 10, 11, and 12 (and remind the rest of us where Murcar's little old railway once ran). The plateau green on 12 is cleverly sited just beyond a ridge on the diagonal, which directs anything underhit on this 386-yarder down into the left-hand bunker. Three good but, in a rare calm, not long two-shotters follow, the green on 13 in a hollow, the green on 14 defended by a curious turf-covered ditch that must be carried, and the green on 15 completely sealed off by a cross bunker. With the fairway concealed beyond a little rise, it is the lighthouse we take aim on from the 15th tee.

The finishing trio are strong medicine. Sixteen, 392 yards, plays from a modestly elevated tee into a rising fairway, happily broad, guarded by sand on the left and gorse on the right. The long second shot, which may well prove to be blind, is played to a narrow green framed left and right by a total of five bunkers. Seventeen plays toward the sea and is 180 yards long. The twin-terrace green is ringed by six bunkers. Hold a perfect 3-iron up into the left-to-right crosswind and you will succeed. The likelihood of failure is high.

The 18th at Balgownie is surely one of the best finishing holes in Scottish golf (in truth, only the home hole at Muirfield, at Carnoustie, at Loch Lomond, and at the Carnegie Course come to mind as its equal). It is 434 yards long. Again the tee is modestly elevated, all the better to reconnoiter the dangers. Bunkers await the pushed or pulled drive, as does gorse and the omnipresent long rough grasses. A very good drive will finish in a dip in the fairway. The long second must carry a steep swale just short of the plateau green. Into the prevailing wind there is little hope of a ball chasing up the face of this bank, much more likelihood of its subsiding into one of the bunkers at the base. Splendid stuff, and a suitable climax to one of the great links.

Ronnie MacAskill, who is not only the head professional but the club's general manager as well, says, "If Balgownie were 500 yards longer, perhaps the Open would be played here. This is a championship course in every respect except length." And Darwin confessed that "it represented a huge gap in my golfing education not to have played Balgownie until now, much more than a good golf course, a noble links."

I urge you to have a simple sandwich-and-beverage lunch in the many-windowed lounge with its view of the starting and finishing holes and the sea. (To eat a cooked meal would find you in the dining room, which does not enjoy such a lovely outlook.) Here, in an atmosphere that is not in the least hushed or stuffy, you will gain some sense of the antiquity and dignity of this fine club. There are old pictures and books, old wood and silver. Women visitors are welcome in this room, notwithstanding the fact that the charming little black and white clubhouse of the Aberdeen Ladies' Golf Club, clearly designed in sympathy with the men's, is all of 150 yards away. So, I might add, is the first tee of the Silverburn eighteen, which the ladies get a great deal of pleasure from and which is in the process of being extensively revamped by Donald Steel in order to make it even more attractive.

Straight through the center of Aberdeen now, that sturdy and confident gray granite city, carrying along beside the harbor—the large oceangoing vessels themselves tied up not 200 yards from the heart of downtown—then out along the Dee and due south some 15 miles along the coast road to Stonehaven, where the most singular golf course covered in this book awaits.

"Stonehaven? Clifftops and railroads," sniffed an American woman golfer to whom I mentioned the course. "Clifftops and railroads."

She was correct—not fair, mind you, but correct, though *railroads* should have been singular. Still, since we walk under the railway viaduct in progressing from the 8th green to the 9th tee, from the 12th green to the 13th tee, from the 13th tee to the 13th fairway, and from the 15th tee to the 15th green, perhaps she can be forgiven for using the plural.

I am afraid that my powers of communication fail before the fantasy that is Stonehaven. I will not be able to make sense of it for you. It is all so hilariously unconventional as to defy analysis. But what extraordinary fun it is! Indeed, here, in all the world, may be the course that merits Darwin's adjective *jolly* above all others.

A few hard facts will doubtless persuade you that in suggesting—no, make that recommending—a round at Stonehaven I must be in my dotage. Nonetheless, here we go. Total yardage from the tips is 5,103. Par is 66. The eighteen holes occupy 62 acres. There is one par five and there are seven par threes, three of these one-shotters in a row on the first nine. The 4th, 5th, and 16th are crisscross holes, but it is the 5th that wins the palm: here the drive from a hilltop tee sails straight toward the sea and, in the bargain, *directly over both the 16th and the 4th fairways!* The aforementioned railway—this is the Dundee/Aberdeen line—features those two-car "sprinters," as the locals refer to them, whipping through the middle of the golf course in the middle of your backswing half a dozen times during the round. The holes are located in three different sectors: on the high meadow beyond the tracks, in the narrow neck beyond the railway viaduct, and, the majority of them, on the precipitously sloping headlands high above the sea. You take them where, and if, you find them—as, one suspects, did Archie Simpson and George Duncan (Open champion in 1920 and briefly Stonehaven's professional at the turn of the century), both of whom had a hand in routing golf holes over this unlikely tract.

I should have known that this was going to be an unusual round when the club's secretary, Robert Blair, greeted my wife and me on a Thursday in early August by saying hospitably, "You've come on quite a nice day." In fact, the wind was blowing at 15 to 20 mph, the leaden skies held little promise of sun (and delivered less), and thermal underwear would not have been amiss as the wind-chill factor hovered about the 50-degree mark. Still, it was not raining.

As you would expect of a very hilly course occupying just 62 acres, there are a number of boundaries and a number of blind shots, three of the latter occurring on par-three holes. Bunkering is light to moderate, and if a shot should find the sand the recovery is easily handled. The greens, which are wonderfully true and keen, are small to medium and, on the whole, not difficult to read. Several of them—one thinks of the 5th, 7th, 8th, and 15th—are uncomfortably close to the cliff's edge. The same is true of a heart-stopping quartet of tees on the first nine—at 2, 6, 7, and 8—which seem to be all but cantilevered dizzyingly out over the wave-washed rocks far below.

The isolated tee on the 203-yard 2nd vies with the launching pad on the 9th at Turnberry's Ailsa for "tee of the world" honors. So totally exposed and so precariously sited is it that—and I say this in all seriousness—we would hesitate before going out there in the 30-, 35-, and 40-mph winds that are common at Stonehaven. It is no place for the faint of heart. As for that blind 203-yard shot, it must first clear the abyss created by a cleft in the cliffs and then a humpy ridge before carrying—or skipping up—a little rise to a wide plateau green bunkered left and right. An original golf hole.

My two particular favorites are also par threes on the outbound nine, the 7th and 8th. For a pairing of spectacle and shot value, the 170-yard 7th can take its place with almost any one-shotter you are likely to play. Again from a soberingly high tee above the sea, the brave shot must be lined for most of its distance out over the cliffs. The merest suggestion of left-to-right spin will find the ball clattering down the rock face to the Skatie Shore below. The 8th, perfectly paralleling the coastline and 10 yards shorter than the 7th, also finds the putting surface raised somewhat above the tee, but this time there is a little breathing space between an amphitheatre green and the cliff's edge. These are two of the best par threes in my experience, and they alone are worth the price of admission.

We had lunch in the quaint old clubhouse that rambles along the hillside. Mr. Blair said to us, "I have to work hard to convince a number of our members that this jewel of a clubhouse should not be leveled and a concrete box put up in its place, but should be carefully preserved and carefully enlarged whenever necessary." I bought a Stonehaven Golf Club necktie, green and white regimental stripes. I am not normally given to that kind of extravagance, but I thought that it might be useful later, something tangible to prove, as it were, that the eighteen at Stonehaven had indeed been real, that I had not dreamed it.

Over the years I have been so busy playing in the Aberdeen environs that my wife and I have done little or nothing in the way of sight-seeing. The city itself, Scotland's third in population, is not without interest, with the great harbor well repaying a walk; also worth visits are St. Andrew's Cathedral (an interior where the white walls and pillars are in striking contrast to the bright coloring of the coats-of-arms on the ceiling) and Provost Skene's House (450 years old and containing several superbly recreated rooms of later periods). Out in the country some 15 miles west, and almost within hailing distance of each other, are Castle Fraser and Crathes Castle, both begun in the midsixteenth century and both in excellent condition today. The gardens at Crathes are among Scotland's most prized.

A word or two on accommodations. Cruden Bay's Kilmarnock Arms, a 200-year-old coaching inn where Bram Stoker used to hole up regularly during summers at the turn of the century, has been refurbished in recent years and is now as cheerful as it is convenient (two minutes' drive from the great links, two minutes' walk from the tiny, deserted harbor). In Newburgh, which is on the way from Cruden Bay to Murcar, is the Udny Arms, a very charming old inn where several of the rooms can be a bit on the cramped side but the cuisine is outstanding. A rung above is Meldrum House, about 15 miles west of Aberdeen. This rambling stone manor, part of which dates to the thirteenth century, has been renovated within the past couple of years. Set in lovely grazing land, it offers a nice sense of times long past, comfortable and homey guest rooms (some with four posters), and very good cooking. In Aberdeenshire, it is as easy to find satisfactory accommodations as it is to find wonderful golf courses.

Chapter Nine

A Very
Mixed Bag

Little more than 30 minutes due south of Stonehaven on the coast road, A92, lie the town and the links of Montrose. A seaside town of some 10,000 residents, Montrose, with rather too much soot-stained stone to be anything like pretty, nevertheless boasts a spacious High Street and dignified buildings such as the Old Church, with its pinnacled square tower and graceful steeple, and the mid-eighteenth-century Old Town Hall. It also boasts two 18-hole municipal courses, the Broomfield, only 4,800 yards long, and the Medal, which reflects the work of Willie Park, Jr., more than that of anyone else.

Montrose ranks with Leith and St. Andrews among the earliest centers of golf, all three looking back more than 400 years. By the mid-nineteenth century Montrose was distinguished by the number of its golf holes, 25, more than any other course has ever had. In October, 1866, a newspaper advertisement referred to an "OPEN GOLF COMPETITION to be held on Montrose Links, Over 25 Holes, being One Round of the Golf Course." By contrast, Musselburgh, for instance, had just 7 holes, and Prestwick, where the Open was born, only 12.

Three principal clubs—Royal Montrose, Caledonia, and Mercantile—play over the links. All of them welcome visitors. Royal Montrose was the first to have its own clubhouse, a spartan cottage that, according to the local newspaper, "the members seemed to like simply because it was . . . defective in every requisite."

Notes from the minutes of members' meetings at the Mercantile Club in 1906, as recorded in William W. Coull's excellent *Golf in Montrose,* also speak of simpler times: "Agreed to buy a bathmat. Mr. Keiller moved we also buy a bath brush. . . . Mr. Robertson moved that we defer the brush just now. On a vote, the motion was carried. . . ."

The Medal Course at Montrose, 6,230 yards from the regular tees against a par of 71, is a delight, though in no sense is it a great links. For one thing, there are three or four prosaic holes, and the splendid duneland through which the first seven holes are routed is in sight but not in play for the last eleven holes. Nonetheless, this is true and natural seaside golf, a combination of imposing sandhills, often violently rumpled fairways, gorse, heather, and long rough grasses. The routing changes direction more than on most links, and the holes are attractively varied. The tee at the par-five 6th provides an indelible memory: It is a tiny platform at the peak of the great dunes, with the flawless beach of tawny sand far below, on the one hand, and the fairway—broad and inviting—far below, on the other.

Curiously, the much less dramatic second nine is perhaps the more testing, containing three par fours of more than 400 yards and a very long par three. It was on the 14th, itself a 401-yarder, the first time I visited Montrose that a couple of young men by the names of Martin and Ian Smith, who had been playing just ahead, invited me to join them. They pointed out that the two men about 300 yards down the fairway were also Smiths, their brother and father. In America this would have been the ideal foursome, a father and his three sons. But so concerned are many British about playing the round with dispatch that four players will often split up, thus saving the biggest part of an hour.

The four Smiths lived in Oxford. Martin, a Ph.D. candidate at Corpus Christi College, went up regularly to London to earn spending money playing trumpet at the Ritz. Ian, several years younger, was studying for his bachelor's at St. Anne's. They played golf only during their annual holiday in Montrose, a family fixture for about ten years. They professed to enjoy the game enormously, and the animated way they talked about shots, together with the aggressive nature of their play—Martin could lace the ball a country mile and, in truth, all over the countryside—seemed to confirm this.

They knew the medal course well and were helpful guides for the final holes, warning of dangers, explaining subtleties. I earned a sincere "Well done, indeed" when I holed a sliding five-footer for three on the 226-yard 16th, a fine one-shotter called "Gully" with a fiendishly undulating green. I also earned a sympathetic "Unlucky" when a putt for par of the same length slipped by on the 410-yard 17th, the course's best hole. It doglegs mildly right through the gorse, and only a perfect approach will find the elevated shelflike green carved out of a dune at the left.

They said that they were not the only English who came to Montrose and pointed out a substantial half-timbered house just beyond the 13th fairway, saying that it had been the holiday home of the head of the Secret Service, whose wife had died some years ago. He had continued to stay there for short periods of time with a woman he did not marry, and when he died the property was left to her. She now occupied it full time. Visions of John Le Carré's world swirled through my head— surely this was a house in which great deceptions and great treacheries had been discussed in a style both pragmatic and sinister, a house now owned by the former mistress of the U.K.'s No. 1 plotter! This was heady stuff.

"If you don't mind my asking," I said, "how do you come to know about this?"

"The piano," Ian replied. "It's the piano. The lady has a concert-grand piano in the drawing room, and she likes to stage little recitals there. Somehow she learned about our musical bent— Martin's trumpet playing is not the whole of it. Father is an accomplished pianist and David plays the violin."

"So we've been to the house a number of times and grown quite friendly with the lady," Martin concluded the explanation.

Clearly, there is more to Montrose than meets the eye.

Some 15 minutes south on the coast road is a course with six deadly dull holes, three to start the round, three to finish it. Nonetheless, Panmure, in Barry, is well worth a visit.

The club celebrated its 150th anniversary in 1995. For the first 50 years its members had played at Monifieth, which is next door, but congestion there forced them to seek their own land. Within a few years of its establishment, the Barry links was so highly regarded that it was selected as the venue for the first Scottish Professional Championship, in 1907. It has been chosen three times as a site for Open qualifying—twice, in 1968 and 1975, when the championship was played at Carnoustie, and once, in 1970, when it was held at St. Andrews. A number of Panmure members live in St. Andrews and are members of the R&A. David Chidley, the secretary at Panmure, said to me when I visited the club for the first time several years ago, "It is fair to view Panmure as a rather prestigious club, on much the same level, if you will, as Muirfield and the R&A. But, of course, we are not nearly so well known." Mr. Chidley also reminded me that to be served refreshments in the members' lounge gentlemen are required to wear jacket and tie and "ladies must be appropriately attired." My wife learned that this meant a dress or skirt—no jeans or trousers of any kind.

Panmure's professional at that time—he has since retired—was Tom Shiel. I spoke with him briefly in his small, well-stocked shop before teeing off. Shortish and silver-haired, with a round, ruddy face, he was an outgoing man who seemed glad to have a little company on this overcast day.

I learned he had twice immigrated to America, and twice he had returned to Carnoustie. He had been 27 when he first came to the United States, in 1954, hoping to find a better living in golf than the Carnoustie area (Barry is only a few miles from Carnoustie) then offered. He worked as an assistant pro at a couple of clubs in the Baltimore area, got married, and returned to Carnoustie a dozen years later with his wife and two children. In the mid-1970s the Shiels were back in the United States, settling in Newport News, Virginia, where he worked at the James River Country Club and at a public course. In 1981, now 54 years old, he again came back to Carnoustie. This time he got the job at Panmure.

It was the health of his parents that had prompted his return to Scotland on both occasions: he was needed to help take care of them. "Both are gone now," he said. "Our children and grandchildren"—he pointed proudly to photos of his two young grandsons displayed on a tiny shelf above the counter— "live in the Washington/Baltimore area. I would like to retire so my wife and I could go back to the States."

He gave me a copy of the "Pro Guide" to the course, a little booklet with detailed distance and hazard information. I promised to check back with him after the round. Was Tom Shiel, I wondered as I headed for the 1st tee, the last in the long tradition of Carnoustie golfers who had immigrated to the United States to seek greener fairways? It is said that in the early years of this century fully half of the golf professionals in America were Carnoustie-born and -bred. The Smiths come immediately to mind, Willie, Alex, and MacDonald. Willie won the U.S. Open in 1899, Alex in 1906 and 1910. The youngest of the three, MacDonald, twice runner-up in the British Open and once in the U.S. Open, is often referred to as the best player who never won either of the two great national titles. Another Carnoustie man, Stewart Maiden, played little competitive golf in America, but his fame is secure, for it was he, having succeeded his brother James as the professional at the Atlanta Athletic Club's East Lake course, who taught Bobby Jones and Alexa Stirling.

Panmure, which measures 6,317 yards against a par of 70 from the medal tees, 6,085 from the regular markers, demands our forbearance. We know it has good golf holes, but we've got to get to them. When the course was laid out, almost a hundred years ago, the clubhouse had to be located within an easy walk of the railroad station at Barry. This ground is flat and uninteresting, and so are the golf holes on it.

A screen of pines serves as a backcloth for the 3rd green. Having putted out on this 377-yarder (the 1st hole is 280 yards, the second 476), we look around for the next tee. It is nowhere to be seen. A path leads through the pines. We follow it optimistically. And when it has led us through this spinney and into the clear, with delight we enter golfing country of character and diversity, of severe beauty and even of surprise. For now it is low ridges of sandhills through which the holes meander. Now the fairways roll and ripple. Now, from time to time, we face an intimidating carry over broken ground, over bent-clad hillocks sometimes dotted with bluebells. Here is the card-wrecking gorse and the throttling heather. Bunkering is light to moderate, but most sandpits have high and deep revetted faces. This is the links golf we have crossed an ocean to play, and we set out upon it enthusiastically.

The final four holes of the first nine are exceptional. Indeed, the 6th, 387 yards and into the prevailing breeze, may fairly be labeled great. It is a test of both nerve and skill. From a tee hidden away in the dunes, our drive must carry a stretch of heather and hillocks that culminates with a disconcerting bunker on the optimum line, well left of center. The landing area is blind and it slopes softly right, inclining to carry the strong, straight drive through the fairway and into mounds and high grass. But the hole curves left. The second shot is played mildly uphill over uneven ground, with slippage to the right, through low sandhills to a plateau green sited uncomfortably close to a boundary on the left. One lonely bunker defends the green, and it is precisely where it ought to be to catch the timorous second, short and right, at the base of the plateau. There is much to think about. Not till the round was over did I learn just how notable a hole the 6th is.

The lovely 7th, 408 yards, runs in the opposite direction, with the long second played up a narrowing dune-framed fairway to a green ensconced among sandhills and gorse.

Eight is an original. We drive downhill over a rolling waste of gorse and long bents to an invisible landing area. Reaching the ball in the fairway, we are forced to wonder whether we have not somehow gone dead wrong. We find ourselves in an enclosed valley, with no sign of the green. Squarely in front of us a sandhill bulks large. A little perplexed reconnoitering reveals that we must hit our 6- or 7-iron over it to reach a green in a clearing ringed by low mounds. Intriguing every step of the way!

As for the 9th, here is a 167-yarder calling for nothing less than a perfectly struck shot as we cross an expanse of rough country—odd-looking hillocks that suggest pumped-up beehives—to a rising green guarded by a bunker at the right front, a big mound and a large bunker on the left. And the ball does not want to stay put.

The first four holes heading home offer invigorating golf,

with the 12th, 343 yards, particularly good. It is a water hole. The Buddon Burn squirrels crazily across the line of play, squeezing the fairway mercilessly some 265 yards off the tee, then looping convulsively forward to imperil the underhit second shot—we are normally playing into the wind here—at a point some 40 yards short of a plateau green at the top of a rise. To cap it all, the green, appearing smaller than it actually is, is positioned boldly on the bias and is guarded by mounds and sand. Terrific stuff, second only to the 6th for that priceless combination of challenge and exhilaration. Again, power is not the key; precision is.

We have reached the end of the club's property. Behind the green and just on the other side of the fence lie the links of Monifieth, a convenient reminder to the Panmure members of their origins and to me of the next game.

Turning about now, we begin the long and essentially straight run to the clubhouse, the breeze our loyal ally. Thirteen is the final hole routed over the marvelous terrain we entered at the 4th, and a fitting farewell it is. From a tee atop the dunes, we strike off downhill over the Buddon Burn. A 400-yarder, this hole calls for a firm second shot slightly uphill and over a ditch. A pronounced tier in the green, running from front left to back right, makes putting—and chipping, for that matter—far from routine.

At 535 yards, 14 is the longest hole on the course, and the railway line accompanies it on the right every foot of the way. The boundary here is not so tight that we feel menaced by it. What we must be wary of is the sudden appearance of those two-car Aberdeen/Dundee "sprinters" that zipped back and forth at Stonehaven. From the 14th tee we get our only glimpse of the Firth of Tay, its waters glinting a tarnished silver in the far distance.

The last four holes—the very long one-shotter 15th (234 yards), followed by three par fours, all about 400 yards—are unremarkable. The chronic slicer must eschew the boundary on 17 and 18, but there is room to spare on the left. The black and gold clock on the captivating Edwardian clubhouse—chimneys, gables, dormers, and a flag-topped turret—reminds us where to aim our drive on the home hole. It also advises us whether we have tarried or moved smartly along.

Time now to report to Tom Shiel. I told him how much I had enjoyed the course, though I felt compelled to note the unpromising start and the unimpressive finish.

"What you say is true enough," he conceded. "There can be no denying it. But," he added with a proud and broad smile, "isn't it the best 'middle course' you've ever played?"

"I'm sure it is," I said. "There are holes—a handful of them—that are wonderful by any standards. The 6th—from the moment you step onto the tee, it—"

"Aye, you've put your finger on it," he interjected. "It's Hogan's Hole. Yes, that's what it's called today. When Ben Hogan won the Open at Carnoustie, in 1953, he played a couple of practice rounds here. He called the 6th one of the best par fours in the world. He said you could put it on any course and it would be outstanding."

Four men's golf clubs—Monifieth, Grange & Dundee, Broughty, and Abertay—and one ladies' club, the Panmure

Ladies' Club, use the two municipal eighteens at Monifieth. The secondary course, Ashludie, measures 5,123 yards against a par of 68. I have not played it, but it is laid out over the same kind of honest golfing ground as the principal eighteen.

I well recall the initial moment of my first visit to Monifieth. I knocked on the door at the Monifieth Golf Club. A steward opened it and advised me to go over to the Abertay club. "It's their turn today to accommodate visitors," he said cheerily. "They handle Thursdays."

The Monifieth Golf Links—6,459 yards long from the regular tees, par 71—has neither the weaknesses nor the strengths of Panmure. The prosaic opening and closing holes next door have no counterparts here. Unfortunately, neither do the marvelous holes through the heart of the round at Panmure. Monifieth is a consistently straightforward, no-nonsense layout. There is nothing capricious or gimmicky about it. You get what you hit, and after the 312-yard opener, be prepared to hit full out. The next three holes measure 405 yards, 419, and 445 from the regular tees, a little longer from the back. If you are a big basher, the 445-yarder is a beauty, bunkers flanking the tee-shot landing area, the green tightly protected by high sand-hills. The hole has been named with a resolute disregard for its severity: "Featherbed."

The first of the par threes follows, a gently falling shot with the Dundee/Aberdeen railway line tight on our right beside the tee and beside the green. No room whatsoever on this 182-yarder for a push or a pull—three bunkers on each side—but, as on all holes except the par-three 14th, the green is open across the front to accommodate a run-on shot.

At the 7th we do an about-face. The first six holes have

played straightaway from the clubhouse in a generally northern direction, the train tracks glittering beside us on the right but rarely in a menacing fashion. Now we bid the railway goodbye, never to return to it, as we tackle this excellent 406-yarder. The drive must avoid the Buddon Burn, the same snaking stream we encountered on the 12th at Panmure. Here it forces a carry of 185 yards on the line to the flag (the less adventurous can steer safely right, but trees pinch the landing area there). Bunkers right and left at the front of the green will snare the wayward second shot. In short, a hole with backbone and interest from start to finish.

The 8th, only 273 yards long, is a distinct birdie opportunity, and the elevated tee here affords a glimpse of the Firth of Tay as well as some distant views of rolling Angus farmland. As for the last hole going out, it's a good par five of 536 yards, where, failing to traverse a deep swale on our second shot, we are left with a blind pitch.

The inward nine is shorter by more than 200 yards (3,111 as

opposed to 3,348 yards), but there is a bit more bunkering, and overall, straighter shots are required. Not only must several drives be put down in narrowing fairways patrolled by gorse, heather, and low dunes, but one green, that of the 370-yard dogleg 15th, is guarded on the right by a mature maple tree. This brings up a key aspect of Monifieth. It is somewhat of a hybrid. It feels like seaside golf (though the Tay is scarcely next door) with its undulating fairways, its gorse, its modest bent-covered sandhills, its greens sometimes nestled in hummocky dells. But it looks almost parkland, thanks to the abundance of trees, generally pines and firs and often in small groves. Only rarely do we enjoy the unimpeded long view.

The round finishes with a hard two-shotter—424 yards and nine bunkers (the pits at Monifieth are penal)—and an easy par five, which, at 519 yards and ever so slightly falling, must yield its share of birdies despite half a dozen bunkers near or at the green.

There is little about Monifieth to make the heart sing or the pulse quicken—no eye-opening surprises, no do-or-die demands, no difficult choices. Still, it is certainly not a bore and we must consistently execute solid shots if we are to produce acceptable figures.

Heavy play still burdens this links, just as it did a hundred years ago when Panmure departed. Harry Nicoll, the grandfatherly links secretary, whom I talked briefly with on this visit, told me, "The five clubs have a total of about 1,500 members. This does not include spouses and children. So both eighteens are often crowded. We've enlarged the greens, which enables us to move the cups around and avoid the compaction of the turf caused by so much traffic in the same spots all the time. The greens are watered, though not the fairways and tees. Water is actually a problem despite all the rain we get because too often the rain is followed by strong winds which whip the course dry in no time."

As I got up to leave, Mr. Nicoll added another piece of information that he thought I should have, though he seemed reluctant to appear boastful. "This is a championship course," he said. "The Scottish Boys' Championship was played here just a few weeks ago. And it has been a qualifying venue when the Open Championship was played at Carnoustie."

He said "was played" and he implied "used to be played." But these words were spoken in 1992. In 1994 the R&A surprised—and pleased—a lot of people by announcing that in 1998, after a 23-year absence, the Open would return to Carnoustie. I must confess that I was not among the pleased. I do not think much of the championship course (there are two other eighteens) at Carnoustie. For the most part, it is routed over poor golfing terrain, and serious efforts during the biggest part of a hundred years, beginning in 1850, by such as Allan Robertson, Willie Park, Jr., Old Tom Morris, and James Braid have failed, in my judgment, to make a silk purse out of a sow's ear.

I am admittedly in a minority, and to give the devil his due I must report what Jack Nicklaus said to me a number of years ago on this subject: "When I first went to Carnoustie in 1967, to play a television match with Arnold [Palmer] and Gary [Player], I thought Carnoustie was the worst golf course I'd ever seen. And by the time I'd finished the Open in 1968, I thought it was the hardest golf course I'd ever seen [Player's 289 was two shots better than Nicklaus and Bob Charles], but a darn good course, and I really had great respect for it. And the last time I went back in '75, I had even greater respect for it. Now Carnoustie is one of my favorites."

There can be little question about it: the Opens held here have been great championships, dramatic, memorable, fiercely contested, the winner in each case—Tommy Armour, Henry Cotton, Ben Hogan (1953, his only appearance in the British Open), Gary Player, Tom Watson—a great player. And there can be even less question about the challenge. This is an extremely demanding course. Against a par of 72, it is almost 6,700 yards long from the *regular* tees, just under 7,000 from the medal tees, and 7,272 yards from the championship tees. When the wind blows, it is brutally hard. But pure difficulty, especially when based largely on length, is scarcely a criterion for excellence, to say nothing of greatness.

The opening holes strike me as quite good. There is a mild upslope on the 1st, 389 yards, which then drops off to a green hidden in a hollow. The superb 2nd, 439 yards, calls for a well-placed drive in order to avoid "Braid's Bunker," in the middle of the fairway at 230 yards, then an equally fine second shot up a cut between low dunes to a tightly bunkered green. The 3rd plays from a raised tee in some modestly hillocky country and, at 336 yards the shortest two-shotter on the course, requires an approach over Jockie's Burn to a small green. These three fairways undulate, and the grass-covered sandhills are functional. We feel that we are on a true links. Indeed, the broad waters of the Firth of Tay can be glimpsed from the 3rd green.

Treasure that glimpse: it is all there is. Treasure those three holes of links golf: they are all there are. Walk to the 4th tee and prepare to enter a vast meadowy plain, a landscape monotonously pedestrian, covered with holes that, too often, are neither memorable nor inviting.

If only the greens had character, we might not be quite so disappointed, but time and again—in truth, on all but three or four holes—they are mere billiard-table extensions of the fairways.

The bunkers? There are some 110 of them, and on the whole they are not capriciously placed. Neither, sadly, is there anything the least natural about them. They have been sited and scooped out in the most calculated and artificial fashion. They tend to rear up from a flat base rather than shelter down into the terrain, as on other courses.

Carnoustie has, of course, a number of holes, perhaps eight or nine, that range from first-rate to outstanding. But it is cursed with three utterly mediocre holes (the 4th, 373 yards; the 7th, 379 yards; and the 11th, 360 yards); two of the inarguably banal one-shotters in the entire British Open rota (the 162-yard 8th and the 145-yard 13th, both of which serve no other useful purpose than as "walkways" betweeen the preceding and the following holes); and two woefully weak par fives, the 12th (476 yards, sometimes played as a par four, in which case it is simply a straightforward slog) and the 14th, just 10 yards longer.

The 14th has gained a certain celebrity over the years. Perhaps 60 yards short of the green there is a sharp swell in the fairway. Into this slope have been cut two bunkers, appropriately named the "Spectacles." They stare hard at you, daring you to attempt to swat your second shot over them and down onto the green. The hole is fun to play and, as you would expect, yields an inordinate number of birdies. Paired with

Player, Nicklaus got his four here in the final round of the 1968 Open, but the South African hit the finest 4-wood of his career to two feet for an eagle, then went on to win by two strokes. Seven years later, this time in an 18-hole playoff, Tom Watson and Australia's Jack Newton came to the "Spectacles" tied. Newton chipped close for his birdie, Watson chipped in for his eagle and went on to win by a stroke.

The 16th at Carnoustie may well be the most overrated par three in the world. It is very long, 235 yards. It is very flat. It has six bunkers, none of them dangerous, none of them truly greenside. Like the entire hole, the green itself is comfortingly level—and all of 12 inches above the fairway. In short, the 16th holds no terror. True, it is easy enough to take a bogey here, but you must be very inventive indeed to come up with anything worse.

In casting about for some explanation as to why this bleak and charmless old links—"sour," someone once called it—should have awed both competitor and observer alike for so many years, I am forced to conclude that it can be summed up in just three words: *the Barry Burn.*

Great water holes are uncommon on links courses, and this stream is a good, old-fashioned, honest-to-God hazard—no mere slit trench. It comes into play on the 414-yard 10th, where it lurks some 50 yards short of the green to snare the badly underhit approach, and on the 17th and 18th. On the last two holes it is satanically thrilling.

The 17th is a 439-yarder called "Island." The burn, some 20 feet wide, snakes across the fairway twice, the second time about 245 yards from the tee. Unless you are a very powerful hitter or the breeze is dead behind you, your tee shot must be placed between the two coils of the burn. This "island" swings generously out on the left, but the long shot into the green from here must clear sentinel hillocks. Drive down the right and you have a much more open approach to the well-bunkered green, but the landing area for your tee shot is dangerously constricted by the water. A wonderful hole, and surely the only one quite like it on the famous courses of the world.

The 18th, at 444 yards, continues our risky flirtation with the burn, but in a more straightforward—and, many days, even more perilous—fashion. Again we must cross the water twice, the first time about 150 yards from the tee, the second time about seven or eight yards from the green. And just to keep us from swinging out of our shoes on both shots, a boundary skirts the entire left side of the hole.

But if the finale is mighty, it serves to point up the prosaic nature of too much that has gone before. This historic links simply sits there, flat, severe, dour. I remember thinking the first time I played it that, like Scotch whisky itself, perhaps Carnoustie is an acquired taste. I told myself then that this must be the case. Surely the next time old Carnoustie would work its spell. Well, I have downed a couple more drams, and for me there is no magic. Still, I urge you to play it. In recent years the turf has improved remarkably, so that Carnoustie is now among the best-conditioned courses in Scotland. As in the case of Willy Loman, "attention must be paid." All the more so, now that the Open is coming back.

Like the oldest of Carnoustie's three eighteens, the newest has an appealing opening stretch and a fine finish. In between, it is, for the most part, ordinary and forgettable.

The Buddon Links measures 5,420 yards against a par of 66.

There are seven short holes and one long hole. There are no great holes.

Whenever we are near the sea, the going is good. The farther we get from it, the less natural and less engaging the course becomes. Dramatizing its desperate stab at contemporaneity are four ponds (at the 4th, 9th, 11th, and 15th), all concealed, all artificial. These efforts to inject drama into what is a pretty drab business do not succeed.

As it turns out, the first four holes are entirely too promising, laid out as they are over attractively wrinkled ground. The two-tier green on the 1st is invitingly elevated; the large, undulating green on the 427-yard 2nd is ideally sited in a dell of low dunes; and on the excellent 4th, 390 yards and into the prevailing wind, our long second shot must carry the Buddon Burn (on yet a third course). Unfortunately, not till we return to the sea to play the excellent final three holes—a par five, a par three, and a par four, all striving to save the day—do we enjoy anything like this pleasure again.

Incidentally, each hole is given the name of a famous battle—Tobruk, El Alamein, Waterloo, etc.—suggesting a heroic quality to the links. It is a bad suggestion.

Well, so far, so disappointing. Is it to be a case of three strikes and you're out, Carnoustie? Emphatically not. The Burnside course is a home run. I let more than 20 years go by before getting around to playing it, but when I finally did, what a treat it was!

There is no doubt about who gets the credit for this gem. It was James Braid who laid it out, in 1926, and 70 years later it remains largely unaltered. The course measures 6,020 yards against a par of 68 (one long hole, five short holes). This is textbook links golf—dunes, gorse, heather, the long bent grasses, some blind shots, and bunkers with ferociously high "bricklayer" faces. There is little in the way of elevation change, but this is, on the whole, splendid golfing ground, ranging from undulating to downright humpy and hillocky, with virtually every hole either a challenger or a charmer or both. Like the golf holes themselves, the greens come in a variety of sizes, shapes, and contours. And as on most true links courses worthy of the name, Burnside offers its share of unpredictability, whimsy, and drama. Bounces can be capricious, and short pitches can be very difficult to control. In short, this eighteen has the gusto that I find missing on the big course next door.

I played Burnside that first time with a couple of retired men, one in his early 60s, the other perhaps 10 years older. The older fellow, Bill Cairns, told me with a twinkle that he had worked all his life as a "commercial traveler," much of eastern Scotland his territory as he sold Carr's biscuits first, then Watney's beer, ale, and stout. He wore knickers in a black watch plaid pattern, dark knee-length hose, a navy polo shirt, and a black traditional golf cap. It is entirely possible that no one on the Burnside course that day was so carefully turned out as Bill Cairns. Ruddy-faced, he was quick to laugh. Carnoustie was his home. He had a history of heart trouble, I was privately advised by his companion, who suggested that Bill Cairns be permitted to move at his own pace and to spend some time looking for a lost ball if he inclined to do so.

The younger man, short and slight and also inclined to take the humorous view of things, was also named Bill, Bill Thoms. His home was Arbroath, just up the coast, and he had been a social worker. "I started out with little children and finished up with the geriatric set," he said, "and along the way I loved every minute of it." On the first tee he said to me, "Oh, I've been playing atrocious stuff, Jim, such awful garbage, and I can't seem to get out of it." But even as he spoke he did not seem distressed. He was simply warning me what I had let myself in for, that's all.

He had already done me a kindness. After the starter had paired me up with the two Bills, I had excused myself to run back to the car for a couple of golf balls. When I returned to the shack to pay my green fee, I learned that it would be 3 pounds 25 pence instead of 13 pounds. Bill Thoms, who held a season ticket for all three Carnoustie courses that carried with it the privilege of inviting guests at a special rate, had advised the starter that I would be playing as his guest and so should be charged the guest green fee. Such a thoughtful thing to do.

I am not sure that either of them broke 110. But it did not matter. They loved the game, they loved this particular golf course, they took considerable pleasure in whatever good shots were hit, and they were eager to point the way for me.

The little light moments came along with some frequency. When a 20-foot putt of mine on the 3rd paused on the very lip of the cup, threatening to fall, the older man cried out imperatively to me, "Do a jig!" When his drive on 10 disappeared beyond the crest in the fairway, he said, in mock sorrow, "It's over the hill—rather like the man who hit it, I'm afraid." And as we were walking up the 12th fairway he took pains to describe for me the problems of the 17th. His companion objected: "Why are you telling Jim about 17 here?" asked Bill Thoms. "Ah," came the response, "I want to take his mind off the perils of this one."

Burnside has three great holes. Two of them are par threes. The green on the 158-yard 5th is all but marooned by a serpentine coil of the Barry Burn, which hugs the front of it, skirts the right side, then turns to come tight around behind it. A bunker awaits at the left to snare the so-called safe stroke.

The 14th, at 228 yards, is among the very best one-shotters I know. There are prominent dunes both left and right of the plateau green and a deep swale in front. Were the shot to be played straight on, at the opening beyond the swale, the hole would be merely wonderful. But, in fact, the tee has been placed cleverly left, perhaps 30 yards left, of where we would expect to find it, with the result that our wood must be hit over the right edge of the left-hand sandhill if we are to have any chance of finding the green, which, appropriately, is generous. It is a brilliant and surprising and, perhaps, unique hole.

The 17th is a cousin of the celebrated 17th next door, and, in fact, the greens are side by side, though the two holes run in opposite directions. This one on Burnside is an even longer par four, a behemoth of a hole at 473 yards, where we cannot reach the Barry Burn, 278 yards out, on our drive, but then must traverse it a second time as it swings left across the fairway some 20 yards short of the green. With the prevailing wind at our back, with the fairway firm and fast, and with two powerful woods, we *may* reach this green in two. Then again, we may not. This is lion-hearted golf. I played the hole as a three-shotter and gladly settled for five. The older of the two Bills was satisfied to make six. Bill Thoms, however, visited the burn three times en route to a nine.

The 18th is a distinct letdown. In the time-honored Scottish tradition of woeful finishing holes, it is a weakling, 307 yards straightaway to a vast green more than 130 feet deep and de-fended half-heartedly by a couple of bunkers at the left front and a couple more on the right side. A boundary rather snug along the right directs the drive to the left side of the generous fairway. Immediately in front of the tee is the Barry Burn.

We had to wait about 10 minutes on the tee for the four-ball ahead to get out of range. The hapless Bill Thoms, having just butchered the 17th, now proceeded to cold-top his drive into the burn. He turned to us, murmuring by way of explanation, "Too long a wait—I had lost my momentum."

We parted in the parking lot, exchanging telephone num-bers and expressing the hope that we might one day get to-gether for a round on Burnside again. I would like that very much. For me, the Burnside course is Carnoustie redeemed, and they were a tonic, an ongoing reminder of the game *as a game,* something I occasionally forget.

I have no sight-seeing suggestions for this coastal strip of Angus. Doubtless there are worthwhile attractions, but we have never sought them out. There must also be good accom-modations, but I am no help there either, having always viewed most of Tayside as within an hour's drive of St. Andrews.

Chapter Ten

A Sampler
of Inland Golf

 With few exceptions so far, I've been concentrating on seaside golf. In this chapter and the next one, the focus is on inland courses, some 10 or 12 of them. I think it's good to have some idea how the other half lives.

Less than 20 minutes from Carnoustie, on a northerly heading, lies Letham Grange, which sounds like a Gothic manor out of Charlotte or Emily Bronte, but which is, in fact, the site of a rather grand Victorian mansion now functioning as both clubhouse and hotel, of two 18-hole golf courses (the Old dates all the way back to 1987, the New to just 1991), and of a splendid four-lane curling rink, "overlooked by the spacious Sweep 'n' Swing lounge where drinks are served in an atmosphere of relaxation and enjoyment." Letham Grange is unusual.

Donald Steel designed the greens but not the course. It was a man named Ken Green who laid out the first eighteen as the central element in his vision of a country-house hotel and golf complex. Like the original developer at Loch Lomond, Mr.

Green ran into grave financial difficulties and is no longer connected with the facility. Trained as an accountant, he had made his money in the commodities market, trading potatoes. Though he loved golf with a passion, he had no experience whatsoever in golf course design when he tackled the laying out of 18 holes at Letham Grange. I say he did a good job of it, and I also say that he showed good judgment in inviting Donald Steel to fashion the greens, which are large, handsome, and varied and putt beautifully.

The original eighteen—I don't think I can bring myself to call it the Old Course—is a big golf course. From the championship tees (the Scottish Amateur was played here in 1994) it measures 6,954 yards; from the medal tees, just over 6,600; and from the regular markers, 6,348. Par is 73—five long holes, four shot holes, nine par fours. For the most part it is glorious "swing-away" golf, where the fairways are broad, the bunkering light (according to my tally, there are just 43 sandpits), and the rough not too punishing. There is a lot of water—ponds at 8, 9, 10, and 15; streams on half a dozen other holes—but, in truth, the water is not all that menacing. The course ranges from rolling—there is not a single flat hole—to hilly. The distances from green to tee can be long and, in a couple of cases (the 9th green to the 10th tee, the 10th green to the 11th tee) steeply uphill in the bargain. Still, one can always choose to ride, for Letham Grange has a little flotilla of 12 golf carts.

There is a decidedly American cast to the golf here. Mr. Green loved the American courses, particularly Augusta National (hilly, light rough, big and complex greens, water, broad fairways), and he aimed to simulate that feeling here in eastern Scotland on a course laid out over what used to be grazing land.

The first six holes are played on essentially open terrain. The next four, routed through woodlands, have a beguilingly secluded quality. The last eight reprise the spacious theme. I enjoyed it enormously. Though there is not a truly great hole on the eighteen, there are no poor holes, and there are at least half a dozen that are excellent, including several that are memorable. The 166-yard 8th, for instance, with a lovely lagoon extending from tee to green and the entire hole framed in tall pines, was obviously inspired by the 16th at Augusta. It is a nice tribute to the original. The 10th, 381 yards, sails steeply downhill through a draw created by slopes and trees to a hidden landing area, from which the approach is played across a pond to a bunkered green set on the bias. The 14th is a 480-yard par five that edges almost indiscernibly left as it climbs along a narrow shelf of fairway to a matching shelf of green carved out of a right-hand hill. The aggressive second shot that is pulled or hooked will tumble off the shelf down into the trees. A 4 is eminently makeable, but so is a 7. This hole does not look like any I can recall.

If you are there on a fine day, you will enjoy lunch in the glass conservatory, with its pretty views down the 18th. You may also want to try the newer course, which, from what I could observe, appears to have some very testing golf holes. It is 5,528 yards long and plays to a par of 67.

Less than half an hour west of Letham Grange lies Kirriemuir. The name itself enchants—we relish the very sound of it, just as we love the sound of Troon and Macrihanish and Carnoustie. Braid designed the 18 here on what is just 75 acres. The course is quite short—5,550 yards, par 68 (14 par fours, 4 par threes). But the setting is beautiful, with the Grampian

Mountains dominating the distant views and land under cultivation alternating with pastures to frame much of the course.

The club was founded in 1908. Holes 3 through 7 were plowed up to serve as a "Victory Garden" (strictly potatoes) during the Second World War. The club wisely chose to enlist its least appealing golf holes in the cause, for it is not till the 8th that the game gets under way in earnest. This is a 156-yarder that plays uphill over a deep hollow to a green bunkered right and left at the front. Only the top of the flagstick is visible.

I was joined at the 10th tee by a director of the club, Jack Alexander, whom I judged to be about 70 and who shoots in the mid-80s. A native of Carnoustie, he saw Hogan play the last two rounds of the 1953 Open there. "I believe it was the best golf I have ever witnessed," he declared.

After we had gone four or five holes, he said to me, "I hit it from left to right, as you can see, but I admit to liking that pull of yours." (And here I'd been believing all these years that "that pull" of mine was a tasty little draw!)

Jack told me that he played three or four days a week, but that he was also an avid fisherman—salmon on the Tay, trout on the North Esk and South Esk. "It was a little more than twenty years ago," he said, "when I was introduced to the joys of salmon fishing on the Tay. I promptly turned my back on golf even though I'd been captain of this club, and I never struck a ball for seven years. Aye, fishing is a disease, a disease it is! Then I came back to the game, but I still do quite a bit of fishing as well."

The second nine, with its narrow fairways often framed by gorse and trees, is both more testing and more engaging than the first. Four of the two-shotters are on the short side, but the pitch must be well-judged if it is to hold the medium-sized greens, which are not imaginatively contoured. What surprised me was that this course, with the beautifully crisp moorland turf on much of it, was as carefully conditioned as virtually any I've ever played in Scotland.

The last two holes at Kirriemuir are marvelous. Seventeen, called "Braid's Gem," lives up to its name. It is a 200-yarder played downhill over tumbling ground to a green slightly angled to the line of play. Two handsome old trees, one right and one left, guard the access, as does a bunker short left and a second bunker in a slope below the right front of the green. It is a beauty, and only a first-class stroke will find the green.

The home hole, almost 400 yards long and tending steadily upward from tee to green, has a big surprise in store for the first-time visitor, who can certainly see the mature tree solidly in the right side of the fairway 260 yards out, but who cannot see the deep swale just short of the green and who could never even imagine the existence of a gathering bunker at the very bottom of this hollow. Fail to clear this alarming dip with your long second shot, almost certainly a wood of some kind, and you will struggle mightily to avoid a double bogey.

But if the golf at Kirriemuir is merely pleasant—and despite those stellar closing moments, that is all it is—I must now confess that it represents for me only half the equation. For it was here, in the village, some five minutes from the golf club, that James M. Barrie was born and here that he is buried. The boy who would grow up to create *Peter Pan* (to say nothing of *The Admirable Crichton, The Little Minister, Quality Street,* and many other novels and plays) was born at "The Tenements," 9

Brechin Road, Kirriemuir, on May 9, 1860. The house, a small and simple whitewashed stone cottage smack on the main road, is owned and operated as a museum by the National Trust for Scotland. It is a fascinating evocation of the circumstances in which a linen-weaver, Barrie's father, and his large family—the author was one of ten children, and "box beds" were the only answer!—lived in Victorian times.

On a very high hill is the steeply terraced Kirriemuir cemetery, which affords magnificent views over the town and the surrounding countryside. A simple five-foot-high gray granite headstone marks the Barrie plot. On it are inscribed the names of eight members of the family, each with the date of birth and death. The seventh reads: "James Matthew Barrie, 9th May 1860—19th June 1937." There is no special prominence given at his grave to the Kirriemuir native who died rich and renowned.

The Alyth Golf Club, about 20 minutes from Kirriemuir on a southwesterly heading, celebrated its centenary in 1994. The golf here is better than at Kirriemuir, but it is not exceptional. Old Tom Morris laid out a nine in 1894. By 1928 there were 13 holes. Six years later Braid came along, adding half a dozen new holes, subtracting a couple of old ones, and revising just about everything else.

The setting is lovely—pastoral Perthshire with its rolling croplands and woodlands, its meadows dotted with grazing cattle and sheep, and all of it against the deep purple backcloth of heather-clad hills. As for the course itself, also nicely rolling, it is enormously pretty, some holes out on more open ground, many in beautiful allées of great firs, majestic pines, and silver birch so old they have gone antique gray. What's more, the springy heathland turf is a joy to walk upon, the holes are admirably varied, the greens generous (the 18th is 50 yards deep, 28 yards wide!) and true.

Regrettably, however, there is not a single outstanding hole at Alyth. There are five or six holes—one thinks instinctively of three consecutive par fours, the 4th, 5th, and 6th—that are quite good, with the teasing burn at the 5th that we just may not be able to carry from the tee and the angled and elevated plateau green combining to pack a lot of challenge into just 329 yards. The well-wooded 10th is also undeniably fine. Here the tee shot wants to slip away to the right off a pronounced slope in the fairway, and even if we manage to avoid that pitfall, the second shot on this 436-yarder must be perfectly struck if it is to find the skillfully bunkered green. But such moments are uncommon. We long for more of the spark, the flair, the sport that only a handful of holes here provide. We are pleased to play Alyth, but we are not delighted.

Some five miles away, again on that southwesterly heading, is a club just five years older than Alyth. Its name is Blairgowrie. A number of Americans have played it over more recent years, for it has popped up in magazine pieces from time to time and it has a lot of golf to offer—two full-length eighteens plus "The Wee Course," a 2,327-yard par-32 all-out charmer. They are batting .666 at Blairgowrie—two out of the three courses are terrific. The third is a pop fly to the second baseman.

It is more than 20 years since my first visit to Blairgowrie, but the memory, like the club's entire property, is evergreen. It was a Saturday morning in late August, my two teenage sons were as eager as I to play the Rosemount course, and we had driven up from St. Andrews with no reserved tee time. The practice putting green was crowded, mostly with members. We were at the mercy of the starter, who also functioned as the green fee collector (£2, more than double the Old Course and Dornoch, but what could one do?). He was cast from the same mold that had stamped out his counterparts at Gullane, St. Andrews, and Carnoustie: short, leather-faced, sixtyish, not given to grinning. It was Saturday morning, he reminded me. We should putt for a bit and he would call us. So we putted for a bit and he did not call us. I thought to try a little sweet talk, and back I went. He was stationed behind the glass in what reminded me of a bay window, an extension of the clubhouse squarely behind the first tee. It was like talking to a cashier at the movies.

"How does it look?" I asked, careful to sound merely inquisitive.

"Not bad," he said. "A while yet, but not bad."

"Oh," I said, "I'm sure you're doing all you can for us. I realize you've got the members to take care of first."

"Aye."

"You know," I said, "I'm told that this is the finest inland course in Scotland."

He looked hard at me for a moment, then replied flatly, "In Britain."

There was nothing else to say.

Within 15 minutes we were off the first tee and on our way to test the validity of this proud boast. Let me say at once that it did not hold up then and that there is even less reason to take it seriously today. Britain aside, the Rosemount course at Blairgowrie is also not the best inland course in Scotland. I can think right off of four that are superior to it, three of which will be discussed in the next chapter. The fourth is Loch Lomond.

Nevertheless, Rosemount is an excellent golf course and, from start to finish, a thoroughgoing treat. Superb moorland turf provides good lies. Each hole affords nearly total isolation as we play down splendid avenues of pine and birch. For the most part the terrain is gently rolling, with even one or two hills. The holes are varied, and the routing of them—we are indebted primarily to Alister Mackenzie (Cypress Point, Augusta National, Royal Melbourne, etc.), secondarily to James Braid—inventive and surprising in the best sense. Most important, the shots to the greens, themselves sited with a becoming naturalness, are consistently testing, in large part because of the adroit bunkering.

The course has two weaknesses, and they are not inconsiderable: the fairways are too broad and the greens are too passive. These are the broadest fairways I've ever seen; landing areas 75 to 90 yards wide are common. Except for two or three holes (the 2nd is one hole that comes to mind), nothing short of a willful effort to go astray will get you into the woods. As for those rather ordinary greens, blame neither Mackenzie nor Braid; following a blight in the early 1960s, they were rebuilt.

The course measures just under 6,600 yards from the medal tees against a par of 72, 6,240 yards from the members' markers. In this second instance par may be 70, 71, or 72, depending on whether a couple of long holes are played as par fours or par fives.

Among the many top-notch holes, which begin with the 1st

(a fine 429-yarder that drifts ever so slightly downhill as it doglegs quietly left and demands two of our best swings rather before we are capable of providing even one in this rarefied category), are the final three.

The 16th is superlative, a 435-yarder that commences with a drive over a corner of Black Loch. Bordered in part by larch and pine, the lake must be a good ten acres. Yet at no point before arriving at the 15th green were we aware of its existence. Not only do we play this course hole by hole, that is precisely how we see it. Rosemount keeps its secrets well. There are no previews of coming attractions.

Where the drive comes to rest on 16 the fairway narrows (by Rosemount standards!), then bends moderately left. With a boundary fence skirting the fairway tight along the left and only a limited access to the distant green, guarded on the right by high mounding, on the left by trees, and on both sides by sand, this second shot is enormously demanding. Though needing to hit full out, we incline to swing defensively.

Seventeen, 165 yards from an elevated tee, is another outstanding hole—across a valley, a marsh on the right, to a spectacular double-tiered green guarded by deep bunkers. One's instinct is to think that because the green is more than 40 yards wide it will gather in most any iron in this part of Perthshire. So it will. But if you are not in the same time zone as the cup, you will inevitably three-putt (or worse).

The 18th is a grand finishing hole, 382 yards long, the first 210 yards flat, but as the hole bends right the fairway dips rather sharply. Two birch trees on sentry duty in the crook of the dogleg force the prudent drive left. The sloping green below is vigorously defended by bunkers front left and front right. A 4 will win the hole much more often than it will lose it.

Twice have important competitions been contested over the Rosemount course, the 1973 British Boys' Championship and the 1977 Martini International, an event that was won by Greg Norman. It marked the first European Tour victory for the then 22-year-old Australian. His 277 total included a course-record 66.

In 1979 a second eighteen opened for play at Blairgowrie. Called the Lansdowne course (the club's land once belonged to the Marquess of Lansdowne), it was designed by Peter Alliss and Dave Thomas. This eighteen is a disappointment. It has the length—6,895 yards from the medal tees, par 72, 6,437 yards from the regular markers, par 71—and it is all very lovely as it wends its way through the same beautiful woodlands and over the same heathery expanses as its elder sister. Oh, the level walk on the resilient turf is a pleasure, but then so is a walk in the park. Where, one asks, is the golf? The course is, with the single exception of the 18th hole—which it pinched from the Rosemount course and which is indisputably the best hole on the Lansdowne—utterly lacking in the one essential ingredient: pleasurable excitement. At 6,900 yards it would doubtless be a taxing slog. At 6,400 yards it is simply dull and easy. No wonder that in 1985, according to the club's centennial history, published in 1989, "a subcommittee . . . was set up to consider ways of improving the playability of Landsdowne. Many recommendations, short and long term, were accepted by the Committee, a number of which have yet to be implemented."

To resurrect a term that passed out of the rules of the game, if not its lexicon, in 1952, I suspect that the club is stymied.

"The Wee Course," on the other hand, is a winner. With a little of it dating back to 1899 and with all of it owing much to the hand of Braid, it is a joy, all 2,327 yards of it. The opener is a cracking one-shotter—flat, yes, but 185 yards long and into the prevailing breeze, to a sternly bunkered and, in the rear, mounded green. The 2nd, 335 yards and called, somewhat preciously, "Faerie Dell," is more than merely charming. It doglegs smoothly right and downhill in the landing area to leave a pitch that must land short of the green just beyond the bunkers well out front but under the two towering firs, right and left, whose limbs all but touch each other as they spread across the line of play before the green. It calls for true shotmaking. The 3rd, much the same length, climbs gently in the early going, heather flanking the fairway, an old-fashioned cross bunker perhaps 20 yards short of the green. And so it goes, one appealing hole after another, with only the 8th, at 415 yards, so long that we may not reach it in regulation. The fierce gorse and the high rough grasses corset the entire length of this hole, making it a genuinely tough proposition.

There are four par threes, no par fives. The greens are large and full of character. No starting times here, as indeed there are on the two eighteens 365 days a year. Just show up, hit off, and enjoy yourself—there are good sport and good fun in a variety of short but worthy golf holes.

Gordon Kinnock, the hospitable head professional at Blairgowrie, said to me, "I get out on the Wee Course as often as I can, even if it's only to play three or four holes. It encourages

me to concentrate on shotmaking rather than just hitting away.
I think it's wonderful."

If you visit Blairgowrie, be sure to have lunch in what some
still call "the new clubhouse." It opened on August 9, 1939, on
the eve of the Second World War. A white pebbledash two-
story structure, Edwardian in feeling, with a number of large
bow windows, it is as comfortable as it is handsome. Eat upstairs in the pretty main dining room and enjoy the views of the
start and the finish of the immensely satisfying Rosemount
course.

Less than half an hour from Blairgowrie, on the outskirts of
Dundee, lies the Downfield Golf Club. This is classic parkland
golf, and how pretty it is. The terrain is pleasantly rolling; a
burn wanders across half the holes; great trees of all kinds, particularly the dense stands of evergreens, isolate the course effectively from the heavily traveled roads and the housing
developments that surround it; and the turf, tee through green,
is superbly conditioned.

There is, in short, much to be grateful for. Yet we could wish
for more bite to it. It is too placid, too equable. Downfield, we
find ourselves musing, where is thy sting? This is a beautiful
course, but too beautifully behaved.

The fairways are broad, so there is little excuse for hitting
into the trees even when they line the hole on both sides, as
they do on 4, 5, 7, 15, and 16. Nor is the rough intimidating.
Out of bounds is not a consideration. Neither are blind shots.
Bunkering is moderate. On the whole, the greens are spacious,
with those on the second nine exhibiting a welcome complex-

ity that is rare indeed on the first nine. As for all that water, it is generally more decorative than daunting.

Though golf has been played at Downfield since the early 1930s, the course we play today dates only to 1964, when it was laid out by the club's greens committee with the assistance of C. K. Cotton (there may have been a little too much gentlemanly compromising along the way). From the medal tees it measures just over 6,800 yards against a par of 73. From the regular tees, it is 6,266 yards against a par of 70. The difference is quite telling—and not simply in distance. The longer layout provides five par fives, four of which will be eaten alive by the strong single-digit player. Birdies on several of these three-shotters—two of them measure 480 yards, another is 491—will conveniently offset bogeys that may crop up on the long par-three 3rd (228 yards) or any of the half-dozen par fours ranging from 407 to 434 yards. But if the regular markers are chosen, only two par fives remain on the card, with the three "convertibles" emerging as excellent and extremely testing two-shotters.

The 11th and 13th are good cases in point. Both are 480-yard par fives from the medal tees. At 434 and 446 yards, both become husky par fours from the regular tees. The 11th is a dandy—and quite memorable. The drive is from a slightly raised tee out in the open. In the landing area the fairway drifts left—a bunker and several trees here—then stretches straight-away toward the water short of the green. We vaguely discern a couple of minuscule islets (a redundancy if ever there was one) in this bulging stream. What we do not discern is the *next* water hazard, a *second* stream some seven or eight paces beyond the first one and all but fronting the green. A curious—indeed, for me, unique—case of double jeopardy. It is precisely this kind of insouciance that we would love to see more of at Downfield.

As for the 13th, a 446-yard par four when played from the regular tees, it doglegs abruptly right in the broad landing area—a couple of bunkers in the elbow—then, on the long up-hill second shot, crosses the burn, which is some 60 yards short of the elevated double-level green. Because the hole plays into the prevailing breeze, that burn, seemingly at a safe remove from the green, can imperil a thinly hit fairway wood. This may be a weak par five, but it is a very strong par four.

Downfield has hosted a number of important competitions since the mid-1960s, including the 1972 Scottish Open, the 1974 British PGA Match Play Championship, and the 1978 Scottish Amateur. Peter Thomson, a five-time British Open champion, whom we will have occasion to hear from in the final chapter, has called Downfield "one of the finest inland courses I've played on anywhere in the world." Either Mr. Thomson has played rather less widely than I believe to be the case or he somehow has developed a regard for Downfield that is out of proportion to its intrinsic merits. This is good, honest golf, mind you, in an exquisite parkland setting, but it is no occasion for hat tossing and dancing in the streets.

Dundee, lying along the north shore of the Firth of Tay and with almost 200,000 inhabitants, is Scotland's fourth largest city. Architecturally undistinguished—much of the old town has been demolished and the new structures are, at best, uninspired—it is notable today, from a visitor's point of view, for the redeveloped waterfront between the rail and the road bridges. A main attraction here is the *Discovery*, in which Robert Falcon Scott sailed to Antarctica in 1901. This triple-masted square-rigger was built in Dundee for that voyage. At the harbor in Victoria Dock sits the *Unicorn*, a frigate of 46 guns which was launched in 1824 and is the oldest British warship still afloat.

As for accommodations, all the courses in this chapter are within an hour of St. Andrews or of what is arguably the single greatest full-facilities golf resort in the world. I think we ought to head for Gleneagles right now.

Chapter Eleven

The Palace in the Glens and the Golf Club in the Village

 One of the charms of going to Auchterarder, where Gleneagles is located, from Dundee (or, for that matter, from Kirriemuir, Alyth, or Blairgowrie) is that your route will almost certainly take you through Perth.

This small city of about 45,000, spread attractively along the banks of the river Tay, is not to be bypassed. Once the capital of Scotland and a royal burgh of great antiquity, it is today a dignified, confident place that repays whatever time you can spend here.

Among the especially worthwhile sights are Balhousie Castle, which dates to the fifteenth century and houses the Museum of the Black Watch Regiment; St. Ninian's Cathedral, a beautiful nineteenth-century Anglican-rite church; and the Fair Maid's House, where a medieval wall may be seen and a gallery with changing exhibitions by Scottish artists is open daily, as is a shop offering high-quality Scottish craftwork and knitwear. Speaking of commerce, there is a section in the center of town marked by graceful hanging flower baskets and a happy absence of cars, where shopping—or just window-shopping—in a variety of attractive stores, some old, some new, is a thoroughly enjoyable experience.

Perth's downtown is a compact area bracketed by two large open parks, the North Inch and the South Inch, both of which front on the Tay. On Moncrieffe Island, opposite the South Inch, is the King James VI Golf Club, which was founded in 1858 and named to commemorate the tradition that the last of the Scottish kings—James VI became James I of England— had played golf in the early seventeenth century "on the Inches of Perth." It was Old Tom Morris who in 1897 laid out the course that is very much in use today. I confess that I have never played it, but I will one day soon. It may well be the only course that occupies an entire island, not merely in the middle of an important tidal river but in the heart of a busy city.

Not 30 minutes south of Perth, just off the A9, lies Gleneagles. By actual count there are some 100 outstanding golf resorts in the world. It would be reckless to rank even one of them above Gleneagles. In truth, perhaps only four or five can be said to be in the same class with this Scottish pleasure dome. In writing about it, I must constantly struggle to avoid sounding like a member of the hotel's public relations staff. I frequently do not succeed.

On the doorstep of the Highlands, Gleneagles boasts a setting of well-nigh flabbergasting beauty—at the head of glorious Glen Devon, with 40-mile vistas to the Ochil Hills in the east and south, to the heather-tinged foothills of the Grampian Mountains in the north and west. The openness, the vastness, the shifting patterns of light and shadow on the distant multihued slopes—the forest green of great firs and pines, the golden beige of hay fields, the gray-green of meadows—this is the Scotland of your dreams. And it is there, all of it, with every shot you play on the three splendid eighteens.

Between them, James Braid and Jack Nicklaus have eight British Opens and three Gleneagles courses to their credit. Braid holds the edge, having won the championship five times and, in 1919, having laid out the first two eighteens, the King's and the Queen's, on this stretch of wild Perthshire moorland. Both courses are no less than wonderful, a collection of arresting golf holes painted with bold brush strokes on a canvas of hills and valleys, of heather and bracken and gorse, of majestic hardwoods and equally majestic evergreens.

Though the King's can be stretched to 6,800 yards for professional events, hotel guests will play it at 6,471 yards (par 70) or 6,125 yards (par 68). In either case, it is all we can cope with, for the handful of oversized par fours—six or seven ranging from 423 to 453 yards—is formidable. And however modest the total yardage may appear on the scorecard, this is big golf—broad fairways, sprawling greens, grand hills, deep bunkers.

There are one or two holes that we may reasonably hope to birdie—for example, the inviting 260-yard par-four 14th, which can be driven—but there is not a weak or indifferent hole on the entire course. Among the most challenging holes are two of the par threes. On the 161-yard 5th the shot is from an elevated tee to a similarly elevated green. Miss this windswept tabletop and you risk ruin in sandy pits far below. Here, indeed, is a shot that stares us out of countenance.

There is no such drama on the 11th, a 221-yarder across scrub and uphill to a green that is heavily bunkered. All it calls for most days is a perfectly struck driver. The 2nd at Shinnecock Hills is its twin, even to the identical yardage.

Two of the many mighty par fours should also be singled out. The 374-yard 3rd climbs steeply up a fairway marked by bold mounds and hollows, the blind second shot surmounting a high ridge and, with any luck, finding the large green concealed in yet another hollow. As for the 13th, called "Braid's Brawest" (*braw* being Scots for *splendid*), it is a 448-yard roller coaster. Only the stoutest drive can carry a ridge studded with a pair of ferocious bunkers, and the second shot, almost as long and over a second great dip, must traverse a cross bunker and avoid, at the left, a steep heathery falloff as well as more sand. It is possible that there is no more splendid two-shotter—seaside or inland—in all of Scotland.

No moment on the Queen's course ascends to quite this level, but there is so much outstanding golf on it that we actually forget the wonders next door. A scan of the scorecard shows total yardage of only 5,965. Par is just 68. Braid must have had an aversion to par fives. This course offers only one, and the King's, when playing at its shorter, par-68 distance, has none. We are grateful to Jack Nicklaus for giving the honorable three-shotter its due—there are five such on the Monarch's.

There is no opportunity to limber up on the Queen's. The 1st hole, spanning a deep swale in front of the tee, moves perceptibly higher, doglegs gently left around the trees to a green that is somewhat smaller than we hoped, measures 409 yards, and is simply too hard for many of us. The 2nd, 146 yards to a pretty plateau isolated by sand and a steep falloff on the right, is yielding, but the 421-yard 3rd is another tartar, the tee-shot landing area confined by a large bunker on the left and a ditch on the right, with six more bunkers—short, left, right—vigorously patrolling the green.

And so it goes, hole after excellent hole. The 9th and 10th are two of the strongest and most compelling dogleg par fours I know. The 9th, which measures 419 yards and plays 460, climbs steadily from tee to green and curves sharply from left to right. The green is tucked up and away behind a high right-hand slope so that it is out of sight for anyone who cannot drive 245 yards on the optimum line. The 10th, which measures 421 and plays 400, is rather the reverse: it falls a bit and it also bends sharply, but from right to left. Here we drive blindly from an elevated tee over a shallow rise faced with bunkers, confident that when we reach the ball all will be revealed to us. We are, however, momentarily perplexed, as on the 8th at Panmure. Finally, down on the left, around the corner, over a high left-hand shoulder of ground, and cloistered in its perfect little dell, we discover the green, concealed almost until the very moment we step onto it. Blocking the direct line is a small spinney of stately pines, which must be cleared with our long second shot if we are to reach this hidden harbor.

The finish on the Queen's is as satisfying as all that went before it. The 17th, at 204 yards, is fiendishly demanding. The tee is high, the green is long (66 *yards* long!) and narrow, and the ground pitches steeply to the right. Our instinct is to aim left, but several small bunkers await there. However, we can recover from them. I cannot promise similar success from that mine shaft lurking beneath the right side of the green. It is about 12 feet deep and with a face so sheer as to be nearly vertical. In fact, I am physically unable to scoop a ball from that sand up onto the putting surface. My best swing finds the ball failing to scale the heights by about a foot, then tumbling all the way back down the bank to come to rest within a club length of where I commenced this ordeal.

The final hole, "Queen's Hame," is a happy climax. Do not be discouraged by the yardage, 412. We drive from the top of a hill, and though there are wetlands at the bottom and gorse in the left-hand rough, the forced carry is within our capacity, the fairway is broad, and the green, under the very windows of the handsome and spacious Dormy House, is hospitably large.

The third in this remarkable triumvirate of courses opened on May 15, 1993. My wife and I had driven over from St. Andrews one day late the previous summer to tour it with Billy Marchbank, the head professional at Gleneagles (his father, Ian, had held the post for the preceding 30 years). Now we returned for what the invitation called "the Opening Weekend celebration of The Monarch's Course." It is possible that we were not the most famous people on hand. The gathering included, in order of importance, Jack and Barbara Nicklaus, Her Royal Highness Princess Anne and her second husband, Commander Tim Laurence, Sean Connery, His Royal Highness Prince Andrew the Duke of York, Gene Hackman, His Royal Highness Prince Abdul Hakeem of Brunei (a legitimate 3-handicapper), Chris de Burgh (his song "The Lady in Red" is no longer high on the charts though still dear to our hearts), Cheryl Ladd (it is nearly 20 years since *Charlie's Angels*), 78-year-old Jessie Valentine (three-time British Ladies' champion, seven-time Curtis Cupper), and Jackie Stewart (the great motor racing champion has a vested interest in Gleneagles).

Over the course of the weekend I made a few notes. Sean Connery is the subject of one of the jottings.

Connery—dark suit, dark shirt, darkly tanned, wisps of silver hair gracing what is essentially a bald head—stood alone in the crowded Glendevon Room as the Friday evening cocktail party rolled into high and convivial gear. He was having none of it. There was a look of frustration, of exasperation, on his lined but still handsome face. He appeared to be hot and bothered. In point of fact, he *was* hot and bothered—literally. I chose this moment to introduce myself. Calling on the only link that could possibly exist between us, I extended my right hand as I said, "Have you been to Pine Valley lately?" The shared club tie gives one a certain cheekiness, even where an *eminenza* such as 007 is concerned. He shook my hand distractedly, but did not respond to my question. "Too damn hot in here," he glowered. "I've got to do something about it. Maybe we can talk later."

With that he wheeled about, leaped up onto a low window sill, and began tugging at a large expanse of plate glass. No one paid the slightest attention. Then, having won that battle for fresh Scottish air, he jumped down and enlisted several waiters in his cause. The Connery forces swept down the length of the room, scoring one brilliant success after another despite the recalcitrance of a couple of their targets. For the great Scot, the place was now habitable. We never did resume our conversation; Connery disappeared into a cluster of people on the far side of the room. And though this intrepid foray into fresh air may not have matched his triumphs over Dr. No or Goldfinger, it was clearly a case of mission accomplished.

The following day, my wife and I had a brush with royalty at the Moet & Chandon Competitors Club near the 18th green (a large green and white tent where champagne and smoked salmon were served all day Saturday). As we approached the door at the end of the red carpet that covered the temporary wooden walkway, a middle-aged woman in raincoat, wellies, and kerchief stood just off to the side, gathering herself after the walk through the cold light rain. My wife preceded me, but now hesitated momentarily, not certain which way the door opened. The woman now stepped in ahead of me and I heard her murmur something. The door swung open, and as I reached out to hold it I recognized the lady between me and my wife as Princess Anne, the Princess Royal. Inside the tent now, I said excitedly to my wife as we headed toward a table, "That was Princess Anne. I heard her speak to you as you went to open the door. What did she say?"

"She said, 'Pull.' "

On a more serious note, the Monarch's course is excellent. From the championship markers, it measures nearly 7,100 yards. From all the way forward it can play as short as 4,300, and in between there are four other choices. Said Billy Marchbank, "We're offering something that every player can be comfortable with. It isn't easy to play to your handicap when you're away. So you choose the length here that makes sense to you and then you enjoy the game."

That accommodating attitude pops up in another context on the Monarch's. Golfers can carry their bag, pull it on a "trolley," take a caddie, or ride in a cart. The paved cart paths—the first such in Scotland—were viewed by many as sacrilegious.

A particularly fine trio of holes in the early going deserves to be singled out. On the 388-yard 3rd, from an elevated tee— Nicklaus likes elevated tees and believes that the world does, too—there is a taxing forced-carry over a pond. The ball lands meekly into an upslope, at which point the hole bends smoothly right and continues climbing to a generous green corseted at the front by bunkers right and left. The *playing* length, as contrasted with the measured length, is a good 415 yards, and the demands on the swing are uncompromising.

The 4th is simplicity itself. If you can hit it 211 yards uphill (240 from the tournament tees), carrying an immense bunker across the face of the green, you will reach this par three in regulation and have a chance—putting on the Monarch's elegantly undulating greens is scarcely automatic—for a 3. Now might be a good time to mention that, as on the other two eighteens, the holes here have been given names ("Crookit Cratur," "Mickle Skelp," "Wimplin Wyne," "Lochan Loup," to cite four of the more cloying), and this monstrous par three has been labeled "Gowden Beastie." It means Golden Bear, and Nicklaus disclaims any complicity in the naming.

At the 5th, a 423-yard par four, we drive blindly over the rise in a saddle-shaped fairway, then thread the long second through trees, striving to avoid wetlands just short of the green on the right. The hole is a beautiful killer.

The second nine, also par 36, is perhaps a shade less stringent. And since it has that happy yet relatively uncommon mixture of three par threes, three par fours, and three par fives, there is what might be called a built-in variety to it. It is also more open than the first nine—I was surprised, coming down the 15th, to spot a hole on another course that was neither the King's nor the Queen's—but then there is a very expansive feeling to the entire eighteen. This stems from two circumstances: the course sprawls across 250 acres (distances from green to tee can be inordinate—thus the appeal of the golf carts) and the

17,000 newly planted shrubs and trees (larch, pine, spruce, oak, beech, rowan, and birch) have yet to make their presence felt.

The overall topography is much like that of the King's and Queen's, which is to say rolling, although the two older courses do possess a couple of dramatic changes in elevation not to be found on the new one. What will be found here is water. Three of the par fives—2, 9, 16—present the long hitter with a common risk/reward situation: go for the green on your second, but chance a dunking if you do.

There are 83 bunkers, some of them embodying an aesthetic vision that may be unprecedented in golf course architecture. A press release advises, "The design incorporates sloping bunker faces, some of them very steep, and the shape of the slopes generally reflects the hills in the distance." I am not sufficiently keen-eyed to appreciate such artistic sensitivity to the surroundings, especially when I am straining to extricate myself from an eight-foot-deep pit with a near-vertical face. Let "the hills in the distance" remain in the distance.

Yes, there is a sculptured look to some of the Monarch's, but there are no sharp features, nothing harsh or jarring. The course looks at home here, nicely compatible with the two wonderful Braid eighteens. From the day it opened, it was a very good golf course. Given a few more years to mature, it may well become a great one. I should think Jack Nicklaus must be proud of what he has done at Gleneagles.

If the golf is superb at Gleneagles—and it is—it is not golf alone that accounts for its preeminence. The hotel itself, which is a handsome hybrid owing more to the Loire Valley chateau than to the Scottish baronial castle, calls up the past, specifically the halcyon days of Edwardian country-house luxury and

privilege. Whether in the public spaces or the guest accommodations, we are endlessly beguiled by the fabrics (half the great
chintzes in the world must be decorating the bedrooms), the
furniture, the wallpapers, the floor coverings, the paneling, the
chandeliers and sconces, the paintings, the *objets d'art.* With
good reason has it been called "the palace in the glens."

But when we begin to tick off the ways to spend our days
here, even this royal ambience must stand aside while we tote it
all up.

It is one thing to provide three superlative 18-hole golf
courses, plus the Wee Course (nine holes of scaled-down golf
that family foursomes find very enjoyable) and the nine-hole
pitch-and-putt course. And we take for granted tennis and
squash courts, croquet lawns, a jogging track, a billiards parlor,
and a health spa—this last, under a vast canopy of bronzed
glass, offering two swimming pools, a solarium, a gymnasium,
Jacuzzi, saunas, Turkish steam and spa baths, hot tubs, massage
and beauty treatment quarters.

But there is more, and it is the more that separates Gleneagles from the rest of the world.

There is the Jackie Stewart Shooting School—clay pigeons
rising above the heath to simulate the flight of 10 game birds
(partridge, pheasant, woodcock, grouse, *et al.*). And the Mark
Phillips Equestrian Centre (Captain Phillips was Princess
Anne's first husband), with a staff of 30; three different arenas,
two of which are enclosed and air-conditioned; more than 30
horses available to guests; and numerous activities ranging
from dressage to polo. And the Gleneagles Off-Road Driving
School, for those who have always dreamed of tooling across the
moors in a Land Rover. And the two beats on the river Tay per-

manently maintained by the hotel for its guests who would like a spot of salmon or sea trout fishing. And the British School of Falconry at Gleneagles, an arcane and aristocratic experience that you can pursue either on horse ("Hawks and Horses," it's called) or on foot. Eight Harris hawks are housed here and two instructors are on hand seven days a week.

On a more mundane note, there is a total of 13 restaurants and bars scattered about the property, and the shopping arcade (for those of us who miss the malls back home) includes such merchants as Burberry's, Georg Jensen, Harvey Nichols, and Mapin & Webb, to name a few who welcome our custom.

Well, I have recited this litany in order to support my contention that Gleneagles is the greatest full-facilities golf resort in the world. It has everything you would expect, many things you would not expect, and all of it on the noblest scale and in a setting of surpassing natural beauty. But what, in my judgment, makes it incomparable is that Gleneagles is not a big hotel. There are 218 bedrooms and 18 suites, so at no time will there be more than about 450 guests. This is not a vast fun factory. There is no point, of course, in claiming that it is an intimate country hideaway either. That would be arrant nonsense. But the madding crowd is absent here. So is the attendant has-

sle. There is a tranquility that, remarkably, coexists with a plenitude of diversion. For those of an active bent with a liking for the good life as epitomized by a great resort, Gleneagles should be experienced at least once.

To come back to earth, I felt obliged to check out that neighboring golf hole I spotted from the 15th on the Monarch's. It turns out to be the 6th at the Auchterarder Golf Club, where they have been playing the game for a quarter of a century longer than at Gleneagles. The club celebrated its hundredth anniversary in 1992.

It was North Berwick's Ben Sayers who laid out the original nine in 1892. Not till 1981 did a second nine open for play. Sayers was one of the greatest characters in turn-of-the-century golf. A renowned clubmaker and an excellent player—he competed in every British Open from 1880 to 1923, coming close to claiming the claret jug on several occasions—the five-foot three-inch Sayers was perhaps golf's first great showman. Trained as an acrobat, he would instinctively turn a cartwheel or execute a series of handsprings after sinking a good-sized putt. By comparison, the matador antics of Chi Chi Rodriguez seem positively subdued.

The newer holes, which can be found on both nines today, are frequently routed over flat ground. Ian Marchbank came over from his shop at Gleneagles to lay out this part of the course, but when the firm that had been engaged to build the holes backed out, it was the members who stepped in: "Every Tuesday and Thursday evening," records the centenary history of the club, "during the next three months people arrived to give their time, firstly in clearing all the brushwood lying on the fairways and strips of woodland. Fires burnt long into the night. The next job was to remove the stones from fairways. This was done like gathering potatoes—a line across the fairway on hands and knees lifted the stones into potato baskets which were loaded onto trailers. . . . For all this hard work, the participants were given sandwiches and one drink from the bar. . . ."

Auchterarder is another short course—5,778 yards, par 69—that has plenty of spunk. I played with Bill Campbell, the club's secretary (its first *paid* secretary), who lived in Edinburgh for many years but now loves this beautiful corner of Perthshire so much that he goes back to the great city, all of an hour away, only to visit his parents. He has relatives and friends in Florida and has enjoyed several holidays there. He said, "I played golf on Christmas Day last year in Tampa wearing only a sport shirt—marvelous!"

He told me that the club gets plenty of visitor play, not infrequently by guests at Gleneagles. The clubhouse, which was built in 1973 to replace the old "Tin Hut," is small but quite smartly furnished and commands striking views of Glen Devon. He also said that a number of Auchterarder's older members are members at Gleneagles as well, where, in contrast to the £140 annual dues here, they pay £1,000. There is a three-year wait to get into Auchterarder.

The golf at Auchterarder is in no sense great. It cannot even be discussed in the same breath with the three neighboring eighteens. But there are a handful of first-rate holes—almost all of them in the Sayers legacy—and the moorland turf is so crisp and springy and the views are so fine that we are delighted to be having a game here.

Except for four or five of the newer holes, the course is beautifully rolling. Bunkering is light and the rough—a very occasional patch of heather catches our eye—is not penal. There is no water and little threat from boundary markers. The greens are perhaps a bit too tame, but they are nicely paced and totally true.

On the face of it, there is not much to stir the blood. Yet the course has merit, and nowhere is it more clearly in evidence than on the final five holes. The finish at Auchterarder is downright rousing. The mix of holes is curious—in fact, I've never encountered anything quite like it. There are one par four, one par five, and three par threes. The two-shotter measures 445 yards, the long hole 513 yards, and the three one-shotters weigh in at 211, 219, and 188. We are not going to salvage a lackluster score on this testing stretch.

On the 14th, 211 yards long, the high face of an old-fashioned cross bunker conceals a long and narrow green in a natural little dell. The excellent 15th, at 513 yards, climbs from the tee, then stretches along pretty much on the level for another 250 yards. A surprising—and surprisingly deep—swale immediately in front of the green significantly complicates the pitch, particularly when the hole is cut toward the front of the green and the breeze is at our back, as is more often than not the case. I can still see the pretty little pitching wedge that my companion finessed over the dip to within three feet of the cup for a birdie. I insisted that only local knowledge made it possible.

The 16th is the finest hole at Auchterarder—and it is a great hole by any standards. It is 219 yards long. The prevailing wind is against us. Looking down Glen Devon, we play from a knob of a tee across a rough valley to a green narrower than by all rights it ought to be and bunkered on both flanks. Please understand, this is no "death or glory" shot, where failure will ruin the round. No, a bogey is easily come by. But to hit this green—a string-straight lifetime driver will surely do the trick—is an enormously satisfying accomplishment.

The 17th, at 445 yards, is terrific. The drive traverses a vast dip in the fairway and the long second sweeps downhill to a generous green that is open across the front.

As for the final hole, this 188-yarder, likely to be played into a left-to-right crosswind and certain to be played over the very heart of the 17th green, all of 35 feet in front of the 18th tee, climbs to a nicely undulating green with sand at the left and a high hedge tight across the back. A finishing hole fraught with possibilities in match play.

Peter Alliss, Lee Trevino, and Ben Crenshaw are honorary members of Auchterarder. In a letter to the club on its centenary, Crenshaw wrote: "Having traveled quite a bit through the world, I have come in contact with many different golf clubs. I would just like to say that there is always a special congenial atmosphere at Auchterarder, and a more hospitable club could not be found."

I feel compelled to make mention of the Crieff Golf Club, founded in 1891 and some 25 minutes drive northwest of Auchterarder, but I wish I could be more positive about the course. John Stark, one of Scotland's most respected golf teachers, is the professional there and is chiefly responsible for the layout of the principal course (there is also a relief nine), seven or eight holes of which were originally fashioned by Braid. The greens are often adroitly sited—on plateaus, on hilltops, in dells—and sometimes attractively framed in trees, but the fairways strike me as much too broad and the entire round is played back and forth on the side of a big hill. What is needed is one leg shorter than the other, but which one?

There are a number of difficult holes, including five par fours ranging from 412 to 467 yards. But there is little to surprise or delight us on this 6,400-yard parkland course that is plain and open and appears to have been developed on a limited budget. I suspect that Stark, who is extremely knowledgeable (to say nothing of articulate, opinionated, and congenial), will probably be tinkering with his offspring, and the result could be a much-improved course the next time I get to Crieff. Needless to say, the views over Perthshire are never less than lovely.

A word or two for the nongolfer. The village of Auchterarder, while scarcely fetching, is pleasant enough and offers several antiques shops. And in Abbey Road is the Glenruthven Weaving Mill, with the only working steam textile engine in Scotland. Weaving is demonstrated for visitors and a shop sells locally woven products. A few miles north of Auchterarder are the Strathallan Aircraft Museum (aircraft and allied equipment dating back to 1930) and, rather at the opposite end of the tourist spectrum, Tullibardine Chapel, a rural fifteenth-century collegiate chapel complete and unaltered.

Chapter Twelve

In the
Kingdom of Fife

We began this journey of very like a thousand miles on the south side of the Firth of Forth, and we have now come pretty close to full circle as we arrive in Fife, here on the north side of the great Firth. In this penultimate chapter, we will look at several Fife courses outside St. Andrews, deferring the cradle of the game till last.

The Crail Golfing Society, which was founded in 1786 and is thus the seventh oldest golf club in the world, plays its golf on a breezy promontory on the eastern tip of Fife, called the Balcomie Links. Of the club's original eleven regulations, one reveals a nice appreciation for the preference of individuals: "That the Captain shall at each meeting of the Society call for the Bill at or before 7 o'clock in the Evening, which Bill being paid, any Member shall be at liberty to go away without being liable for any expenses that may be further incurred during that Meeting."

It was in 1874 that Crail made a lasting contribution to the

art of greenkeeping, then rather primitive. In the minutes
dated August 7 the Society agreed that "iron cases be got for
the eight holes on the links to prevent the holes from being de-
stroyed." There exists no earlier record at any course of the in-
sertion of metal cups into the holes.

Old Tom Morris designed the course at Balcomie, the first
nine in 1895, the second four years later. Though there have
been some changes over the years, the eighteen we play today is
still in large measure the one that he laid out a hundred years
ago. In 1961, when the club decided to install a sprinkler system for the greens, it was the members themselves—in the tradition of self-sufficiency that we saw at Machrihanish and at
Auchterarder—who carried out the task of laying the piping to
all 18 greens.

The clubhouse, a contemporary structure sited at the highest
point of the club's hilly property, takes full advantage of the
magnificent views. On a pretty day you will want to pick a
table for lunch or a drink that looks down on the final four holes
to the rocky foreshore and, across miles of royal blue sea flashed
with whitecaps, to Bass Rock and Berwick Law, patches of Gullane and Muirfield visible on the horizon. This is one of the extraordinary clubhouse vistas of the world.

Over the years I have become friendly with Crail's head professional, Graeme Lennie, who must be about 40. A strong
player—he holds the course record here, 63—he is also a member of the British Golf Collectors' Society. "I'm building a little
library of my own," he said, "but the older golf books, the ones
I'm most interested in reading, have gotten to be very expensive. But I keep my eye out for them in the shops. Sometimes
you get lucky." Here is a golf professional for whom the game

is more than giving lessons, selling equipment, and keeping the members happy. Golf is his avocation as well as his vocation. He loves it for its history, its tradition, and its lore, and perhaps—this is purely speculative—for its mystery as well.

"We've got golfers at Crail from all walks of life," he told me, "everybody from joiners to brain surgeons. And there are no cliques—it's really very democratic. We do have some international members, particularly Scandinavians, who don't live all that far away. An international member pays a £200 entrance fee, but his annual subscription is only £24, not much more than a green fee. In the case of the local members, the annual subscription for men was recently raised from £89 to £97." A smile crossed his face as he added, "This caused four suicides and a hundred and twelve resignations."

Total yardage at Balcomie—and this from the back tees—is all of 5,922 against a par of 69. Two of the six par fours on the outbound nine measure 459 and 442 yards. The other four range from 306 to 348. The second nine is a crazy quilt of golf holes. There are only three par fours. The second one we come to, 15, is a flat, straightaway 265-yarder where the green just sits there waiting to be driven. The other one, 17, is 200 yards longer and plays from a hilltop tee down to a level fairway that seems, at least relatively, to go on forever. There are back-to-back par fives, which also happen to be side by side, the uphill 11th and the downhill 12th. So if you've been counting, you know that we are left with four par threes. Three of them are more than 200 yards long, including the home hole at 203.

On the 1st tee we get a feel for the entire course because so much of it is spread out below us. What we observe is a vast, treeless meadow sweeping down, in vaguely terraced formation, to the sea. There appears to be little separation between holes and little definition to the holes. Flagsticks help to guide our puzzled gaze, but the holes are sometimes so tightly clustered that the first-time visitor is understandably confused. It is all too much of a piece. Were it not for the bunkers, infrequent and artificial, it would look like the world's biggest practice range.

All right, then, what is the appeal of Balcomie? Principally a single circumstance: every hole is played within sight of the sea. The walk over rolling, sometimes hilly terrain is a glorious treat, so enthralling are the views. Simply to be out on Balcomie is cause for rejoicing.

But, you insist, that is hardly enough. Wherein lies the test? Again, principally in a single circumstance: the wind. No hole is sheltered from it. On a course where conventional hazards—bunkers, burns, boundaries—rarely harass us, the wind vexes us relentlessly.

The 2nd, 3rd, 4th, and 5th all play along and above the sea, with the drives of 4 and 5 daring us to bite off large chunks of these perilous doglegs, disaster waiting on the wave-washed rocks below. At 459 yards, the par-four 5th, with the sea endangering both of our all-out swings, is a genuinely heroic hole and, in fact, the strongest on the course.

The next eight holes, tucked in from the Firth, are nevertheless peppery, with the final hole in this stretch a particular favorite of mine. A 207-yarder, the 13th plays emphatically uphill over a rocky escarpment smothered in long rough grasses. The climb itself looks daunting, and into the wind the shot is fearsome. The green is not visible, though the flag is.

There is room beyond the clifftop on this fine and thrilling hole. It is always a driver for me.

And now that we have played straight up, we turn our back to the nearby clubhouse and, from the 14th tee, play straight down, 149 yards, to a green far below ringed by six bunkers. On the right is the added peril of the beach, which is out of bounds. The entrancing world of Balcomie lies all around us, links and sand and sea inviting—nay, importuning—us to pause and drink it all in. Then, of course, there is a shot still to be played, a mere flick of a 7-iron perhaps, but unsettling in a snapping breeze.

It is a good walk—the biggest part of 200 yards, I should guess, and a pleasant walk near the sea—from the 14th green around to the four "back holes." So close to the sea is the 15th tee that there are times in winter when waves engulf it. The only problem on this 265-yard par four is timing our swing between the waves breaking on the shore. They are a distraction.

Sixteen, a short cousin of the estimable 13th, requires a solidly struck iron—the 163 yards plays closer to 180—up the steep slope. The 17th, at 461 yards, is a rigorous two-shotter by most standards, and 18, though hospitably open across the green's broad front, is, at 209 yards, difficult to par when par is what we must have to save our bacon.

Well, the game is over, and full of fun it was from start to finish. What we imbibed out there for three hours was the intoxicating nectar of pure holiday golf, where the sea was always in view, the target was generally within reach, and the penalty for failure was rarely stringent. Wonder of wonders, we may even have played to our handicap!

Each year in September Crail hosts a tournament that is a test of endurance, the Ranken Todd Bowl, itself a huge ribbed silver vessel that looks to be worth the crown jewels. Some eight or nine local clubs, including St. Andrews, Leven, Lundin, and Elie, are invited to send a four-man team. Each team plays only two balls, both balls counting. A qualifying round is held in the morning to eliminate all but four teams. The semifinals are contested in the afternoon, and in the evening the final 18 is played. The world is full of 54-hole invitational tournaments, but this may be the only one that is settled in one day.

A few miles west of Crail, itself the most eastern of Fife's East Neuk ("neck") fishing villages, lies Anstruther. Its golf club dates back to 1890. At 2,072 yards, par 31, the nine-hole course, with its five par threes and four par fours, is in no sense serious. But, laid out for the most part on the headlands above the Firth, with splendid views of Bass Rock, Berwick Law, the Isle of May, and much of the East Lothian coast in the distance, and, in the foreground, Anstruther and its harbor, it is an invigorating place to walk while swinging a golf club. Its fifth hole, called "Rockies," is one of the most difficult, one of the most exciting, and one of the most eccentric par threes in the world. The hole is 236 yards long, it parallels the shoreline (the sea is on our left), and it plays from a clifftop tee downhill over broken ground to a green tucked away to the right beyond a small outcrop. The green is hidden, the shot is blind. Indeed, for all but the truly powerful hitter, the hole, generally played into or across the prevailing wind, is a *dogleg*. That's right, a dogleg par three. First we hit out to the left—the so-called fairway slopes strongly left down to the rocky foreshore—then we turn right and pitch back to the green in the lee of the great headlands. It is mad and mighty stuff, a fantasy of a golf hole.

Not incidentally, this is followed by two more par threes, which crisscross each other and which, with their sharp changes in elevation and whimsically sited greens, are further proof—if proof be needed—that Anstruther is the beau ideal of antic golf.

A 10-minute drive farther along the coast uncovers seaside golf of a more traditional nature, though the club itself is not without a couple of endearingly quirky moments. Its very name—The Golf House Club, Elie—calls for some explanation. In the latter part of the nineteenth century several clubs played over this links, but one, perhaps a shade tonier than its counterparts, decided to erect a golf house. It was this decision that gave the club its peculiar name, which distinguished it from those clubs that did not have a clubhouse and so met in pubs or inns.

The clubhouse today is the result of several extensions to the original structure, which was erected in 1876. A one-story building, it is white with a bright green trim, all of it so spruce, sparkling, and spiffy we would have sworn that the painters must have folded up their ladders and slipped away not 10 minutes before we arrived. With its unpredictable roof lines, its numerous chimneys and gables, to say nothing of the many and assorted long windows—some arched, some squared off, and more than 20 of them giving on the 1st tee—it may take a little getting used to. There is a fanciful nature to it, a sunny, holiday spirit that is directly at odds with, for example, the massive and brooding clubhouse of the R&A. Elie's golf house hymns the joy of the game. My good friend Alec Beveridge, a longtime member, calls it "couthie," a Scottish word that suggests niceness, a hospitable niceness, if you will, that inspires affection.

As for the interior, like those of Western Gailes, Prestwick, and Royal Aberdeen, it is that comfortable and reassuring combination of old wood, old silver, and old leather. Amusingly, in a club where women seem to enjoy equality with men, the clubhouse has a main entrance that the ladies are prohibited from using before 7 P.M.; the door opens directly into the men's locker room.

For all its undeniable charm, the clubhouse at Elie may not make the enduring impression on visitors that the starter's hut does. This shack is one of the great curios in the world of golf. Mounted within it and thrusting boldly up out of it toward the

very heavens is, of all things, a submarine periscope. Presented to the club in 1966, the periscope, dubbed "Excalibur," enables the starter to see over the hill that rises precipitously in front of the first tee to make certain that the players who have disappeared beyond the crest are now out of range. There is a delightful story told in the club's history about a lady golfer whom the then starter, Freddie Berwick, had been on good terms with until one day when, thanks to his treetop-tall "eye," he happened to observe her *throwing* her ball out of a bunker onto the first green. When she arrived to play the following day, he remarked, "I see your bunker play has got a lot better recently." To which she replied, "I don't think you're a friend of mine anymore, Mr. Berwick."

The course we play today was laid out by Old Tom Morris in 1895, with revisions by James Braid in the 1920s. It was here in Elie that Braid was born and reared and here that he learned to play the game.

A look at the scorecard reveals that from the medal tees the course measures 6,233 yards against a par of 70. Sounds about right. A closer look, however, discloses that there are no par fives and only two par threes. With 16 par fours, Elie runs the risk of being boring. In fact, that's the last thing it is. These two-shotters range from 252 to 466 yards, the holes run to every point of the compass, the wind here is frustratingly fickle, blind shots—beginning with the opening stroke—pop up with bewildering frequency, the greens are full of fun, the bunkers are full of woe, and the topography overall is wonderfully varied, never more so than where the old coal-mining operations have imparted some bizarre wrinkles to the fairways.

Except for the opening and closing holes, the sea is in view throughout the round, and often, as from the lofty 3rd tee, it is the same majestic panorama over the Firth of Forth to the East Lothian coast that so enthralled us at Crail and Anstruther.

There is a cluster of four holes out at the far end of the links that is characteristically Elie, cunning and old-fashioned, on the one hand, classic and rigorous, on the other. The 10th is a 267-yard par four. If the wind is with us, we may putt for an eagle. The blind drive heads up a steep hill and then down an even steeper one, perhaps to finish on the sloping green above the beach. Here the seabirds strut on the rocks at the water's edge, an old seal slithers out on these same rocks in warm weather to sun himself and bark, and holiday makers picnic on the sand. It is all very diverting, perhaps a bit too diverting for most of us, who need to keep our minds on the business at hand.

Next comes the course's second—and last—par three, this one, at only 120 yards, little more than half as long as the 225-yard 3rd. The green on "Sea Hole" slopes wickedly from right to left, and the sea wall is a scant few yards from the green's left edge. Only the flag is visible, a circumstance that in days gone by prompted the caddies, who were stationed on the rocks beside the green, to fabricate holes-in-one in the hope of pocketing a bigger tip. When a shot would finish quite close to the cup, but out of sight of the player, three of the four boys would leap up cheering and gesticulating while the smallest was stealing onto the green and popping the ball into the hole.

The 12th, at 466 yards from a tiny tee just above the strand, clings to the curving shoreline. It is a great and difficult hole.

None but the brave will cut off enough of the beach to get home in two, and a deep greenside bunker at the right will give even them pause.

Thirteen is a superb hole. In a flight of hyperbole, Braid called it "the finest hole in all the country." At 380 yards, it is not forbiddingly long, but the second shot, generally into a left-to-right wind off the bay, rises to an angled green that is 190 feet wide! Defending it is a deep swale across the front. Time and again it swallows even the slightly underhit second shot, including shots that actually land on the front of the green. Immediately behind the putting surface is a steep bank, which can be counted on for a kindly roll if we are wise enough to overclub.

The final five holes—all, needless to say, par fours—provide considerable length (three are more than 400 yards), terrain that ranges from flattish to hilly, an occasional boundary, and a blind shot or two. We are not likely to make up strokes as we head for the "golf house," unless perhaps on the home hole itself, which is 359 yards long and presents an immense and essentially level green once we have passed a miniature "Valley of Sin."

It was on this hole in 1935 that a saddler by the name of Ken Foster made what may well be the most remarkable double bogey the game has ever known. After a strong drive into the breeze, he flew his second shot dead left through a pane of one of the clubhouse windows. He dropped another ball and, now playing four, flew it through the same window. He then dropped a third ball and knocked it into the cup for a six.

A footnote to the Elie story that, in truth, ought to be a

headline: not once in its long history has this golf course ever been closed. Among the countless reasons for loving "The Golf House Club," surely this one must be included.

The first time I visited the Lundin Golf Club, not 15 minutes farther down this same coast road we've been skimming along since Crail, was some 17 or 18 years ago. As I was putting on my golf shoes that November day in the simple changing room, I could not help but overhear a conversation between two quite elderly members who had just completed their round. One was recalling a match that saw "Jimmie whip Sandy" after appearing to be out of it "when his drive on seventeen caught that bunker on the left," from which he played a wonderful 4-iron "to within six feet of the cup and holed for his birdie, turning what had looked like a certain loss into a certain win."

Not many minutes later, in the lounge, the storyteller came up as I was chatting with the then secretary, R. M. Taylor. Mr. Taylor introduced me to Fred Horne, the club's oldest active member, 86 years of age and a member of the Lundin Golf Club since 1910. I said that, having overhead him talking about that match which, I gathered, had taken place some years ago, I could not help but wonder about the identity of "Jimmie."

"Braid, it was," he said, "Jimmie Braid. Over at Elie."

"You knew him?" I asked.

"Indeed I knew him," the old man replied. "There was a time when I would have a game with him once a year over at Elie. But, of course, he's been gone for some years now." Braid died in 1950.

Fred Horne turned now to the secretary. "What is it that's

going on here tonight? Looks as though it's all set up for a big dinner."

"It's the annual dinner for awarding the prizes," the secretary answered.

"Why wasn't I invited?"

"You could have bought a ticket like everyone else."

"*Bought* a ticket? I could have *bought* a ticket?"

"Now, Fred," the secretary said firmly, a small smile taking the edge off his words, "I know you're a Life Member, but that doesn't entitle you to a free meal." They laughed and I joined in. Then Mr. Horne turned suddenly to me and asked whether I had yet played Elie. I said I had not, but that I intended to to-morrow.

"You'll like Elie," he said. "It's quite good. Not better than Lundin, you understand, but quite good all the same."

I have been content to agree and to leave it at that ever since.

What a splendid start at Lundin, bracing as only a first hole can be that is hard by the sea, in this case with the tee high above it on a ridge of sandhills, commanding the whole of Largo Bay, from Roddon's Point in the east to the tall chimneys of Methil in the west, the view on a clear day spanning the waters of the Firth to the far shore, where the old links at North Berwick may just be visible. And what a good swing must be executed, for the hole is 424 yards long, and though the drive is a falling shot to a fairway shared with the 18th, the second is a rising one, back up the great duney ridge to where a large green awaits. When I first made its acquaintance, this green undulated improbably, but in recent years it has been squashed to a disappointing blandness. Heaven preserve us from the depredations of a Greens Committee!

Continuing along the coast, we catch our breath on the 2nd and 3rd, a couple of shortish (346 and 335 yards) and engaging two-shotters also played from high above the beach. And then, for the demanding 4th, we are once again atop the ridge, but this time we make no descent. Instead, we play straight along this generously wide and gently rolling plateau beside the shore till, 452 yards later, we arrive at the green. But, I fear, not often in two shots, notwithstanding the fact that this is a par four, for roughly 25 yards short of the putting surface there is a sharp and narrow dip across the fairway and at the bottom of this cut is a sliver of burn. Are you man enough to hit the gambling 3-wood into the prevailing breeze? Or do you lay up, content to accept a bogey and walk meekly to the next tee? This is a true "death or glory" hole: the great second shot produces a chance at a 3; the almost great second shot produces the likelihood of a 6.

Having proceeded on pretty much a straight line from the clubhouse out along the seashore, we have, all of a sudden, come to a dead end. More specifically, we have come to Mile Dyke, which we will not cross despite the fact that, staring at us from the other side of it, are more golf holes like the four we have just played, stretching away along the strand into the distance. But they do not belong to the Lundin Golf Club—not today, though once they did, or, to be precise about it, Lundin was once a co-owner of these holes. Now they are the property of the Leven Golf Club.

How this came to pass is, I believe, worth explaining. When the Lundin club was founded in 1868, it shared an 18-hole course with Leven. The links, like the Old Course and Western Gailes and Royal Aberdeen, was essentially two fairways wide and nine holes long, with the entire course shoehorned between the sea and the railroad.

Now, as we've seen, there is nothing unusual in Scotland about two golf clubs playing over the same golf course. What was out of the ordinary in this situation is that Leven's headquarters was at the west end of the links and the Lundin clubhouse at the east end. Play on this one eighteen began at *both* clubhouses, which were some two miles apart. Yes, east was east and west was west and often the twain did meet!

As the game grew in popularity, this arrangement, however convivial, became impractical. In 1909 a judgment of Solomon divided the baby in half. Lundin and Leven each took the nine holes on its respective side of Mile Dyke. Then, in order to come up with nine more holes, each club spilled over onto the landward side of the railway. It was at this time that James Braid was called in by the Lundin club to lay out new holes and incorporate them into an eighteen. The course we play today is little changed from Braid's plan of more than 85 years ago.

So after tackling the 140-yard 5th, tucked in at the end of the club property, at a right angle to the line of the 4th hole, where both sand and water bedevil us, we now cross the abandoned railway line and play the nine "new holes" on what might be described as a cross between links and parkland in turf and topography. The next three holes, all par fours, run beside the old railway embankment (out of bounds here on the right every foot of the way), and the first nine concludes on a prodigious par five, 560 yards into the prevailing wind.

At the 161-yard 12th the play is steeply uphill, and we now find ourselves on an immense plateau that hosts the 12th green, the 512-yard 13th (the green on this dogleg right tucked away prettily in a stand of evergreens), and the 14th tee, all of it with views of the entire links far below and of Largo Bay that fairly take our breath away.

The last four holes (418 yards, 314, 345, and 442) mark a return to the clubs' (Leven's as well as Lundin's) original property, with its characteristically heaving and tossing ground. Thanks to the hillocky nature of this territory and the need to cross a couple of burns, there is plenty of variety, surprise, and challenge here. The final hole, 442 yards long, is rigorous. The landing area for the drive is broad, but the long, narrow green is sited in a kind of saddle between the sea ridge on the right and a road, which is out of bounds, on the left. Bunkers in the right-hand slope preclude bouncing the shot in safely from that side. The player who would get home in two has no choice but to flirt with the road as he makes a full-blooded stroke that must advance the ball more than 200 yards with little deviation from dead straight.

All things considered, Lundin may well be among the half-dozen most spirited courses in Scotland. Serenity is not in the context of the game here. There is a lot going on in this 6,377 yards (par 71), a whole lot. Omnipresent is, of course, the breeze, which, light or heavy, takes its toll on a links where the play is so markedly a point-to-point business. Then there are the bunkers (uncomfortably more than a hundred of them, many quite penal), the burns, the bents, the boundaries, and the "blinds." Blind driving is a problem here at 6, 7, 10, 11, and 15. So are blind or semiblind shots to the green, as on the 1st, 12th, 15th, and 17th. The burns give us a little something to think about on eight holes. And thanks chiefly to the abandoned railway line, out of bounds ranges from a remote possibility to a clear and present danger on 16 holes. Obviously, we must keep our wits about us at all times, which may help to explain why this relatively short course has, over the last 25 years, hosted the Scottish Professional Championship, the British Seniors, the World Seniors, the Scottish Amateur Stroke Play Championship, the East of Scotland Amateur, and, perhaps most telling of all, final qualifying for the British Open.

Next door—immediately next door, as we have seen—lies the links of Leven, home of the Leven Golfing Society, which dates back to 1820. It was one of the Society's officers, Tom Anderson, who was kind enough to take me in tow on my first visit. A small, wiry, animated man whom I judged to be in his early 60s, he was clearly proud of his golf club and eager to make certain that its worth be appreciated. He regretted that the secretary was not on hand, but vowed to do the honors to the best of his ability.

I told him that I was quite impressed by the clubhouse. A three-story red brick building erected a little more than a hundred years ago, it has a stately look to it. The rooms are gracious and high-ceilinged, and though the furnishings are in no sense opulent, they are very comfortable. I thought it must once have been the residence of a well-to-do Leven burgher, but Tom quickly corrected that notion. "Purpose built to be just what it is," he said, "a clubhouse for golfers. Only one or two—the R&A, of course—older than it and in continuous use as a clubhouse right down till today."

Leven has an impressive collection of trophies—loving cups,

medals, and the like—including one that was first competed
for in 1870. Tom pointed out this handsome gold medal and
said, "That's the prize for the oldest open amateur tournament
in the world. In the beginning it was restricted to players from
local golf clubs. But today they come to Leven from all over the
country to play for it. The tournament actually goes back fifteen years before the Amateur Championship itself." It was an
insurance company that put up the medal, and the competition
today is still known as the Standard Life Gold Medal. Commercial sponsorship of golf tournaments in Britain—the Dun-
hill British Masters, Toyota Match Play, Bell's Scottish Open,
and others—has a long and honorable lineage.

Tom now escorted me upstairs to the billiards room, with its
one sturdy table. He rolled a couple of balls across the felt to
dramatize the trueness of the surface. "The greens may not
quite measure up to it," he chuckled, "but they are very good."
Then he raised a small panel in the wall to reveal a dumbwaiter.
"No need to run up and down the stairs to get a pint. A man
can concentrate on the snooker."

At Leven as we stand on the 1st tee there is little to delight
the eye, to lift the spirits. The Firth of Forth is at hand, surely
not a hundred yards off to the right, but some low and unat-
tractive structures block it from sight. Unfortunately, nothing
blocks out the trailer park and attendant hodgepodge of buildings in full view along the right side of the 2nd and 3rd holes.
There are a couple of low, duney ridges in the heart of this au-
thentic linksland, but there is nothing even remotely resembling a hill. We play on a compact rectangle between the
Scoonie Burn and Mile Dyke. Much of it lies spread out there
before us, gray-green, austere, with an occasional flag, yellow or

red, contributing a welcome note of color. Leven has much the same limited aesthetic appeal as the Old Course, itself no visual feast. But perhaps, I thought, like the Old Course, there is more here than is at first apparent. After all, Open qualifying is conducted from time to time on this links when St. Andrews is the venue for the championship.

We begin on the clubhouse side of the Scoonie Burn (only a near whiff can fail to clear it) and march straight out, parallel to the sea, for the first four holes. All are par fours, two of them, the 1st and 4th, quite demanding at 413 and 449 yards, respectively. On the opener itself, rising ground just short of the green, like the swell of a gentle wave, hides the putting surface and introduces an element of anxiety into the first testing shot we are called upon to execute. The 5th hole, just under 160 yards and parallel to the short 5th at Lundin on the other side of the fence, and the 6th, almost 570 yards, with a boundary to fret the slicer much of the way, introduce a nice variety to the routing. Seven is a turnabout and, at 184 yards to a smallish green defended by both sand and hillocks, a strong par three. The 8th, a medium-length par four, brings that nettlesome boundary on the right back into play, and the 9th is yet another par three, the third in the space of just five holes. This one reveals only the flag.

I was playing alone this afternoon of my initial visit—Tom Anderson had invited me to join him for a game later in the day, but I had to get back to St. Andrews—and on the 9th had an experience that I have no wish to repeat. I scored a hole-in-one, but my scorecard shows 3.

This 173-yarder, which climbs only very gently, was playing into the breeze. I pushed a 4-wood wildly right and over the rise, a shot so dreadful as to be inexplicable. I teed up another ball. This one I hit perfectly—as it turned out, *perfectly* in the literal sense of the word. I could detect a mild hubbub from the direction of the 10th tee and one voice exclaiming, "It's in! It's in! He's holed it!" I could see nothing but the waving flag.

I shouldered my bag, took a couple of steps, then stopped. The force of the quandary had struck me. If I crested the little slope on a diagonal that was obviously carrying me toward the thicket and the boundary, the threesome ahead would sense at once what had happened, and the bloom would be off the rose. They would probably extend condolences instead of congratulations. If, on the other hand, I strode directly to the cup and collected that ball, I would be exercising my right to declare the first ball lost. I would also be giving up the chance of finding the wayward ball (not something I do lightly) and, unless I chose to make a clean breast of it, I would be deceiving the threesome ahead.

I decided to hunt for the first ball. There was no one behind me. I could spend as much time as I wished in the search. If I were sufficiently patient, I could probably avoid any exchange with the group ahead. Let them think what they wished. The perfect shot had doubtless brightened their day. Why acknowledge the wretched one? Indeed, why did I have to say anything? I was playing alone and therefore accountable to no one but myself.

I went on prowling through the rough—in vain, as it turned out—till I could see that they had disappeared down the 10th fairway. Then, at last, I walked to the green and picked the second ball out of the hole. One thing was certain: I had discovered a new way for this most complex of games to harry me. Sometimes golf is entirely too much like life.

The more I played Leven, the more my affection for it grew. Unlike Crail and Elie and Lundin, it is no charmer, but it is honest and it calls for good swings. Both gorse and heather must be shunned, to say nothing of the long bent grasses cloaking the ridges. The rumpled fairways sometimes produce awkward stances and lies. Bunkering is not heavy but a lot of the pits are deep. As for blind shots—on the 325-yard 10th, for example, both drive and approach are aimed at unseen targets— they may surface rather too often to suit the purist, but there is nothing contrived about them. They simply reflect the natural flow of the ancient linksland.

There are consecutive par fives of indentical length on the second nine, which is laid out within the first nine (3,006 yards, par 34) and which measures 3,429 yards against a par of 37. The 12th and 13th are both 482 yards long, and since they run in opposite directions, one or the other, depending on the breeze, will provide a good birdie opportunity. Picking up that stroke will come in handy at the end, for the last four holes are difficult. The 15th, rising almost imperceptibly, is 188 yards, with the green, on a ridge, imaginatively shaped and inhospitable. Prepare to chip your second shot. The 386-yard 16th, in the same direction and again slightly uphill, finishes within a few steps of the Leven Bowling Club's green. Seventeen, showing 414 yards on the card, plays shorter thanks to the modestly falling nature of the second shot. Eighteen is the toughest hole on the course. In fact, it is one of the toughest par fours I've ever played. Barring a tornado at my back and a rock-hard fairway, I cannot imagine being able to reach it in two. It is 475 yards long, and the Scoonie Burn, which we've not seen since the game began, now reappears to cross in front of the green and then slink down the right side. Here even the powerful and accomplished player—and *only* here on the entire course—faces a true "death or glory" shot.

Back in the clubhouse after the round, I spotted a sign posted at the bar that strongly implied that though the secretary might not have been on hand that afternoon, his vigilance could not be questioned:

N O T I C E

The Suggestion Book will now be kept behind the bar and available therefore from the staff, who have been instructed not to release the book to members who have been drinking excessively.

John Bennett
Secretary

Future suggestions, I fear, are unlikely to be quite so creative as some in the past.

Among the many other courses in Fife outside St. Andrews are two that are somewhat well known, Scotscraig and Ladybank, and two that are little known, Aberdour and Charleton. A few words about each might be useful.

Located in Tayport, the Scotscraig Golf Club was founded in 1817. The course appears to be nearly a mile from the sea.

There is not much change in elevation over the 18 holes, which, from the medal tees, add up to almost 6,500 yards against a par of 71. Scotscraig is a hybrid, partly seaside, partly parkland. The first nine, where the links feeling is most in evidence, possesses five very good par fours, with the 8th hole particularly fine as it moves slightly uphill along a dune-framed valley to an extremely undulating green. The second nine has an attractive variety to the holes, but there is a meadowy effect to some of it and no real distinction to any of it. Overall, however, the fairways ripple, the greens are swift and true, the gorse will swallow you alive, and the heather and the long rough grasses take their toll. And if the trees tend to detract from the linkslike aspect of the course, they do heighten our aesthetic pleasure in the round.

The Ladybank Golf Club, near Annsmuir, was founded in 1879. Its par-71 course, 6,271 yards from the regular markers, can be stretched to 6,461 yards. A flat and wooded heathland layout, Ladybank has about it a sweet sense of seclusion and solitude. There are pines and silver birch, heather and gorse. The fairways are wide, the greens are large and occasionally of interest. The greenside bunkering is skillful and serious. Ladybank has a bit more variety and appeal than the Lansdowne course at Blairgowrie, which it instantly calls to mind. But there is, again, that unfortunate blandness resulting in a number of forgettable holes. Still, this course is used from time to time as a final qualifying site for the Open when it is played at St. Andrews.

In 1983 Ladybank had its moment in the sun when, as a last-minute substitute venue, it hosted an exhibition match between Jack Nicklaus and Seve Ballesteros. The occasion was the

launch in St. Andrews of the Old Course Golf and Country
Club (a reincarnation of the Old Course Hotel, which sits
neatly in the crook of the dogleg on the infamous Road Hole).
The very staging of the match became a cause célèbre. Frank
Sheridan, new owner of the hotel club, had assumed that if he
brought to St. Andrews, at considerable expense, the two greatest players in the world for a friendly round of golf, that round
would be played on the Old Course. But the St. Andrews Links
management and the R&A did not see it that way. So the two
British Open champions—Jack had won at Muirfield in 1966
and at St. Andrews in 1970 and 1978; Seve, victor in 1979 at
Royal Lytham, would win on the Old Course in 1984—and
their enthusiastic gallery of 5,000 were forced to commemorate
the opening of the Old Course Golf and Country Club, not on
the Old Course, but 10 miles down the road at Ladybank. The
tabloids had a field day.

Aberdour, where golf has been played since 1897, is for fun
and for views. A parkland course (mature trees of all kinds) at
the sea, it starts with a pair of memorable 160-yarders, goes on
to provide good sport throughout the first ten, then, rather
sheepishly, one suspects, offers an open rolling meadow that
contains no more than three worthy shots over the final eight
holes. It measures all of 5,460 yards (par 67: six short holes, one
long hole). I do not urge you to make the one-hour drive from
St. Andrews down the coast, well beyond Leven, but I do say
you would enjoy the first ten holes thoroughly and be bowled
over by the first two.

The opening hole mesmerizes. From an elevated tee we play
a medium iron—or a medium *wood* if the wind is head on!—
downhill 160 yards to a sloping green. A stone wall saves the

pull or hook from tumbling onto the rocky shore. All very nice, you concede, but scarcely unprecedented or hypnotic. It is the backstop and the backdrop that are so arresting. Immediately behind the green bulks the biggest rock I've ever seen on a golf course. And immediately behind this boulder lies the Firth of Forth in all its grandeur, this time with Edinburgh itself in full view on the far side of the water, complete with the Castle and Arthur's Seat and, on the horizon, the Lammermuir Hills and the Pentland Hills. In the foreground are sailboats, Inch Island, and Inchcolm Island, with the ruins of twelfth-century St. Colm's Abbey. Striking a golf ball seems incidental.

The 2nd tee is squarely beside the 1st green. It is marked by another monstrous rock. On this one-shotter we must travel the same distance, but not on the same line. Instead, we fire boldly across a corner of Hawk's Bay, from our elevated tee to an equally elevated shelf of green carved out of a right-hand hill well above the beach. It is a thrilling shot and, at 160 yards, one that we are fully capable of executing. Aberdour is the only course I've played that commences with two par threes, and what splendid creations they are. It simply was not possible for the rest of the eighteen to measure up to this extraordinary beginning.

On May 15, 1994, a new golf course, called Charleton, opened in Fife. Just outside Colinsburgh, and about 15 minutes from St. Andrews, it is the brainchild of Baron St. Clair Bonde, who believed that some of his 1,000-acre estate could be more profitably put to use as a public golf course. It was not an expensive course to build—there are no hazards, natural or man-made—and it is not an expensive course to play. Vowed the Baron in a display of *noblesse oblige* at the time the course opened, "I am determined I will charge no more than £12 a round this year and I will try to keep the fees down to at least half of what is being charged by the established golf clubs here in Fife."

The eighteen was laid out by John Salvesen, a former captain of the R&A who learned his trade under Donald Steel. It ranges from rolling to hilly, the pastoral views are gorgeous, and at 6,132 yards against a par of 72, it offers holes that, with the exception of the 434-yard 13th, we can reach in regulation. But, lacking hazards, it requires a stiff breeze to make it testing. Still, Mr. Salvesen has "boxed the compass," and we rarely know in which direction the next hole will take us. The green complexes, with their framing mounds and their vigorously undulating and sloping putting surfaces (the 2nd and 16th, two very short par fours, slope boldly away from the pitch, downhill from front to back), are the salient features of the course. There is generally room to swing freely, though this is not a treeless expanse of pastureland. Worth noting is the charming little chalet of a clubhouse, which looks as though it must have sat there forever but is actually not a day older than the golf course.

The Kingdom of Fife is full of places to see and things to do. The East Neuk fishing villages—Crail, Anstruther, Pittenweem, St. Monance, Elie, Largo—are picturesque without being precious. The trick for the visitor is to keep them straight. If you had to settle on just one as the most attractive example of the genre, it would probably be Crail. Here you find it all: the handsome and spacious town square, called Marketgate;

narrow, cobbled lanes spilling down to the pretty, protected harbor; seventeenth- and eighteenth-century stone cottages, with their crow-stepped red tile roofs; and the Collegiate Church of St. Mary, in part reaching back to the twelfth or thirteenth century.

Fife also has its share of great houses open to the public. Of those my wife and I have visited over the years, three stand out. Earlshall Castle, just outside Leuchars and some 10 minutes from St. Andrews, is the sixteenth-century home of the Baron (he collects swords) and Baroness (she collects mugs) of Earlshall, who seem honestly pleased to have people roaming through their house and gardens. The flowers, incidentally, are one thing—roses in every conceivable hue are a feast for the eye—but it is the topiary yews we especially remember. They have been shaped and sheared in the form of chessmen and they are colossal, a display of wit and sophistication worthy of Villandry and Versailles.

Little more than a mile outside the village of Ceres, itself quite attractive, is a grand Edwardian manor called Hill of Tarvit Mansionhouse. A property of the National Trust for Scotland, it is a showcase for the late Frederick Sharp's collection of Flemish tapestries, Chinese porcelains and bronzes, French and Regency furniture, European paintings, and more. The extensive gardens are still carefully maintained, but gone are the curling pond, the croquet lawn, the tennis court, and the nine-hole golf course. Sharp, an ardent golfer, had made his course available free of charge to the residents of Ceres seven days a week.

Kellie Castle, some three miles northwest of Pittenweem, also belongs to the National Trust for Scotland. Built of a variegated local sandstone, and with lovely views across farmland and woodland to the Firth of Forth, Kellie Castle is above all a tower house. Its three massive towers were erected, beginning in the fourteenth century, over a period of 300 years. The impression, if only from the exterior, is more of a fortress than a mansion.

Two eating places are particularly worthy of note, and both of them are in Anstruther. For lunch, the Dreel Tavern: low beamed ceilings, dark paneling, three fireplaces. The food is decent, the prices reasonable, and the atmosphere wonderful. On pretty days you can eat outside in a simple garden above the Dreel Burn, a stream that runs through the heart of Anstruther but is easy to miss. For dinner, try the Cellar, which, as it happens, is also easy to miss. I can tell you that it's near the children's amusement pier, that its regulars claim it to be the best seafood restaurant in Scotland, that it may well be just that, and that it is expensive. Still, it is well worth the 20-minute drive from St. Andrews, where our pilgrimage has brought us at last.

Chapter Thirteen

St. Andrews

 St. Andrews has a lot of golf holes: 117 of them, 99 at or near the sea plus the spanking new eighteen a couple of miles inland at Craigtoun Park. There is something here for everybody. And make no mistake about it: everybody is here. I recall walking up North Street from Golf Place a summer or two ago, passing visitors like myself, most of them in groups of two or three or four, many of them engaged in conversation. In the space of two blocks I never heard a word of English. I heard German, Italian, French, Swedish, Japanese, and what I took to be a middle-European tongue that I could not identify. I was astonished at the international buzz.

Now, you may well ask, were they all here to play the Old Course? The answer is no, although it might seem that way when you try to make a reservation for a tee time or put your name on the ballot for tomorrow's play. Actually, a number of visitors are here simply because, the golf aside, St. Andrews is irresistible: it is a beguiling seaside resort, the repository of a thousand years of history (some of it quite violent), and the home of an ancient and eminent university. Anyone who has allotted more time for his or her visit than it takes to play the Old Course—about 3 hours and 40 minutes—will quickly sense the royal burgh's charms and be captivated by them. Perhaps, heretical as it may be to suggest it, the golfer on pilgrimage to St. Andrews may find the old town even more appealing than the Old Course.

That is chiefly because the Old Course takes a bit of getting used to. It is no beauty. What's more, it is shamelessly deceitful and capricious. And it can be—from its only water hazard (the Swilcan Burn, fronting the 1st green) to the Valley of Sin (a hollow in the left forepart of the last green)—supremely frustrating. Nonetheless, it is truly the fount of man's best game; some form of golf, however rudimentary, has been played over this ground for perhaps 500 years. And virtually every great champion from Old Tom Morris to "young" Tom Watson has on this storied links experienced triumph or tragedy. Here the British Open has been contested 25 times and the Walker Cup 8 times; and here, from its imposing, foursquare, many-chimneyed clubhouse smack against the 1st tee, the Royal and Ancient Golf Club of St. Andrews commands the links (and, one sometimes suspects, the world). But the R&A does not *own* the links. Golf in St. Andrews is municipal golf: the courses belong to the town, just as Dyker Beach belongs to New York City and Harding Park belongs to San Francisco and Cobbs Creek belongs to Philadelphia. The consequence of this is that the R&A, far and away the most powerful golf club in the world, does not own a golf course. Not even a nine-hole one. Nor a practice putting green. R&A members play their golf on the Old Course or the New, the Eden or the Jubilee, the Strathtyrum or the Balgove, but they do not own any of them. The courses belong to St. Andrews, and the game upon them belongs to the world.

Standing in front of the squat bulk of the familiar sandstone clubhouse, the golfer finds himself gazing out over a monotonous, treeless stretch of flattish and featureless ground. There is little to please the eye. Sam Snead's reaction on first sighting the Old Course was not atypical: "What the devil is that?" he asked in all seriousness. "It looks like an old, abandoned golf course."

That was in 1946, a year after the end of World War II, and today no one is likely to make the same mistake. Still, it does look primitive and bleak. There seems to be no definition to the holes. It also looks flat. It does not play flat.

Out on the Old Course, which from the regular tees measures 6,566 yards against a par of 72, we find ourselves abroad in a sea of heaving turf: all humpy and hillocky, tousled and cranky and crumpled, with ripples, ridges, maniacal mounds (like the "igloo" blockading the entrance to the 4th green), gullies, hollows, plateaus, dells, and swales (the "gorge" in front of the 5th green). I once asked Jack Nicklaus whether the Old Course posed the most difficult shots to the green of any British Open course.

"I wouldn't say the most difficult," he replied. "I think *awkward* might be a better word."

There are other words one might use about the Old Course: *irritating, frustrating, infuriating,* especially when it comes to the bunkers. So diabolically shaped and sited are these hazards that even the green is no safe haven. In the 1978 Open, Tommy

Nakajima, one of the finest players to come out of Japan, reached the 17th green (466 yards) with his second shot, yet was forced to write a 9 on his scorecard. No, he did not seven-putt. Attempting to negotiate a fearful undulation with his lag putt from perhaps 70 feet, he watched stoically as the gluttonous Road Bunker, which eats into the left side of this long, narrow putting surface, swallowed his ball. He then failed—again and again and again and again—to execute the delicate little splash shot required from behind the vertical face of this sandy pot. Some wag suggested that the Road Bunker be renamed the "Sands of Nakajima."

Not incidentally, each of the 112 bunkers on the Old Course has its own name. Some names must have been prompted by an amusing—or at least interesting—story: Wig, Mrs. Kruger, Principal's Nose. Others are merely ominous: Coffin, Grave, Hell.

As for the greens, there are only 11 of them—four (1, 9, 17, 18) with one hole, seven containing two holes. These fabled double greens are immense. For most of us, they are, in truth, inconceivably vast. They average about three-quarters of an acre, some 33,000 square feet. Contrast that with the greens at Merion's East course, which average 5,500 square feet. If we grant each of the two holes on a typical St. Andrews green its half measure, it is still three times the size of a typical Merion green. Several years ago I paced off the distance from the cup for the 7th hole to the cup for its "partner," the 11th. It came to 96 yards, or, since putts are usually measured in feet, 288 feet—so a shot hit wildly left on the 7th or wildly right on the 11th could set the stage for a putt the length of a football field! It is advisable to bring along a sense of humor when you tackle the Old Course.

It need scarcely be added that these greens are not level. The undulations are not only pronounced, they can also be very abrupt, creating hollows deep enough to hide your partner in if, just as you turn to take your putter from the caddie, he should elect to lie down *in your line* but, as it happens, *out of your sight.*

Like the greens, the fairways are also doubly wide, but only for the player who hits it left. On hole after hole, with the exception of 8, 9, and 10—here, after having marched pretty much straightaway from the clubhouse for the first seven holes, we are now making the loop that gets us turned about to march pretty much straight back—there are acres and acres to accommodate a hook, but not 10 paces to save the chestnuts of a player who slices. Heather, gorse, out of bounds—in short, calamity—await the ball launched to starboard. Now it must be noted that, from the standpoint of opening up the green for the second shot, the right side of the fairway is the ideal place for the drive. But pursuing this path takes skill and courage. To the left lies safety—and, as befits the faint of heart, a discouraging string of bogeys.

Still, the fantastical greens, the unreliable bounces, the whimsical stances and lies, the scandalously sited bunkers (the expression "fairway bunker" is traditionally used to denote sand hazards that frame a fairway; at St. Andrews a fairway bunker— for instance, at the 5th, 9th, 12th, 14th, 16th—is too often literally that, smack in the heart of the fairway, precisely where we dream of placing our drive), the unpredictably shifting winds—all of these we might somehow cope with if only the Old Course were not also mysterious. But it is. First, there are the blind shots—on the outbound nine in particular, driving seems to be nothing but a lottery. We hit and hold our breath, rarely seeing the ball land, even more rarely seeing it roll to a stop. As for the shots to the green, the flag may be there in the distance, but there is nothing to serve as a backdrop for it, nothing to give us an idea of how far away it actually is. There are no yardage markers. Of inestimable worth is a professional caddie—not, you understand, a mere bag carrier, though both are available, the latter at half the cost ($20 as opposed to $40). But be forewarned: if you hire a caddie, you will do well simply to accept the club he proffers and execute your swing. You probably should not attempt—at least not the first time around—to get a feel for the shot, for how much ground lies between you and the hole, and for how the ball, in flight or on the ground, can be expected to behave. Often there is a shimmering, miragelike quality to what it is your vision encompasses, with the green itself, despite its enormity—indeed, perhaps because of it—so maddeningly ill-defined. The subleties are staggering, and only likely to be grasped after playing the Old Course over and over. Even then, uncertainty may creep into your thinking and your swing, with disastrous results.

Admittedly, it is all so strange, so puzzling, so idiosyncratic, that we risk losing sight of a fundamental truth about the Old Course: it possesses a number of unassailably great golf holes, all of which, as it happens, are on the second nine. This is not to suggest that the outward half is weak or dull. With the exception of the 8th, when played from the lower tee, and the bland 307-yard 9th, the holes here are good or very good, beginning with that tantalizing approach shot over the Swilcan Burn to the 1st green. But there is a sameness to four of the par fours—2, 3, 4, and 6—all heading in the same direction, all with blind or semiblind drives menaced by gorse on the right and bunkers heaven knows where, that makes it difficult to tell one hole from another. Happily, the lengths of these two-shotters do vary, or we would have no luck at all keeping them straight.

We face no such problem on the incoming nine, surely one of the half-dozen great nines of the world. Here the holes are remarkably individual, and the challenge, as a consequence, is wonderfully varied. And when we respond successfully to that challenge, we experience a deep and rare satisfaction. The 170-yard 11th—there are only two short holes on the course, just as there are only two long ones—from its elevated tee plays across the 7th fairway to the elevated green above the Eden estuary. It is grand and thrilling. Hill Bunker, some 10 feet deep, guards the left side of the green. Strath Bunker, shallower but with an essentially vertical forward wall, eats into the right side. Both are gathering pits—this is a case of Scylla and Charybdis. Oh, there is room between them, but the breeze will play havoc with a ball that has even a hint of sidespin on it. Moreover, the green is tilted sharply down from back to front, so that if we make our good swing from the tee and wind up above the cup the likelihood of getting down in two putts is remote. It is a hole that has been copied all over the world, but the original remains the most testing.

Step off the back of the 11th green and you are standing on the 12th tee, which is modestly elevated. It could reasonably be claimed that in all the world of golf this is the place to be. Turn your back on the 12th hole and you gaze down upon the broad Eden estuary as it stretches away to merge with the North Sea. Face left and, beyond the flags for 7 and 11, you survey the New Course and the Jubilee, almost certainly thronged with golfers, and beyond these two eighteens the lightly capped waters of St. Andrews Bay rolling toward the West Sands. To your right is the Eden Course and, next to it, the Strathtyrum. More golfers here, many more golfers. What a vast playing field it all is—links, links, links, gray-green and rippling, studded with low dunes and heather and gorse and fearsome sandpits, not beautiful in the generally accepted sense perhaps, but supremely natural, with scarcely a nod toward the hand of man for any of its charm. But look dead ahead now, beyond the flag on 12, and there, in the far distance, stands the beloved town itself, above the rocks and sea on its gentle escarpment, its low, gray silhouette punctuated by four or five church spires. With each stroke we draw closer to it as we play our way straight home over these last seven holes.

And what splendid holes they are! The 12th, only 316 yards, has seen its share of 2s—oh, yes, it is driven from time to time when the breeze is at the big basher's back—and its share of 6s. The hole poses two problems: a quartet of very penal bunkers, invisible from the tee and in the center of the fairway just where we would normally expect to land our good drive, and then a shallow shelf of a plateau green that can be the very devil to hit and hold. So even on this short par four, the complexities of this unique course put us on the defensive.

The 13th is a splendid and unusual two-shotter, about 400 yards long, where the target for the drive is a rectangle of fairway framed by gorse on the right, bunkers on the left (the Coffin among them) and rough-covered little "foothills" at the far end. Place your drive in this preferred spot and you now face a blind shot, first over those "foothills," then over badly broken ground, that must carry 180 yards and avoid the ferocious Hole o' Cross Bunker, a greenside pit behind which the cup is often cut. Is there no surcease? Well, the putting—you are now on the largest green in the world, very like 45,000 square feet, this home for the flags on 5 and 13—will probably be a fairly straightforward business.

The 14th, 523 yards, may be the greatest par five in the world. Day in and day out, it is the most destructive hole on the Old Course (not surprising when you realize that it is entirely possible to clear the massive Hell Bunker only to wind up in the lethal Grave Bunker). Littered by some 15 bunkers and bordered tight on the right by a low stone boundary wall, the 14th, "Long Hole In," appears at first to be classically penal. In fact, it is classically strategic, and staunchly supports the claim that this is the ultimate strategic golf course, where the thinking may be even more important than the hitting. There are three separate routes to the 14th green: left for safety, straight for a chance of getting nearly home in two if you can carry the Hell Bunker, right for taking the sand out of play but flirting with the boundary. Nicklaus elected the conservative route, driving left into the 5th fairway ("Long Hole Out"), in the final round of the 1978 Open and won the championship for the third time. In the final round of the 1933 Open, Gene Sarazen followed a beautiful drive with a risky brassie that, caught a shade inside, just failed to clear the hidden Hell Bunker. He buried his third shot in the front wall of the hazard and capped the disaster with three putts for an 8. A 7 would have gained him the playoff with Craig Wood and Denny Shute.

In the first round of the 1995 Open, Nicklaus also caught Hell Bunker with his second shot. He failed to get out on his third, his fourth, and his fifth. The lies were indeed "awkward."

Free at last on his sixth shot, he now pitched to the green and three-putted for a 10. For the remainder of the 1995 season, visitor after visitor came to the 14th, bent on seizing this one opportunity to "beat Jack Nicklaus." I actually played the hole with a number of those giant killers. I remember one fellow who also found himself in Hell, struggled manfully to extricate himself, finally reached the green in 8 and holed a 14-foot curler for 9. He was ecstatic.

It was a prudent 7 here that helped Peter Thomson win the 1955 championship. Twice on this hole in the final round—first from one of the deep little pits called the Beardies, following his drive, then from a greenside bunker—he chose to play out of the sand backward. Leading at the time by three or four strokes and bowing to the categorical imperative of bunker play at St. Andrews ("If you get in, *get out*"), he took his medicine calmly, wrote down 7 on the card, and went on to win by two strokes. It was this incident that prompted an amusing definition of the Old Course by Gerald Micklem, a former British Walker Cupper and longtime golf administrator: "A place where you play backward twice on a hole because it is the smartest way to become Open champion."

I also recall playing the hole a few years ago with a couple of strapping Australian lads. This was their first game on the Old Course and they attacked it with a flourish, bombing unimaginably long tee shots to every point of the compass despite my well-meaning directions and counsel. Several times on the outbound nine they unintentionally visited the New Course. On the 14th the more powerful of the two shrugged off my cautionary advice and cracked a 275-yarder into the right side of the fairway, not a dozen yards from the stone boundary wall.

From there he launched an even more impressive 3-wood that scurried up the steep front bank of the green, obligingly ran out of steam as it crested the terrace, and drifted down to stop some 22 feet from the cup. I am pleased to report that he did not make the eagle, for it was quite enough that this reckless slasher from down under had made a mockery of a hole that has consistently cowed the best players in the history of the game.

The 15th is a much simpler matter. It is quite long enough—and at 401 yards, it can be a little too long for many of us as the prevailing wind comes off the port bow (though these Fifeshire breezes are notoriously fickle). There is gorse on the right and sand on the left, including the pesky little Sutherland Bunker—hidden, of course—at about 200 yards, but there is also a fair and flattish piece of ground out there to accept the decent drive, and the immense green (coupled with the 3rd) is defended only by a solitary pot bunker at the front left. There is nothing automatic about a 4 on this hole, but at least you will not get into a stew contemplating its complexities and mulling your options.

The 16th is decidedly less hospitable. Indeed, it is hostile. Only 351 yards long, it is fraught with danger. A tight cluster of three bunkers, called the Principal's Nose, lies exactly where we would like to drop our drive, in the left center of the fairway. Right of this triune hazard is a patch of fairway some 29 yards wide and marked on the right by a boundary fence that indicates the old railway line. As ever, the breathing room for the drive is to the left, but from there the second shot is threatened by the Wig Bunker, knifing into the left front of the green. Steer right of Wig, however, with your 6- or 7-iron and you are in danger of that boundary fence, which lurks only a few feet from the right edge of the green. A decidedly dicey business, this 16th, from start to finish.

One's instinct, when confronted with the obligation to play it or the requirement to write about it, is to dodge the 17th hole. It is simply too difficult to play, and for decades it has been done to death by golf's scriveners. Ben Crenshaw was right when he said that the 17th, called the "Road Hole," is the hardest par four in the world because it's really a par five. In fact, it was a three-shotter until some point in the 1950s.

The facts about it can be stated simply enough: it is 466 yards long; neither fairway nor green is visible from the tee; the blind drive must wing its way over a corner of the Old Course Hotel, in the crook of the right-hand dogleg, to land we know not where; the green, sited diagonally across the second shot and built up onto a plateau three or four feet above the fairway, is quite long from left to right and quite shallow from front to rear; a devouring and claustrophobic pot bunker invades the left side of the putting surface; the right and rear of the green are guarded by a paved road and attendant stone wall, both of which are in play. No free drop here.

To label this hole harsh and inhuman would be understatement. It is an instrument of torture. It is an ogre, a monster, a villain of darkest hue. And coming where it does in the round, the penultimate hole, it can be—and so often has been—ruinous.

Perhaps no historic moment on the Road Hole is more vivid in our memories than the climax of the 1984 Open, when Tom Watson came to the 17th tee in the final round tied with Seve Ballesteros and needing a four here to carry the battle to the home hole. He did not make it. His drive was not so strong as he had hoped, and now he found himself faced with a 2-iron to that mocking target. It was simply too difficult a shot in those circumstances. So difficult, in fact, that neither he nor any other world-class player can bring it off 50 percent of the time with the Open Championship on the line. The distance is too long, the target is too elusive, the penalty for failure is too great, and the stakes are too high. And so we should not have been taken aback to see that low 2-iron dart away to the right and come to rest on the far side of the paving and almost against the stone wall. Watson did well to salvage a five, but it was four he had to have, and when Ballesteros, playing just ahead, learned of Watson's failure, he rolled in a 12-footer on the 18th for a three to shut the door emphatically. The 17th had once again proved fatal to a player's aspirations, and this time to the aspirations of a champion who had won the Open five times but never at St. Andrews.

And at last we have arrived at the home hole, named for Old Tom Morris. It is friendly—that broadest of all fairways (shared with the 1st), that immense single green (55 yards wide and nearly 40 yards deep), not a bunker to be found anywhere, a manageable 354 yards to be covered from tee to cup. A four is highly likely, a three much more than a remote possibility. We drive solidly up the left side, aiming for the great red and gold clock on the R&A clubhouse, giving a wide berth to the boundary that edges the right side of the fairway along The Links, with its parade of shops, clubs, private homes, and Rusack's Hotel. We troop over the old stone footbridge that spans the Swilcan Burn, reminding ourselves of the harmless legend that claims knights of old crossed it on their way to the Crusades. Our drive has finished just short of Granny Clark's Wynd, leaving a shot of perhaps 125 yards to the center of the green, where, as luck would have it, the hole has been cut. Mindful of the consequences of leaving our approach short in the Valley of Sin, we go a trifle past the flag, perhaps 35 feet. The putt is downhill, but not intimidatingly so. Leaning over the railing behind the green are 15 or 20 spectators. We notice them for the first time. They are, in truth, a fixture at the home green of the Old Course, a few of them doubtless St. Andreans who have taken up this vigil on occasions great and small. They have, it occurs to us, seen this green three-putted more than once, and by famous players at that. The collective gaze we feel focusing upon us is one of resigned skepticism. Our frailty is about to be exposed. But perhaps it need not be. The lag is not really unsettling. Let us put a smooth, unhurried stroke on the ball and surely it will feed its way down and expire somewhere within the sanctuary of that cherished two-foot circle. And so, indeed, it does. We tap in for a four—and exhale slowly.

There is not a hint of greatness in the hole. On the other hand, neither is there anything in the least mundane about it. It is like no finishing hole on any great course in the world. But then, the Old Course is unlike any other great course in the world. It is *sui generis*, a law unto itself, and so extraordinary—its subtleties beyond calculation, its mysteries unfathomable—that, in the end, it defies conventional analysis. But it consistently challenges the keenest thinking, the finest strokes, and the stoutest heart that a truly great player can summon.

The wise Francis Ouimet, who defeated Harry Vardon and Ted Ray in a playoff for the 1913 U.S. Open at Brookline, chose not to rationalize the enduring appeal of the Old Course. As nonplaying captain of our Walker Cup team competing at St. Andrews in 1947, he instructed each of his young charges, if asked an opinion of the Old Course, to reply simply, "I'm mad about it."

The Other Courses

There is an inclination on the part of visitors to give short shrift to the other eighteens here at St. Andrews; after all, golfers have come to experience the Old Course, and anything else must inevitably play second fiddle. This tendency dates back at least to 1910, when Bernard Darwin's seminal *The Golf Courses of the British Isles* was published. The master was not much taken with the New Course, which Old Tom Morris laid out in 1895 and which has, except for the improved quality of its turf, changed little over the years. Darwin writes that, in contrast to the Old, "the new course is infinitely more ordinary, and that this comparative commonplaceness . . . resolves itself largely into the fact that there are not nearly so many good natural greens. . . . It has 'relief course' plainly written all over it."

The New enjoys essentially the same type of undulating linksland as the Old, which is right beside it, but the exasperating cants and cambers that afflict so many of the stances and lies on the ancient layout are less common here. The New is thus less quirky, less contrary, and less likely to produce excitement, pleasurable or otherwise. There are no high-risk shots that can result in either birdie or double-bogey. It is quite straightforward, but the gorse does make us hesitate, and at 6,604 yards against a par of 71, there is a need for hitting.

Out at the far end of the links, in the charming dune country bordering the Eden estuary, there is an especially attractive trio of holes that show the New at its best: the par-five 8th, with the narrow opening between two sandhills, cart-gate fashion, defining the approach to a largely concealed green; the 225-yard 9th, above and along the water, where an overzealous wood hit left can drown; and the splendid 10th, where, as we now head for home, we need all the help the elevated tee can provide if we are to have any chance of reaching this 464-yard par four in regulation.

Over the years I have found myself listening, from time to time, to those who prefer the New to the Old, claiming that the New is more honest, less capricious, that it presents its demands fairly, that the visitor has a chance here, that, in short, it is the better course. There is considerable truth in this brief, but not in its conclusion. Yes, the New is good golf, at times very good golf. But it is not great golf. It does not extract from us anything like the thinking and the shotmaking demanded, hole after hole, on the Old. And when we apply to the New that harshest of standards—"Would you cross an ocean to play it?"—the answer must be no.

On the other side of the New, which is to say nearer the sea, lies the Jubilee Course, which opened in 1897 on the day Queen Victoria celebrated her Diamond Jubilee. Then it was only 12 holes and was, as Pat Ward-Thomas tells us in *The Royal and Ancient,* "regarded as the Ladies Course, an alternative to the gentler challenge of the Ladies Putting Green." The powers that be have been tinkering with it for about a hundred years, and they have finally gotten it right. Donald Steel, golf architect and writer, can take a bow for his ambitious and imaginative makeover of a course that I once believed to be the second worst in the world (the U.S. Navy's layout at Guantanamo Bay took the palm).

The opening hole on the new Jubilee is the opening hole on the old Jubilee, a par four that stretches straight and far—it is 454 yards long—to a broad and open green. It is a dispiriting start—an unlikely par, an unprepossessing hole. But the 2nd, one of Steel's new holes, is charming, a 336-yarder doglegging right, the short approach shot rising to an adroitly bunkered bilevel green in the dunes. This, we say to ourself, is more like it. And there is a great deal more like it lying in wait.

Steel has taken the stepchild of St. Andrews and imbued it with character and attractiveness and variety, principally by using to advantage two parallel spines of sandhills. Threading a number of holes though these low dunes, he has sited greens and tees with an admirable naturalness that is characteristic of the entire routing plan.

The par threes in particular are superb. On the 5th, 162 yards, we play to a green cocked up invitingly in the dunes. The green is actually quite large, but fail to place your shot in the sector containing the cup and three putts will almost certainly follow. The 9th, 192 yards, puts us in mind of the fabled 11th on the Old Course, an elevated tee to a slightly less elevated green, marvelous views in all directions. All that is required here is a perfect stroke.

These days on the Jubilee, the game is very lively, very exacting. And, at 6,805 yards against a par of 72, very long. The net of it is that this once-despised eighteen is now the strongest test in town. But don't be put off by that: this is also thoroughly enjoyable links golf, with the muffled sound of the breaking waves wafting over it from the far side of the sandhills.

Donald Steel's revisionist strategies can also be seen over on the Eden Course, which Harry Colt, the first golf architect who was not a golf professional, designed in 1912. Steel has certainly toughened it—any effort that would rid us of the weak original opening and closing two-shotters (for big hitters, they were both often one-shotters) was to be applauded—but the best holes still belong to Colt, and they are on the first nine, where two delightful short par fours play beside the Eden to plateau greens perched perilously above the estuary, and where the three long par fours, averaging about 420 yards, call for first-class hitting if we are to have any chance of reaching the skillfully sited greens in two. The old Colt greens, it should be noted, give the course much of its backbone and its appeal. These often fantastically contoured—indeed, sometimes even billowing—concoctions make clear the influence of the Old Course on the architect. The change in elevation from front (low) to rear (high) on the green of the par-three 8th, for example, cannot be less than eight feet.

Two of Steel's new holes, 14 and 15, a par four and a par three, play across a pond that he dug. This artificial hazard is jarring, so unexpected is it in a landscape whose abiding naturalness has always been its chief virtue. But we will doubtless get used to it, and it does call for a couple of fairly demanding iron shots.

The Eden measures 6,112 yards against a par of 70. Do not be misled by these amiable figures: this is a good test. You may want to keep in mind that the 9th green here, unlike its counterparts on the Old, New, and Jubilee, actually finds us within a few hundred yards of the changing rooms.

The relatively new Strathtyrum Course, which opened on July 1, 1993, also gets back to these same changing rooms at both 9 and 18. This time Mr. Steel started from scratch, but there was actually very little opportunity for him to display any artistry. The Strathtyrum, all of 5,094 yards yet boasting a par of 69 (somewhat of a stretch there, since one par five is 456 yards and the other is 447), was designed with women and the elderly in mind. Unless you are heading into a fresh breeze, there is minimal challenge from tee to green on the majority of holes. The 18th, at 390 yards the longest of the par fours, can call for a couple of strong swings; it is unique in this respect. The fairways are wide, the bunkering is light, and there is a lot of backing and forthing on what strikes us as rather more a meadow than a links.

Still, the Strathtyrum is not totally devoid of interest, for the greens are imaginatively contoured, the undulations can be tricky, and, as targets for an iron shot, these putting surfaces are not particularly generous. This last prompts the requirement for some deft chipping. The Strathtyrum, which just may turn out to have a broader appeal than was originally envisioned (golfers love to post a good score, no matter how it is arrived at), will certainly serve to take some of the pressure off the other eighteens.

Adjacent to the Strathtyrum is a little nine-hole course called Balgove. Designed for beginners and youngsters, it consists of six par threes and three par fours. There are very few hazards and the greens are small. It is an ideal place to enjoy one's first taste of the game.

Time now to head for the hills, which are in very short supply on these coastal courses. But a couple of miles inland, at Craigtoun Park, there is land that is much more than gently rolling. On it, at the behest of the owners of the Old Course Hotel, Peter Thomson has fashioned an eighteen that is certain to delight visitors to St. Andrews for generations to come.

Thomson, a native of Melbourne, Australia, was one of the outstanding players during the second half of the twentieth century. Between 1952 and 1958 he won the British Open four times and finished second three times. In 1965 he won the championship for the fifth and last time. Twenty years later he utterly dominated the Senior PGA Tour in America, amassing nine victories in one year, 1985. We know him as a player, but we do not know him as a golf course architect. The courses he has designed or redesigned—and there are about a hundred of them—are in Australia, Japan, the Far East. There are no Peter Thomson courses in the United States.

I have played the Duke's Course, as it was named, once, late in the summer of 1995, when it was open only to 15 or 20 golfers a day while the turf was establishing itself. By May of 1996, a full schedule of play is expected to be in effect. And though guests at the Old Course Hotel will have priority, there should be ample starting times for all others.

But though I have played the Duke's just once, I have examined it closely twice. The first time was in the summer of 1994, when I spent more than two hours at Craigtoun with Thomson in his tiny, mud-spattered white Fiat, as we followed the routing plan. The sites for the tees and the greens, the outline of the fairways, and the location of the bunkers, all were clearly evident on this lively junket from the 1st tee to the 18th green. Thomson had a lot of real estate to work with here, so much, in fact, that the first thought was to build three nines. You are immediately struck by the expanse of his canvas, and as you work your way around the course it becomes obvious that this truly is big golf, beginning with the length from the tournament tees, 7,110 yards. Here we find big fairways (they average a good 50 yards in width), big greens, big elevation changes (the overall change is 155 feet, which, on a championship course, is very great indeed), and big vistas. You get the impression that this course will surely host important tournaments, quite possibly on an annual basis. Par, it should be noted, is 72, with the traditional mix of ten par fours, four par threes, and four par fives. Though parts of the property are heavily wooded, only four or five holes are isolated in a framework of trees. Most holes have a considerably more open aspect.

Now in his mid-60s, Thomson is a man of wide-ranging interests and of considerable cultivation (he is a writer, a painter, a student of classic literature, a lover of classical music, and a connoisseur of vintage wines). His demeanor is restrained, gentlemanly, even donnish, with an overlay of wry amusement. He loves the Old Course above all, insisting that it demands more discipline and skill than any other course. When it comes to designing golf courses, he has equally firm convictions.

"I do not see a tract of land as a file of topographical maps, to be used as the basis for some sort of computer-generated design. I don't believe in predetermined contours. By and large, you want to take what the land gives you. That's why the architect has to be on the scene if he is going to achieve a natural form and feel to it all."

As far as hazards are concerned, the Craigtoun course will have no lakes or ponds calling for forced carries. "I'm now rating courses by the number of balls you need to play them. This will be a one-ball course, which I think is ideal. I think a twelve-ball course is nonsense." It need scarcely be added that Peter Thomson considers island greens silly, an affront to reason. He is not opposed to water *per se,* merely the intemperate use of it. At Craigtoun there are a couple of foxy little burns.

Bunkers constitute the principal hazard here. "There are eighty," he told me, "and there will *not* be any added later." These pits are sculpted, with the turf descending well down the face and the sand generally confined to the bottom. Some are quite deep, and all are penal to one degree or another. "None of them is hidden," he said. "They actually confront the player boldly, but they can be avoided. So I believe the golfer should be penalized for hitting into them." But they are used sparingly, he added, pointing out that the long par-four 2nd hole, 465 yards from the back tees, 415 yards from the regular markers, has no sand. Its length, together with the siting and the shape of the green, makes bunkers redundant.

Though the greens are large, the contouring is conservative. Thomson is typically firm on this point. "Putting should be fun on generally flat surfaces, just as you find on classic golf courses. You notice that on the Old Course, with those immense double greens and some very dramatic rolls, nevertheless, the particular area where the cup is cut is quite level, and there is nothing at all excessive in the fifteen or twenty feet around the hole."

None of this, of course, precludes the bilevel green, even, as at the 18th, one with three levels—"like the last hole at Augusta," Thomson said to me in an aside as he discussed with the green shaper how he wanted this particular putting surface to be contoured. The hole itself also suggests the 18th at Augusta in its flow—uphill all the way—and in its length, 400 yards from the competition tees. (In the end, I noticed a year later, this green would have only two levels.) Thomson knows the great courses well, and there is inevitably, perhaps consciously, an element of the eclectic in his designs. He had earlier pointed out the 3rd, a falling and shortish par three over a scrubby wasteland, as having a Pine Valley feeling.

The 13th tee is the highest point of the course. I had no sense that we had been climbing steeply as we worked our way up to it (the little Fiat may be the reason), but now here we were, and the view from this pinnacle was transfixing: the ancient royal burgh, a portion of the links, St. Andrews Bay, the Angus coast as far as Montrose, even the vague outline of the Grampian Mountains. A panorama to take its place with those at Gullane, Turnberry, and Aberdour.

The 13th, measuring 355 yards from the regular tees and playing less as it falls steeply and swings to the right, prompted Thomson to say that the most difficult task for an architect is to design a really first-rate downhill hole, so most architects avoid them. This brought us to the 14th tee and the second half of this descent from the heights. And here was Peter Thomson, in the face of his own dictum, laying out *consecutive* downhillers.

The 13th is beautiful and uncomplicated. The 14th is also a beauty, but there is more going on here as it sweeps down the lower half of the great hill, bending almost indiscernibly right much of the way. This is a very long par four, 480 yards from the back, 425 yards for us mere mortals. Central to the situation here are a lone old tree in the fairway and a surprising little burn, both entering the equation in the tee-shot landing area. The burn comes in from the left, the tree stands sentinel on the right. The perfect drive is placed between the burn and the tree, but this is a confined space. The shot to the green from here is long; however, the green is open across the front. Alternatively, the drive can be played safely away from the burn to a broad landing area well left, but this leaves an even longer second shot and one that is semiblind (the flag in view, but not the green), that must carry over several mounds and then find a green set at an unaccommodating angle. The strategic considerations are candidly set forth from start to finish.

"I think," Thomson said, "it may be the best hole on the course. It is demanding but also fair, and it requires the player to think well and to swing well if he is to make par." There was no hint of smug self-satisfaction, but the pleasure he took in the hole was unmistakable and altogether winning.

He also used this hole to stress one of his principal tenets, which is rooted in the style of the earliest British courses. "I believe," he said, "that half the game should be played along the ground, with shots to be run onto the green from well out in front of it."

You can do just that at Craigtoun. The greens are never sealed off by water, and only in the rarest instances by sand. It is a course that manages that most elusive of all feats: it truly welcomes players of every skill level, while at the same time unveiling a series of holes that range from good to great. It also makes St. Andrews the only place I know where a player can enjoy true links golf on one of the half-dozen greatest seaside courses in the world and, just two miles away, superlative inland golf in a setting of extraordinary natural beauty.

Each month during the season the St. Andrews Links management publishes a free newsletter called *Links News.* It is full of easy-to-get-at information about playing golf in St. Andrews, information that anyone spending a few days or more here would find useful. Virtually everything you might want to know is contained in it, including green fees on the various courses (pay by cash or credit card), course opening hours, how to obtain a starting time, how to get on the daily ballot for an Old Course tee time, what a lone golfer should do in order to play, what condition the individual courses are in, how heavily prebooked each course is during that particular month, and plenty of additional information that could make golf at St. Andrews more enjoyable. The newsletter even gives you a phone number to call if you wish to lodge a complaint. Obviously, the links management wants satisfied customers.

No matter how rigidly golf-centered your holiday, you should take whatever steps are necessary to spend a few hours making the town's acquaintance. It is neither postcard pretty nor quaint—no Portofino or Perouges or Stow-on-the-Wold or Adare—but there is a solid handsomeness to it and no little nobility. What's more, since the heart of St. Andrews is less than a square mile, and since that compact area is essentially level, it is a walker's paradise, and you will find yourself, even with only a morning or an afternoon at your disposal, coming willy-nilly upon many of its most treasured moments. Simply begin to roam, up any of the three principal streets—North, South, or Market—which parallel each other. There is a pervasive sense of times long past, what with the sixteenth-, seventeenth-, and eighteenth-century stone dwellings of South Street (the step-gabled roofs help to give the town an almost Flemish air); the roofless remains of Blackfriars Chapel (1525); Queen Mary's House; the Pends (a fourteenth-century arched stone gateway leading to the Cathedral precincts that, legend has it, will collapse when the wisest man in Christendom walks through it; the Pends still stands); St. Mary's College (dating to 1552 and with a tranquil old quadrangle that may lack the formal elegance of the great enclosures at, say, Cambridge or Oxford, but its gentle embrace is nonetheless warm and sheltering). And, of course, the Cathedral of St. Andrews, begun in 1160 and consecrated in 1318.

In a town where so much that is old has been carefully preserved, the single most important—and imposing (it was the second longest cathedral in all of Britain, Norwich being the longest)—monument is in ruins. But with its great tower still standing, what splendid and evocative ruins they are! And how majestic the setting, on a promontory above the sea. The remarkable assortment of tombstones in the Cathedral graveyard continues to intrigue the curious. Old Tom Morris is buried here. So is Young Tom.

On the upper part of North Street, beyond the cinema (built in 1931 and still operating under the name "New Picture House") and the Crawford Centre for the Arts, you may find yourself standing before Younger Graduation Hall, set back from the street, with its own forecourt. Almost 40 years ago it served as the setting for what may have been the most moving moment in the annals of golf.

When Bobby Jones came back to St. Andrews in 1958 as nonplaying captain of the American squad in the World Amateur Team Championship, the town fathers seized the opportunity to make him a Freeman of the Burgh of St. Andrews. Only Jones had won both the Open (1927) and the Amateur (1930) on the Old Course, an achievement that is not likely to be equaled. No foreigner ever captured the heart of St. Andreans as did Jones, whose fineness of character and gentlemanly demeanor registered as strongly upon them as did his love for links golf and his flair for playing it. Now crippled by a spinal disease—he needed a powered golf cart to get around—he was to be honored by St. Andrews as only one other American had been, Benjamin Franklin, 200 years earlier.

More than 2,000 people, the great majority of them townsfolk, crammed Younger Hall that evening. After the provost spoke of the abiding friendship between Jones and the residents of St. Andrews, Bobby edged his way painstakingly along a supporting table to the lectern. Without benefit of script or notes, he talked earnestly and informally (we are indebted to Herbert Warren Wind for his firsthand report of the occasion) in his Georgia drawl. He recounted both the high points and the low of the tournaments in which he had competed on the Old Course. "I could take out of my life everything except my experiences at St. Andrews," he said, "and I would still have had a rich and full life." He concluded by speaking of friendship: "When you have made me aware on many occasions that you have a kindly feeling toward me, and when you have honored me by every means at your command, then when I call you my friend I am at once affirming my high regard and affection for you and trust in the sincerity of your expression. And so, my fellow citizens of St. Andrews, it is with this appreciation of the full sense of the word that I salute you as my friends."

He then climbed into what he called "my electric buggy" and guided it slowly down the center aisle. As he did, the entire gathering rose to its feet and broke into an unutterably poignant rendition of the old Scottish song "Will Ye No Come Back Again?" As it happened, he never would.

If you can spare some time for good old-fashioned crass commerce, there is, on The Links, a humdinger of an outlet store called the St. Andrews Woolen Mill. In addition to a staggering assortment of tweeds, shetlands, sheepskins, mohairs, cashmeres (I recall fingering a sweater priced at $775), it also offers picture books and shortbreads, heather seeds and heather keyrings and heather boutonnieres, tartan piper dolls, travel rugs, cut crystal, Scottish jewelry, and golf umbrellas. And as Bob Philip (he and his brother Raymond own the place) once told me, "We've got a gimmick upstairs—free coffee, tea, or lemonade, and a marvelous view overlooking the eighteenth green of the Old Course."

A Word or Two About
Dining and Accommodations

Dining can be both varied and excellent in St. Andrews and its environs. At one end of the price scale are the Chinese take-outs, the pizza parlors, the wine bars, and the delis—after all, this is a university town.

My favorite restaurants include the Grange (rustic charm on a hill just south of town, with eagle-eye views of St. Andrews:

moderately priced); the Niblick (an intimate beamed-ceiling room at 1 Golf Place, where the Partan Bree, a smooth shellfish soup, is outstanding: moderately priced); the top-floor dining room at the Old Course Hotel (distinguished international cuisine, chic and luxurious setting, magnificent views of sea and town: expensive); and the Peat Inn (10 minutes from town, where David Wilson, one of Britain's celebrated chefs, offers what he modestly calls "good cooking in the middle of nowhere" and a very extensive wine list: expensive).

Since St. Andrews is, as much as anything, a seaside resort, it provides a variety of places to stay. You can find a room in a university dorm (with bath, in many cases) or in one of the countless B&Bs, a number of them on Murray Park or Murray Place. Among the hotels that my wife and I have found very satisfying over the years are Rufflets (a country-house hotel set in beautiful topiary gardens a couple of miles out of town on the Strathkinness Road—Jack Nicklaus's choice for himself and his family: moderately priced); Rusack's Hotel (Bobby Jones's choice—attractive English country decor, relaxed atmosphere; room 218, hanging over the home hole of the Old Course, may well be a serious golfer's favorite accommodation in all the world: moderate to expensive); the Old Course Hotel (stylish and supremely comfortable; world-class decor, amenities, cuisine, and views: expensive); the Peat Inn (eight spiffy minisuites to go with that marvelous food: moderate to expensive); the Scores Hotel (traditional haven for golfers, on a rise above the R&A clubhouse—sparkling and comfortable; lovely views of the bay and the West Sands from the front rooms, 38-second walk to the 1st tee of the Old Course: moderate).

Speaking of walks, my wife and I customarily stroll the

Scores (the hotel takes its name from the street) after dinner, as you might a boardwalk. It extends from the R&A clubhouse to the Castle, which, like the Cathedral, is today a romantic ruin. We sit for a few moments on a bench under the embowering trees, gazing absently toward the Castle, which is protected on the north and east by the cliffs and the sea. It has served variously as a prison, a fortress, and the palace of the Archbishop of St. Andrews. It was the setting for high and bloody drama on more than one occasion, the most chilling being the assassination of the Cardinal Archbishop David Beaton, whose allegiance to Rome was unshakable. In 1546 Henry VIII's Protestant adherents entered the Castle disguised as stonemasons, stabbed the prelate to death, and suspended his cadaver from a window by an arm and a leg. It is not easy to reconcile the violence of the past, much of it engendered by religious conflict, with the tranquility of the present in St. Andrews. Today such struggles as do take place here are confined to the golf links and the University Debating Society.

I remember the night some years ago—it was a crisp November evening—when, on the return leg of our walk, we discovered a back way into St. Salvator's College. A high stone wall almost flush with the sidewalk encloses the college grounds, cutting off not only our access but our view. I suggested we walk down Butts Wynd, a narrow lane connecting the Scores with North Street, in the hope of finding a gateway in the wall. It is indeed there, and we entered to find ourselves in the beautiful quadrangle of St. Salvator's. Shadows and silence—the great collegiate church mantled in darkness, its cloistering scarcely discernible, and, on the far side of that perfect lawn now dampened with early dew, a light or two in the

Jacobean facade of Lower College Hall. There is no getting away from it: ancient universities, bewitching and timeless by day, can be even more enchanting by night. No student stirred as we stood there for a moment, picking out a detail here and there in this cherished seat of learning, peering up at the graceful spire, its pinnacle soaring above North Street and now lost in the night. Then we retreated to the narrow gateway in the wall and down Butts Wynd to the Scores.

We were heading back toward the Old Course now, the sea close below on our right. Beyond the bay and the estuary of the Eden, on the far side of the Firth of Tay, the lights on the Angus coast—Carnoustie, Monifieth, Barry—glow softly golden in the distance. The only sound was the shushing of the surf on the boulders at the base of the bluff. It was sweet indeed.

Golf Clubs, Golf Courses

In telephoning Scotland, the country code is 44. Last line of address is the phone number.

ABERDOUR GOLF CLUB
Seaside Place
Aberdour
Fife KY3 OTX
01383 860688

ALYTH GOLF CLUB
Alyth, Blairgowrie
Perthshire PH11 8JJ
01828 32268

ANSTRUTHER GOLF CLUB
Marsfield, Shore Road
Anstruther
Fife
01333 310956

AUCHTERARDER GOLF CLUB
Ochil Road
Auchterarder
Perthshire PH3 1LS
01764 662804

BLAIRGOWRIE GOLF CLUB
Rosemount, Blairgowrie
Perthshire PH10 6LG
01250 872622

BRAIDS NO. 1, NO. 2
Braid Hills
Edinburgh
0131 4476666

BRORA GOLF CLUB
Golf Road
Brora
Sutherland KW9 6QS
01408 621417

BRUNTSFIELD LINKS
32 Barnton Ave.
Davidson's Mains
Edinburgh EH4 6JH
0131 3362006

CARNEGIE CLUB
Skibo Castle
Dornoch
Sutherland IV25 3RQ
01862 894600

CARNOUSTIE GOLF LINKS
Links Parade
Carnoustie
Angus DD7 7JE
01241 853789

CHARLETON GOLF COURSE
Colinsburgh
Fife KY9 1HG
01333 340505

CRAIL GOLFING SOCIETY
Balcomie, Fifeness
Crail
Fife KY10 3XN
01333 450278

CRIEFF GOLF CLUB
Perth Road
Crieff
Perthshire PH7 3LR
01764 2909

CRUDEN BAY GOLF CLUB
Cruden Bay
Aberdeenshire AB42 7NN
01779 812285

DALMAHOY HOTEL, GOLF &
COUNTRY CLUB
Kirknewton
Lothian EH27 8EB
0131 3331845

DOWNFIELD GOLF CLUB
Turnberry Ave.
Dundee
Angus DD2 3QP
01382 825595

DUDDINGSTON GOLF CLUB
Duddingston Road West
Edinburgh E15 3QD
0131 6617688

THE DUKE'S COURSE
Craigtoun Park
St. Andrews
Fife
01334 474371

DUNAVERTY GOLF CLUB
Southend, by Campbeltown
Argyll
01586 83677

DUNBAR GOLF CLUB
East Links
Dunbar
East Lothian EH42 1LP
01368 862317

ELIE, THE GOLF HOUSE CLUB
Elie
Fife KY9 1AS
01333 330301

GLENEAGLES HOTEL
Auchterarder
Perthshire PH3 1NF
01764 663543

GOLSPIE GOLF CLUB
Ferry Road
Golspie
Sutherland KW10 5RS
01408 633266

GREENOCK GOLF CLUB
Forsyth Street
Greenock
Renfrewshire PA16 8RE
01475 720793

GULLANE GOLF CLUB
Gullane
East Lothian EH31 2BB
01620 842255

HONOURABLE COMPANY OF
EDINBURGH GOLFERS
Muirfield
Gullane
East Lothian EH31 2EG
01620 842123

KING JAMES VI GOLF CLUB
Moncrieffe Island
Perth
Perthshire
01738 25170

KIRRIEMUIR GOLF CLUB
Northmuir
Kirriemuir
Angus DD8 4LN
01575 573317

LADYBANK GOLF CLUB
Annsmuir
Ladybank
Fife KY7 7RA
01337 830814

LETHAM GRANGE GOLF CLUB
Colliston
Arbroath
Angus DD11 4RL
01241 890373

LEVEN LINKS
Promenade
Leven
Fife KY8 4HS
01333 428859

LOCH LOMOND GOLF CLUB
Luss, by Alexandria
Dunbartonshire G83 8NT
01436 860223

LUFFNESS NEW GOLF CLUB
Aberlady
East Lothian EH32 0QA
01620 843114

LUNDIN GOLF CLUB
Golf Road
Lundin Links
Fife KY8 6BA
01333 320202

MACHRIE HOTEL GOLF COURSE
Machrie, Port Ellen
Isle of Islay
Argyll PA42 7AN
01496 2310

MACHRIHANISH GOLF CLUB
Machrihanish,
by Campbeltown
Argyll
01586 81213

MONIFIETH GOLF LINKS
The Links
Monifieth, Dundee
Angus DD5 4AW
01382 532767

MONTROSE LINKS TRUST
Traill Drive
Montrose
Angus DD10 8SW
01674 672932

MUIRFIELD (Honourable
Company of Edinburgh
Golfers)
Gullane
East Lothian EH31 2EG
01620 842123

MURCAR GOLF CLUB
Bridge of Don
Aberdeenshire AB23 8BD
01224 704354

MUSSELBURGH GOLF CLUB
Monktonhall
Musselburgh
Lothian EH21 6SA
0131 6652005

NAIRN GOLF CLUB
Seabank Road
Nairn
Nairnshire IV12 48B
01667 453208

NAIRN DUNBAR GOLF CLUB
Lochloy Road
Nairn
Nairnshire IV12 5AE
01667 452741

NORTH BERWICK GOLF CLUB
West Links
Beach Road
North Berwick
East Lothian EH39 4BB
01620 5040

NORTH BERWICK GOLF LINKS
East Links
North Berwick
East Lothian EH39 4LE
01620 2221

PANMURE GOLF CLUB
Burnside Road
Barry, by Carnoustie
Angus
01241 853120

PETERHEAD GOLF CLUB
Craigewan Links
Peterhead
Aberdeenshire
01779 72149

POWFOOT GOLF CLUB
Cummertrees, Annan
Dumfriesshire
014617 227

PRESTWICK GOLF CLUB
2 Links Road
Prestwick
Ayrshire KA9 1QG
01292 77404

ROYAL ABERDEEN GOLF CLUB
Links Road
Balgownie, Bridge of Don
Aberdeenshire
01224 702571

ROYAL BURGESS GOLFING
SOCIETY
181 Whitehouse Road
Barnton, Edinburgh EH4
6BY
0131 3392075

ROYAL DORNOCH GOLF CLUB
Golf Road
Dornoch
Sutherland IV25 3LW
01862 810219

ROYAL MUSSELBURGH GOLF
CLUB
Prestongrange House
Prestonpans
Lothian EH32 9RP
01875 810276

ROYAL TROON GOLF CLUB
Craigend Road
Troon
Ayrshire KA10 6LD
01292 311555

SCOTSCRAIG GOLF CLUB
Golf Road
Tayport
Fife DD6 9DZ
01382 552515

ST. ANDREWS LINKS
St. Andrews
Fife KY16 9JA
01334 475757
(For information on all
courses—Old, New, Eden,
Jubilee, Strathtyrum, Bal-
gove—and for starting times)

ST. ANDREWS
The Duke's Course
Craigtoun Park
St. Andrews
Fife
01334 474371

SOUTHERNESS GOLF CLUB
Southerness
Dumfriesshire DG2 8AZ
01387 88677

STONEHAVEN GOLF CLUB
Cowie, Stonehaven
Kincardineshire AB3 2RH
01569 762124

TAIN GOLF CLUB
Chapel Road
Tain
Ross-shire IV19 1PA
01862 892314

TURNBERRY HOTEL COURSES
Turnberry
Ayrshire KA26 9LT
01655 331000

WESTERN GAILES GOLF CLUB
Gailes, Irvine
Ayrshire KA11 5AE
01294 311649

WHITEKIRK GOLF CLUB
Whitekirk, Dunbar
East Lothian EH42 1SX
01620 870300

Appendix B

Hotels

ARDSHEAL HOUSE
Kentallin of Appin
Argyll PA38 4BX
0163 174227

BALCARY BAY HOTEL
Auchencairn
Dumfries & Galloway DG7
1QZ
01556 640217

BALMORAL HOTEL
Princes Street
Edinburgh EH2 2EQ
0131 5562414

BLENHEIM HOUSE HOTEL
Westgate
North Berwick
East Lothian
01620 2385

BURGHFIELD HOUSE HOTEL
Dornoch
Sutherland IV25 3HN
01862 810212

CALEDONIAN HOTEL
Princes Street
Edinburgh EH1 2AB
0131 2252433

CAMERON HOUSE
Loch Lomond, Alexandria
Dunbartonshire GH3 8QZ
01389 55625

CARNEGIE CLUB
Skibo Castle
Dornoch
Sutherland IV25 3RQ
01862 894600

CULZEAN CASTLE APARTMENTS
Culzean Castle
Maybole
Ayrshire KA19 8LE
01655 760274

DALHOUSIE CASTLE HOTEL
Bonnyrigg, Edinburgh
Lothian EH19 3JB
01875 820153

DORNOCH CASTLE HOTEL
Dornoch
Sutherland IV25 3SD
01862 810216

GEORGE HOTEL
George Street
Edinburgh EH2 2PB
0131 2251251

GLENEAGLES HOTEL
Auchterarder
Perthshire PH3 19F
01764 62231

GOLF VIEW HOTEL
Seabank Road
Nairn
Nairnshire IV12 4HD
01667 52301

GREYWALLS
Gullane
East Lothian EH31 2EG
01620 842144

KILMARNOCK ARMS HOTEL
Cruden Bay
Aberdeenshire AB4 7ND
01779 812213

THE LINKS HOTEL
Golf Road
Brora
Sutherland KW9 6QS
01408 621225

MACHRIE HOTEL
Machrie
Isle of Islay
Argyll PA42 7AN
01496 2310

MARINE HOTEL
Cromwell Road
North Berwick
East Lothian EH39 4LZ
01620 2406

MARINE HIGHLAND HOTEL
Troon
Ayrshire KA10 6HE
01292 314444

MELDRUM HOUSE
Oldmeldrum
Aberdeenshire AB51 0AE
01651 872294

THE NEWTON HOTEL
Nairn
Nairnshire
01667 53144

OATFIELD HOUSE
Southend Road
Near Campbeltown
Argyll PA28 6PH
01586 554893

OLD COURSE HOTEL
St. Andrews
Fife KY16 9SP
01334 74371

OPEN ARMS INN
Dirleton
East Lothian
01620 850241

THE PEAT INN
Peat Inn
Cupar
Fife KY15 5LH
01334 84206

POINT GARRY HOTEL
West Bay Road
North Berwick
East Lothian EH39 4AW
01620 2380

PRESTONFIELD HOUSE
Priestfield Road
Edinburgh EH16 5VT
0131 6683346

ROSSLYN CASTLE
Roslin
Lothian

(administered by Landmark
Trust, Maidenhead,
England—telephone
0628 825925)

ROYAL GOLF HOTEL
Dornoch
Sutherland
01862 810283

RUFFLETS HOTEL
Strathkinness Low Road
St. Andrews
Fife KY16 9TX
01334 72594

RUSACK'S HOTEL
Pilmour Links
St. Andrews
Fife KY16 9JQ
01334 74321

THE SCORES HOTEL
The Scores
St. Andrews
Fife KY19 9BB
01334 72451

SEAHOUSE
Gullane
East Lothian
(for information, call this
New York City number: 212
696 4750)

SHORE COTTAGE
Saddell
Argyll
(administered by Landmark
Trust, Maidenhead,
England—telephone
0628 825925)

TURNBERRY HOTEL, GOLF
COURSES AND SPA
Turnberry
Ayrshire KA26 9LT
01655 331000

UDNY ARMS HOTEL
Newburg, Ellon
Aberdeenshire AB4 0BL
01358 789444

WHITEKIRK MAINS
Whitekirk, Dunbar
East Lothian EH42 1SX
01620 870245

Printed in the United States
By Bookmasters